THE
DICTIONARY OF
GRAPHIC
IMAGES

THE DICTIONARY OF GRAPHIC IMAGES

PHILIP THOMPSON & PETER DAVENPORT

Foreword by George Lois

ST. MARTIN'S PRESS
NEW YORK

Manufactured in the United States of America
Set in Monotype Baskerville by Bedford Typesetters Ltd.
Designed by Philip Thompson & Peter Davenport

First published by Bergstrom & Boyle Books Limited
31 Foubert's Place, London W1V THE

Library of Congress Cataloging in Publication Data

Thompson, Philip.
    Dictionary of graphic images.

    1.   Symbolism (Psychology)—Dictionaries.
2.   Signs and symbols—Dictionaries.   I.   Davenport,
Peter, joint author.   II.   Title.
BF458.T46   1981   704.9′46′0321   80-28163
ISBN 0-312-20108-7   AACR1

Authors' Note

We started compiling this dictionary in 1974. We suddenly realised there was a gap between the numerous dictionaries of historic symbols and the living visual language that artists and designers had been evolving during the last fifty years or so.

We apologise to all those whose work is missing from this book who in our opinion as well as theirs might have had a claim to representation. Our original criterion for selection was what we considered an imaginative use of cliché. Beyond this, inevitably the choice was arbitrary. We were tempted daily to open a new category entitled, Because We Love It, but this would have delayed publication by years.

We have credited each illustration with the country in which it was published followed by the date of publication and the name of the person most responsible for the work. We have striven to date and credit work accurately and spell names correctly. We apologise for any errors or omissions but sources of such information are often inconsistent.

Words set in small capitals, eg ABACUS, ZZZ, indicate entries which can be referred to elsewhere in the book.

Our thanks are due to the photographer Jon Stewart for his help in the early stages and to Colin Forbes, Alan Fletcher and John McConnell of Pentagram Design who encouraged us and published our original thoughts on the subject in the *ABC of Graphic Clichés*. Our thanks are also due to Maxwell Proctor of the library of the Central School of Art and Design and to our editor Veronica Pratt who wisely discouraged us from writing a Dictionary of Everything (a much heavier volume). This book could hardly have been written without Zoe Davenport who lightened our task with her resourcefulness and devotion and Pat Huntley who put our disorganised thoughts into manageable form. Our special thanks are due to George Lois for his foreword. Finally we would like to thank all the contributors for their kindness in allowing us to reproduce their work and for their generous help and encouragement.

Foreword by George Lois

This is a dictionary of visual images, of graphic clichés. It is vital to repeat the authors' distinction that while the cliché is a derogatory word in literary circles, the visual cliché is essential in the world of graphic communicators. 'Without it there is little communication,' claim the perceptive duo, Philip Thompson and Peter Davenport. I would go further. I would say that without the visual cliché there would be virtually no communication on the printed page or on television.

The visual cliché can immediately give life to an idea. It gives clear meaning to what could be an abstraction. In posters, package design and magazine covers, words can often be unnecessary—at times even excess baggage. (How's that for a well placed verbal and visual cliché!)

A photograph of Muhammad Ali in boxing trunks, with arrows piercing his body, suggested at once in the 1960s that he was a martyr because of his refusal to fight in an unjust war. Here was an act of extraordinary moral valour—of modern martyrdom—that stripped Ali of his championship title and deprived him of his right to fight during three years of his prime. He was surely the St Sebastian of the Vietnam era. (See illustration under SAINTS' SYMBOLISM.)

A graffiti moustache, starkly drawn on the saintlike photo of Stalin's daughter Svetlana (à la Duchamp's Mona Lisa) reminded too many uncritical worshippers of America's newest media-made darling that if she were Stalin's daughter, she probably couldn't really be Joan of Arc—while conjuring that deliciously derisive street epithet, 'Your father's moustache!', an urban cliché that translates into the more frontal, 'Up yours!'. (See illustration under WOMEN WITH MOUSTACHES.)

I superimposed a movie marquee across the entrance to Saint Patrick's Cathedral for an *Esquire* issue devoted to youth-orientated motion pictures to make the point that movies had become a new religion to America's youth. (See illustration under BUILDING.)

Visual imagery can also be made without a 'picture'. An ad campaign to dramatise Qwip, an American telecopier with a consciously misspelled name, used just bold type that said, 'The sanest offices are Qwip qwazy!' Another ad urged the use of Qwip rather than the mails by saying, 'Are you Qwazy? Don't mail it. Use the Qwip!' The misspelled 'qwazy' dramatised and clarified the potentially confusing spelling of the product. (See CAPITAL OUT OF ERROR.)

Exactly the reverse of Qwip was my Wolfschmidt Vodka campaign in which words simply enhanced an overpowering visual statement. One hardly had to read the words being said by the Wolfschmidt bottle lying on its side to know that the bottle (a graphic cliché for the phallus) intended to seduce the orange (a graphic cliché for the female) to make a 'screw-

v

driver' (the graphic/verbal cliché/climax to all this innuendo/imagery). (See FRUIT and illustration under PERSONIFICATION.)

What separates a brilliant idea from the pedestrian pack is that element of surprise. A fresh, human, disarming point is pursued by the creative thinker. The use of strong visual imagery plus a few brilliantly arranged words combines to form a message that vastly exceeds the sum of its parts. One plus one can indeed add up to three.

The raison d'etre of an advertising thinker is to entrance consumers with a visual image that fuses with an unforgettable verbal theme. Most advertising is simply invisible. You can read through a magazine and discover that seconds later you are hard pressed to remember a single ad in the publication. Most have no visual or verbal imagery, and those that use imagery treat it as a cliché in the literal sense, as a 'hackneyed literary phrase' without imagination to redeem it. The creative fusion of visual and verbal imagery is rare and becoming rarer—just as the dominance of the television medium cries out for imaginative intelligence.

In creating a television commercial, the advertising thinker must produce a continuing fusion between the visual image and the audio dimension (the verbal image) to keep viewers from getting up and lurching out for a beer when the commercial comes on. The television public has a love-hate relationship with commercials; they love to hate them, and for ample reason, but they also love to love them, given some substance to love. That substance is the graphic cliché, creatively transformed into a spellbinding interlude that lingers far beyond its 30-second life.

In print and television, that elusive, magical combination of words and pictures is at the heart of the most persuasive and memorable advertising. Classic example: a red chair on a burnished wooden floor is photographed against a deep red background. Wedged disturbingly under one of its well-carved legs is a white matchbook. The headline reads: 'If your Harvey Probber chair wobbles, straighten your floor.' The thought is communicated that a Probber chair is never made imperfectly. The matchbook imagery (the graphic cliché for a wedge) is unforgettable. For years after this ad ran, a white matchbook was wedged under each chair in the Probber showroom.

The Dictionary of Visual Language comes to us at a time when art directors seem to be less and less aware of the world's rich, limitless lode of imagery, and of its awesome potential for communicating with spirit and style. It is to be hoped that this wonderful, needed volume will stir new interest in this enormous reservoir of creative 'tools'.

With the advent of the Creative Revolution in American advertising in the early 1960s, a whole generation of young art directors moved to centre stage in their advertising agencies, not simply as newly appreciated creators, but also as businessmen. Art directors, heady with power, went through a bizarre metamorphosis: they became writers as well as artists, marketers as well as writers, and inevitably, communicators of 'information' as well as marketers. They soon lost touch with their creative roots, with their essential source of creative originality: visual imagery. They studied annual reports with more intensity than they should have studied the history of art and design.

But a few art directors, aware that their craft depended on a passionate intimacy with the myths and symbols of man's fumblings and triumphs throughout history, remained loyal to the idea that visual imagery was the language of humanity. They understood that artists needed to work with writers, almost symbiotically, to bring about that electric fusion between image and word. That's what creative communicating is all about. That's why this book is so important. Perhaps it will reawaken the world's dozing talents.

Introduction by Philip Thompson

In the beginning the communication of ideas and the formation of concepts was achieved through the representation of objects and biological forms. Later this developed into symbolic and hieroglyphic writing. With the development of language and writing these tokens of the visual world became buried in the spoken and written word to remain undiscovered for centuries while semantic differences proliferated. It is the designer's task to exhume these tokens and reinstate them as images.

Graphic design is a language. Like other languages it has a vocabulary, grammar, syntax, rhetoric. It also has its cliché, but this is where the analogy ends. The dictionary defines cliché as a 'hackneyed literary phrase'. Frank Binder in his *Dialectic 1932* says, '. . . there is no bigger peril either to education or to thinking than the popular phrase'. Clearly in literary circles the cliché's stock is low. In our use of the word as applied to the graphic language we do not intend a derogatory tone. We suggest that its overuse is its greatest virtue for then we can assume a wide area of common acceptance. Without it there is little communication.

One example of a basic cliché is the representation of the twin Greek masks of comedy and drama to symbolise the theatre. Another is the heart representing love and affection. Their hackneyed reproductions on countless theatre programmes and Valentine cards devoid of any humour, irony or imagination are well known. Yet they persist because they contain an essential truth that appeals to our collective sense of myth and form.

It is this international and trans-cultural acceptance of the visual cliché that is its greatest virtue. It enables the designer to breathe new life into the dried husk knowing that the basic symbolism is within common experience.

A vast armoury of technique is available to help with its resuscitation and thus propagate new ideas. Some of this technique is analogous to the rhetorical figures of speech of literature and oratory, a great deal of which translates into the visual field. There is one figure however which is peculiar to graphic communication and probably one of its most important; this is known as 'fusion'. This is effected by a near-metaphysical union of two or more basic clichés. The nearest equivalent in literature or poetry is the bringing together of two common words from disparate sources which revitalise each other to create a new idea, like the 'fearful symmetry' of Blake.

We have arrived at this dictionary empirically: that is we have analysed the graphic language over the last four decades and have found that a universal grammar emerges.

Our universe is overlaid with many interpretive symbolic systems; religious, artistic, erotic, psychological, etc. It is not the visual communicator's purpose to categorise them. He has total access to all of them and may correlate and fuse the relevant imagery from different systems as he thinks appropriate.

McLuhan has said that the new is unacceptable; that every new idea has to be supported by nine old ideas in order to be accepted. This thesis supports the existence of visual cliché and the fact that the designer introduces new concepts on the backs of old.

Some clichés like the acorn or anchor seem to belong to a system of civic or heraldic symbolism which has flowered and declined. One is tempted at times to regard them as discredited or beyond redemption. But it is then that they may receive the kiss of life and reveal truths as if for the first time.

For June

Abacus. At one time a trade-sign for money lenders. A calculating frame. Apart from its obvious use in relation to subjects of elementary education and arithmetic it is also used as a general symbol for thinking or reasoning sometimes superimposed on a CRANIUM.

Book jacket, Thoughts on Design. *USA 1946 Paul Rand*

Abacus used as scoring device. See also BED. *France 1951 André François*

Accumulated Graphics. Objects that pick up their graphics through time and space like the PARCEL, PASSPORT, POSTCARD, backs of lorries, etc. Essentially a collection of overprinted and random demotic marks. See also FRANKING, HANDWRITING, LABEL, STAMP.

Simulated parcel is a book jacket for a history of the Post Office. UK 1961 Gerald Wilkinson

Magazine cover. A parcel of the work of Pentagram to be published in Graphis *was sent through the mail and allowed to pick up the random overprinting and accidents associated with the mail. UK 1965 Pentagram*

Acorn. An unofficial symbol of the English countryside. No particular historic significance but used by investment money-lending firms as a symbol of growth from its habit of growing into oak trees.

Acorn represents growth (of a series of gramophone records). Each sleeve decorated with the appropriate number of acorns. USA 1955 Erik Nitsche

Acrobat. A symbol of the reversal of the established order: form into chaos, meekness into aggression, beauty into ugliness and so on. Any distortion or deviation from the norm (like the long-legged man who advertises the circus) is a natural focal point of attention. See also CLOWN, JUGGLER.

Cover of Graphis *introducing an article on the artist's work. In effect this is a piece of fine art and reflects the artist's use of the acrobat as part of his own personal iconography. The upside-down figure features largely in Shahn's work. In this attitude the acrobat has strong associations with the hanged man in the Tarot cards. USA 1955 Ben Shahn*

Adam and Eve. A symbol for the origin of personal identity and of the human race. Popular with the rag trade where oblique reference is made to nakedness (as in fig-leaf images and 'Nothing to wear?' type headlines). See also APPLE, FIG LEAF.

Adam and Eve myth demonstrates woman's duplicity.
UK 1952 André François

From The Alphabet of Creation.
USA 1953 Ben Shahn

Address Book. The image of an opened address book or desk diary is a popular device and appeals to the inquisitive due to its verisimilitude. See also DIARY.

Aerial. One of the characteristics of TELEVISION is the aerial (reception symbol), unlike radio which is strongly associated with the MICROPHONE (transmission symbol).

Aerial landscape as a guide to affluence.
USA 1955 Ben Shahn

'The last house in the street.' Aerial as a guide for street musicians.
UK 1956 André François

Aeroplane. The mechanised bird Symbol of freedom and aspiration 20th century technology turned th fantasy and mythology of our ances tors into fact. Closely connected witl the symbolism of ascension anc levitation. See also HELICOPTER.

Condensed profile of aeroplane signifying death dive.
USA 1957 Joan Kahn

The aeroplane as a symbol of travel: the headline reads 'The Cardinal moves from Boston to Vienna'. See also NEWSPAPER, TORN PAPER.
USA 1964 Saul Bass

The runway and surreal sense of terror is an obsession shared by Hitchcock in North by Northwest. *Typical of the contrived photographic situations of the 1960s.*
UK 1967 Helmut Newton

Airmail Stripes. The dual-colour diagonal stripes on airmail envelopes are a powerful graphic device. Sometimes used to symbolise the concept of airborne or international.

Large painting. See also FRANKING.
UK 1961 Derek Boshier

TIME INTERNATIONAL
Advertising Offices: London,
Paris, Düsseldorf, Amsterdam,
Stockholm, Zürich, Milan.

Symbol for 'International'. Book cover for Time.
UK 1963 Bob Gill

ENGLISH BY AIR H A CARTLEDGE

BRITISH BROADCASTING CORPORATION

ENGLISH BY AIR
H.A. CARTLEDGE

BBC

Booklet cover for BBC. Visual pun on words 'by air'. See also LABEL.
UK 1970 Philip Thompson

Album. A characteristic object of childhood where the owner is required to contribute collected elements. High involvement factor which accounts for its popularity as an image. Evocative, although the symbolism is indeterminate. See also CORNERS.

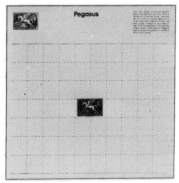

Pegasus

The characteristic appearance of a stamp album as a cover for a house organ. A real STAMP *is stuck on the cover.*
UK 1969 Derek Birdsall

The characteristic appearance of a cigarette card album is used for a letterhead. A real card is slotted-in on each sheet.
UK 1973 Arnold Schwartzman

Alphabet. The use of the total alphabet or part of it as the main image in a design.

ABC. This suggests an elementary guide to a particular subject.

'*ABC of modern furniture*' *runs the copy. A universal symbol of simplicity combined with comprehensiveness. See also* CHILDREN'S BRICKS.
USA 1955 George Tscherny

A to B. Associated with basic travelling (getting from one point to another).

Advertisement for a motor car.
UK 1969 Brian Byfield

A to Z. This suggests the ultimate and definitive version.

See also ZEBRA.
USA 1961 Kurt Weihs

Letterhead for a man of letters.
UK 1968 Derek Birdsall

Sequential. Used for clients whose initials are sequential such as KLM (airlines) or VW (automobiles).

Trademark for George Hoy.
UK 1964 Bob Gill

Total Alphabet. Usually has overt literary associations in the sense that it constitutes the whole of literature.

'*Your public library has these arranged in ways that can make you cry, giggle, love, hate, wonder, ponder and understand.*'
USA 1961 Charles Piccirillo

XYZ. This suggests the refined details for sophisticated readers.

Ampersand. The word is a corruption of 'and per se (by itself) "and" '. The sign is a typographic condensation of the Latin 'et'. Historically the subject of typographic and calligraphic embroidery.

Poster for art exhibition. Emphasis by disposition.
Switzerland 1950 Max Bill

Trademark for Benton & Bowles Inc. It is also a REBUS.
USA 1960 Gene Federico

Trademark for Goods & Chattels. The goods and chattels either side of the ampersand constantly change consistent with the nature of the firm.
UK 1962 Fletcher/Forbes/Gill

The ampersand featured widely in a series of advertisements from 1958 onwards for a printer to emphasise the conjunction of two names (Alfieri & Lacroix).
Italy 1966 Franco Grignani

Skywritten version for a Belgian airline.
See also MARKS AND TRACKS.
Belgium 1966 Julian Key

Ampersand assumes human proportions.
See also SCALE.
UK 1966 Designer unknown

Analogy. Much graphic design is a reasoning process from parallel cases or situations. Sometimes there is a straight functional resemblance; at other times the similarities are supported verbally.

The owner of the new VW is saying that it is like his 1929 model A Ford for reliability.
USA 1963 Helmut Krone

Bunch of asparagus as analogy for crowd of people. Isolated asparagus doesn't 'run with the bunch' – that is, he shops with discrimination.
USA 1963 Arnold Varga

Analogy continued

Christmas card.
France 1966 Savignac

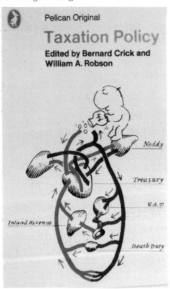

Similarity of function between circulation
of blood and circulation of money.
UK 1970 Mel Calman/Philip Thompson

Anchor. A Christian symbol of hope. At one time popular with marine insurance companies because of its association with security. A general maritime symbol. It has formal associations with the ankh, the Egyptian symbol of life. It is the main feature of many civic coats of arms, particularly ports.

Angel. A symbol of invisible forces. More specifically a divine messenger. See also WINGS.

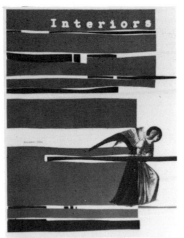

Christmas issue of magazine.
USA 1954 Aldo Giurgola

Angel as divine messenger. See also
CROWN, TRUMPET.
USA 1954 Paul Rand

The 'saintly' Dr Schweitzer gets an angel
on his Bach record sleeve.
USA 1955 Ben Shahn

Animals. Of prime importance in symbolism because of their characteristics, shape, colour and movement and because of their relationship with man. Most quadrupeds, fish, insects and birds throughout history have been the subject of myth or legend or imbued with symbolic significance. Some of this originated in religious or magical ritual or some aspect of folk culture. Some was due to the obvious attributes of the particular animals; the strength of the horse, the industry of the ant. In the struggles between different animals some spiritual hierarchy was implied as in the eagle fighting a snake which represented the baser instincts being subdued. The invention of FABULOUS BEASTS which took attributes from different animals deepened the symbolism. These complex strands of meaning still inform the thinking of the present-day designer. See animals and birds by name.

Animals represent human counterparts:
old goat, lion, chicken, etc. Common use of
WINDOW *to explore disparate elements.*
USA 1969 André François

Annotated Figure. A necessary device from text books where individual parts of a figure are annotated. The dotted line is a characteristic element. The application is invariably a humorous transference.

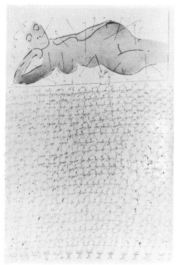

Illustration from a magazine article 'How to get along with your wife'. Here the text-book method of annotating diagrams is transferred to the area of judgement and assessment.
USA 1960 R.O.Blechman

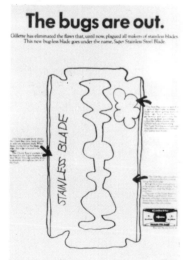

Annotations refer to improvements in cutting edge, improved coating etc.
USA 1966 Robert Wilvers

Antlers. Popular at Christmas. In graphics (as in real life) they double as coat-hangers and occasionally as candle holders. See also TROPHY.

Antlers double as TREE.
France 1978 André François

Anvil/Hammer. The anvil is a fundamental earth (female) symbol, the HAMMER represents the potent male figure. In some mythologies the blacksmith is the creator of the world – literally fashioning it out of FIRE. In general they are a symbol of fashioning or policy-making, literally hammering it out.

Anvil and hammer visually interpreting headline.
USA 1961 Seymour Chwast

One of a series of posters accompanying the 1968 student revolt in Paris.
France 1968 Atelier Populaire

Apple. One of the most popular of images in the last forty years or so. A symbol of earthly desires and materialism. In the middle ages the symbolism was mixed. In the ADAM AND EVE myth it represented the fruit of the tree of knowledge, at other times it signified Christ's mercy in his redemption of mankind. In modern times the association with original sin is strong although the treatment is usually flippant and concentrates on the more obvious features of sexual attraction. A natural substitute for BREASTS and rosy cheeks. The fact that it is shaped like the world and can be peeled and bitten into with characteristic effect contributes to its fascination. By association it sometimes symbolises elementary education as in 'an apple for the teacher' (American) and 'A is for apple' references.

Better books aid concentration.
UK 1954 André François

Inevitably arrows (see ARROW) are linked with apples.
USA 1961 Henry Wolf

The William Tell myth of accuracy is often referred to in designers' use of apples. Copy says 'There are times when you cannot afford to miss'.
USA 1965 Lou Dorfsman

Real apples replace model's BREASTS.
UK 1973 Sam Haskins

Arch. The triumphal arch was for the ancient Romans a symbol of heaven. They were erected in thanksgiving for military victories. Cartoonists use it satirically in connection with political victories.

Arithmetical Signs. As with many other sign systems, many arithmetical signs have been absorbed into the common currency of the visual language, e.g. plus, minus and multiplication signs.

Signs turn into painting. From a booklet spread on applied science.
USA 1956 Milton Herder

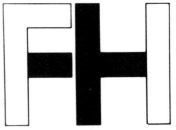

Trademark for Fédération Horlogère Bienne (Association of Clockmakers). The design is a treble visual pun – a MONOGRAM FH, the Swiss flag (see FLAG) and the plus and minus signs which signify the slow and fast clock regulator.
Switzerland 1958 Gerstner + Kutter

Plus sign used as ampersand substitute.
UK 1963 Derek Birdsall

The plus signs are mathematical ampersands. With the copy they suggest an infinity of paper and board products from wood cellulose. See also TREE TRUNK. *USA 1963 Bradbury Thompson*

Ark. Symbol of refuge and providing for the future.

Ark as a rainy-day symbol. USA 1965 Gennaro Andreozzi

Arm. The disembodied arm is a symbol of strength in trade-union activities or political legislation. This is borne out in colloquial speech in such phrases as 'political muscle'. It is also popular as a symbol of industrial power (the human element behind the scenes) and as a symbol of military aggression. See also BODY LANGUAGE, FIST, HAND.

Anti-war poster. Germany 1924 Käthe Kollwitz

The brawny arm and fist as a symbol of raw power. USA 1930 McKnight Kauffer

Poster. Aid for Spanish Republican Committee. Spain 1936 Miró

The Future Is Ours, Comrade

Joseph Novak

Ironic comment on communism; communist salute from arm of PUPPET. *USA 1964 Milton Glaser*

Armour. A man in armour or a suit of armour or helmet is sometimes a symbol of reliance, protection and invincibility. Much loved by insurance companies and other firms concerned with security. Armour is sometimes humorously associated with tin cans and the necessity for using tin-openers. Being protected is close to being imprisoned. See also KNIGHT, SHIELD.

Logical association of armour reinforces idea of protecting one's health with mineral water. See also BOTTLE TOP.
France 1962 Savignac

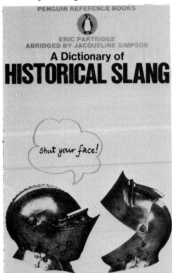

The vizor is a mouth substitute. Armour is a generalised symbol for the idea of medieval history. See also SPEECH BALLOON.
UK 1972 Mel Calman/Philip Thompson

Arrow. One of the most constantly used graphic devices in both its forms; the feathered variety and the formal SQUARE and TRIANGLE which is the mechanised version of the printer's fist (see FIST). (Invented by Paul Klee?) The arrow is a distinctly phallic symbol (seen in its pure form in the botanical male bloom sign, the astronomical sign for Mars and the chemical sign for copiapite). This partly accounts for its popularity, not least among graffiti artists (see GRAFFITI). Paradoxically its symbolism is both precise and indeterminate, designers tending to overload it with their own subjectivity. It is frequently found in conjunction with receptive (female) figures like the APPLE, CIRCLE, HEART and TARGET. See also DANCE DIAGRAM, DIMENSIONS, GAMES AND BATTLES.

For an exhibition of posters by the artist. The poster is literally symbolised as an eye-catching object.
France 1936 Cassandre

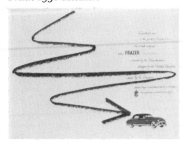

The dynamic arrow also bears evidence of its tracks. See also MARKS AND TRACKS.
USA 1949 Paul Rand

In the 1930s and 1940s there was a fashion for paper-thin undulating arrows similar to those used by Paul Klee in his paintings twenty years earlier. There was also an affinity with the soft objects of Dali which were contemporary. See also EYE, MAP.
UK 1948 Hans Schleger

The arrows here symbolise the strands of human experience that make up a 'hero's life' (Ein Heldenleben) by Richard Strauss. The music itself quotes from the composer's earlier works and the arrows suggest this.
USA 1952 Eric Nitsche

For a symposium exploring advertising.
USA 1957 Arnold Varga

Los Angeles goes up the charts.
USA 1958 Tom Courtos

Symbol for British Rail.
UK 1965 Design Research Unit

Poster for art exhibition. In addition to
normal poster sites these were situated
within the London Underground whose
house style it parodied. This gave it an
added 'double-take' dimension.
UK 1967 Bob Gill

Still from the film, The Theatre of
Mr and Mrs Kabal.
Poland 1968 Walerian Borowczyk

Poster for an architectural conference.
USA 1969 Folon

Art. The use of art by industry to lend
prestige to an otherwise indifferent
product is widespread. There are
thousands of products which use the
MONA LISA as a trademark to suggest
excellence. Sometimes original art is
specially commissioned as in the case
of *Bubbles* by Millais for Pears soap.
This use of art as a sort of cultural
talisman persists. As an antidote to
this, art is sometimes used ironically
or as a basis for parody.

President Johnson as Mona Lisa.
USA 1967 Paul Davis

Jane Fonda as Venus in Botticelli's Birth
of Venus.
USA 1968 Seymour Chwast

Atlas. The image of the Greek god
supporting the world on his back,
much loved by insurance companies.
Symbol of strength.

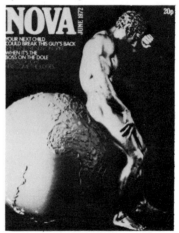

One of a series of photographs for an
article on population growth and decline.
The GLOBE literally increases and
decreases accordingly.
UK 1972 David Hillman

Atomic Cloud (Mushroom Cloud).
In the post-1945 cold war years this was popular with designers of peace posters. Too specific for use outside of its prime meaning.

Poster for nuclear disarmament. See also
SKULL.
Switzerland 1954 Hans Erni

Book jacket.
USA 1960 Chermayeff & Geismar

Atomic Structure. Mathematical models of atomic structure and micro-photography discovered by designers during the 1940s reached its apotheosis in the 1951 Festival of Britain. Still popular at the 1958 Brussels fair, Expo '58.

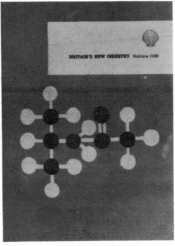

Book cover for Shell chemicals.
UK 1951 Henrion

Visual representation of atomic energy based on a nuclear fission chain-reaction diagram. Sir John Cockroft (who wrote the article concerned) pencilled the identifying symbols on the finished artwork at Games' invitation.
UK 1954 Abram Games

Auto-create. A graphic device which is a joke on the nature of drawing. Given a graphic respectability by such as Steinberg it was probably discovered by early cave dwellers.

USA 1950 Ben Shahn

An example of simultaneous auto-create and auto-erase.
Germany 1969 Hans Hillman

Axe. Fairly complex historical symbolism. In language to axe something implies cutting expenditure.

Figurative use of axe to suggest cutting education costs.
UK 1977 George Him

Baby. Often a photographic interpretation as authenticity is important. Popular because it melts the heart of the most hard-bitten consumer. An ad-man's last ditch solution. Consequently, babies (apart from promoting baby products) have been used to sell everything from soap to heavy industry.

The baby reference is linked to buying for Mother's Day. The bricks reinforce the baby theme and provide a flexible graphic element to spell out the message. See also CHILDREN'S BRICKS.
USA 1948 Paul Rand

Advertisement for a drug house. Condensation of baby image and hospital name tag as a symbol for hospital concern.
USA 1964 Herman McCray

Badge. The badge is the distinguishing mark. Essentially graphic, self-proclaiming, it is the natural aid to identification. See also ROSETTE.

The idea of political allegiance is transferred to the PIN-UP.
USA 1956 Henry Wolf

Painting. Epiphany. (48 ins diameter).
UK 1964 Richard Hamilton

Bag. See also BASKET, BOX, CASE, DUSTBIN.

An ordinary craft paper bag is the piece of direct mail for a packaging specialist.
USA 1958 Tony Palladino

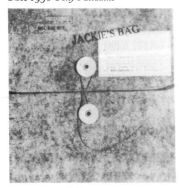

Bag as a record sleeve.
USA 1961 Reid Miles

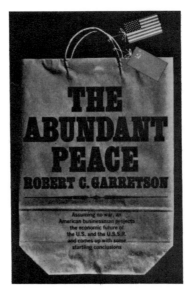

Bag as a book jacket.
USA 1965 S.Neil Fujita

Five foot high construction of a paper bag.
USA 1968 Alex Hay

Bagpipes. Although a musical instrument of antiquity found in many parts of the world its association with Scotland is strong to the point of exclusivity.

Ball. The game is naturally epitomised and symbolised by the appropriate ball. Visually characteristic according to the nature of the game (golf ball's dimples are aerodynamic) and the economics of their manufacture.

Five games symbolised by the relevant ball. The CBS eye acts as a formal simile.
USA 1960 John Burrell/Arnold Blumberg

See also STARS AND STRIPES.
USA 1962 Richard Gangel

Rugby ball and letter O as a visual pun. A protest poster against racialism in sport.
UK 1969 Robin Fior

Ball and Chain. Primary association with convicts. More generally a symbol for limitation on personal freedom and movement. Sometimes the symbolism is stretched to suggest limitations on one's life-style and capacity for decision-making.

Balloon. A compelling symbol because of its tension and airborne aspiration. Sexual overtones. One of the many objects of childhood associated with pleasurable memories. These memories are invoked when applied to adult interests and products. Various characteristics of the balloon may be alluded to such as inflation and lightness.

Banana. An obsessive phallic symbol. The verbal expression 'banana-skin humour' derives from films and comics where characters slip on the discarded item.

Bandage. The bandage is a strong and unmistakable symbol for an accident. The single bandage around a finger or nose is similarly a powerful symbol for pain or discomfort. These ideas can be metaphorically transferred to inanimate objects like buildings that are in a state of disrepair.

Painting: Chiquita Banana.
USA 1964 Mel Ramos

Cause and effect.
France 1951 André François

Copy reads, 'How about this inflation?'
USA 1946 Paul Rand

The original American record sleeve had a printed (unpeeled) banana on the cover with a printed stuck-on banana skin over it.
USA 1968 Andy Warhol

Film title (One, Two, Three) *determines image but there remains an ambivalence about* BREASTS *and censorship (see* CANCELLATION MARKS*). The long black glove is an erotic adjunct.*
USA 1961 Saul Bass

Ballot Box. Useful symbol for elections or the concept of democracy. Not much use outside of its prime meaning.

Life-size photographic image. Seminal example of such verisimilitude which became the norm in mid-1960s. See also EYE.
USA 1951 Irving Miller

Muybridge is the basis for a kinetic image incorporating the well-known banana-skin reference.
USA 1977 R.O.Blechman

Banner (Graphic). The diagonal strip (usually red) on the corner of magazines and other graphic media is an indispensable device, unsophisticated in origin but with a great sense of urgency. The message at an angle of forty-five degrees was a dynamic learnt from the Futurists and reached epidemic proportions in the 1930s and 1940s.

Early use of this hardy design element.
Belgium 1897 Emile Berchmans

Banner (Real). A device for making public declarations of one's views, allegiances, loves and so on. One of the most primitive and direct of advertising techniques.

Three horsemen with knightly (see KNIGHT) *associations proclaim the merits of a health salts.*
UK 1927 Ashley Havinden

Poster.
USA 1946 Ben Shahn

Bar Diagram. Comparative device. More useful than the 'cake' when the tolerances are finer. See CAKE DIAGRAM.

Fusion of bottle tops (see BOTTLE TOP) *and bar diagram.*
USA 1960 Brownjohn, Chermayeff & Geismar

Barbed Wire. Extremely tactile image. A 'keep out' symbol. Also associated with danger, division and imprisonment. Its war associations are often referred to. Sometimes more imaginatively it is used to evoke (by juxtaposition) the opposite quality of fragility.

Holland 1961 H.P.Doebele

Ironic Christmas parcel on a magazine cover. See also BULLET HOLES.
USA 1940 Paul Rand

Barometer. Used in relation to its prime meaning (weather) and to convey the general concept of measuring pressure or simply measuring. The word 'barometer' has associations with measuring opinion.

Barrel. A natural symbol for alcoholic drink. The tap is visually very characteristic. More abstractly it is sometimes used to symbolise the idea of shedding one's worldly goods – the person with minimal living requirements wears or lives in the barrel. The reference is to Diogenes.

Basket. Usually the meaning is closely associated with its prime function. For instance, the idea of rejection with a waste-paper basket or consumer spending with shopping or supermarket baskets, a modern-day horn of plenty. See also BAG, BOX, CASE, DUSTBIN.

Waiting, empty supermarket baskets as a symbol for consumerism.
USA 1957 Ben Shahn

Copy asks 'Need cash to pay taxes?'.
USA 1956 Howard Wilcox

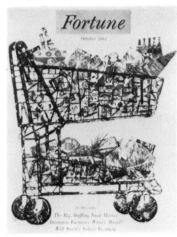

A full supermarket basket as a symbol for consumerism.
USA 1953 Jerome Snyder

'Esquire's Christmas gift guide.' Ironic Christmas comment.
USA 1957 Henry Wolf

Copy suggests impoverishment (resorting to barrel living) due to excessive expenditure on heating bills.
UK 1971 Philip Gough

Copy begins, 'Bad printed matter is invariably doomed'. The typography echoes the lines of movement derived from comic books. See also LINES OF MOTION.
Italy 1955 Franco Grignani

Bath. The old-fashioned bath with claw feet and large exposed taps has a hypnotic interest for illustrators far exceeding its voyeuristic associations. The act of bathing has associations with purification and initiation rites.

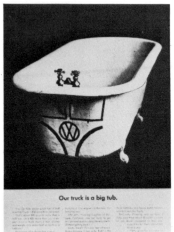

Tub-shape of VW van referred to in the copy is emphasised by GRAFFITI. *USA 1962 David Larson*

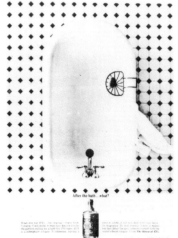

Erotic implications suggested by copy 'After the bath . . . what?'. An advertisement for a woman's cologne. See also EUPHEMISM, PLAN VIEW. *USA 1963 Bob Miller*

Bayonet. Aggressive, brutal, its symbolism is nearer the DAGGER than the SWORD. A reminder of the personalised aspect of war its associations are horrific rather than glorious.

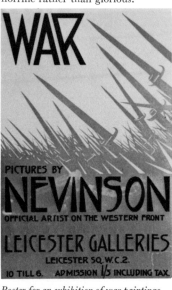

Poster for an exhibition of war paintings. UK 1918 C.W.R.Nevinson

Poster, 'The spirit of Geneva', an ironic comment on the League of Nations. See also DOVE. *Germany 1932 John Heartfield*

Beach. The beach as a contrasting setting has been a hardy standby for photographers. Particularly popular with car advertisements where the sea adds a further dimension of romantic time/space. Also popular for still life groups notably delicate glass where ironically the material is returning to its source. A symbol of freedom and liberation.

Characteristic wedge of sea describes the environment. UK 1912 John Hassall

Contrast between delicacy of shoes and hard stones. (Oxymoron - juxtaposition of opposites.) USA 1956 Art Kane/Bert Stern

Bed. It has profound connections with birth, love and death. Especially in light-hearted contexts we are aware of its ambivalence.

Bed as a symbol of rest and contentment. See also CIGAR, FRANKING, SANTA CLAUS, STAMP.
France 1958 André François

Bed as a symbol of illness. A semantic transference is made : an 'ill' pound is a devalued pound (see POUND SIGN).
UK 1970 Mel Calman

Bed of nails. In cartoon situations a strong symbol of insouciance.

Sustenance in an extreme situation.
UK 1959 Maureen Roffey

Bee. A traditional symbol of busyness and co-operative enterprise. It appears on many coats of arms of towns. Sometimes oblique reference is made to it as a 'lover' symbol (birds and bees). See also CELL, HONEYCOMB.

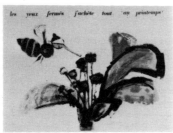

'I can get everything at Au Printemps (store) with my eyes closed'. A blindfolded bee fumbles a spring flower.
France 1960 André François

Before and After. A basic cliché of folk and popular advertising, usually associated with quick medicinal cures. The basic idea was given a facelift in the 1960s.

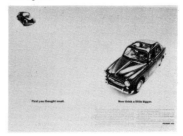

Copy says, 'First you thought small. Now think a little bigger'.
USA 1961 George Lois

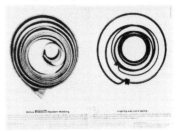

The copy reads, 'Before Pirelli resilient webbing . . . a spring was just a spring'. This characteristic (1960s) approach to copywriting derives from the landscape format of the double-spread.
UK 1964 Crosby/Fletcher/Forbes/Gill

Beggarman/Poorman. The comic book convention of patched trousers and open-toed shoes is a useful shorthand.

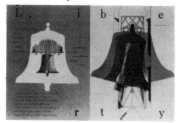

France 1951 André François

Bell. Traditionally a symbol for an announcement of joy or sorrow or a summons. It has great symbolic meaning in all cultures summoning people to church, meals, school and the market square.

Formalistic design for a non-hard-sell client. Highly characteristic of the 1950s. Quotation from Milton with reference to 'liberty'. Visual pun for 'Liberty' bell. USA 1953 Bradbury Thompson

Bicycle. The defiance of gravity and feeling of personal freedom and mobility characterise the bicycle. These qualities together with its strong compositional value account for its popularity among painters (Leger, Robert Medley et al) and designers. In the early days of bicycling it was closely associated with certain aspects of female liberation.

SUBSTITUTION *of typography for wheels. USA 1954 Gene Federico*

A visual metonymy: the bicycle represents the postman who was the hero of the film Jour de Fête. *UK 1962 Norman Vertigan*

One of a series of posters for a bookshop. The city mentioned is the City of London which is symbolised by the traditional City dress: BOWLER HAT *and* UMBRELLA. *The penny-farthing supports the Dickensian 'City of London' theme. UK 1963 John Sewell*

Ironic comment on 20th century youth: long hair and bicycle. Bicycle as a symbol for out-of-dateness. USA 1965 André François

Binoculars. Binoculars, in common with other optical instruments, enable us to be in two places at once. This apparently magical phenomenon is often an early childhood experience. See also MICROSCOPE, PERISCOPE, TELESCOPE.

Bird. Like the rest of the animal world, historically individual birds have been used as symbols throughout history and in many cultures. The dove is a symbol for the Holy Ghost. Because of its nature it is associated with gentleness and therefore peace. The stork is a symbol of fertility and parental affection. The eagle is a symbol of authority and power and has been used by various countries to represent nationhood. It is often depicted imperialistically straddling the world. In general birds have an affectionate hold on the imaginations of designers and poster artists partly for these symbolic attributes and partly for their graphic flexibility. See birds by name.

Symbol for Lufthansa. The design has remained unaltered since its inception.
Germany 1919 Otto Firle/Walther Mackenthun

Transition from fine art Vorticism *to commercial poster art. Key work in the development of graphic design's formal processes. Although this was done as a painting, it was bought by the* Daily Herald *who added lettering and chose to be associated with its modernity.*
USA 1919 McKnight Kauffer

Original design for Imperial Airways, later taken over by BOAC and then by British Airways.
UK 1932 Theyne Lee-Elliott

Textile birds demonstrate popular use of this image in the 1940s.
UK 1949 Ettinger

Uses the universal association with the PHOTOGRAPHER *of 'watch the birdie' request.*
France 1950 André François

Exhibition poster for artist's work.
France 1956 Braque

Substitution of three birds (free-wheeling, extemporising) for three friends.
USA 1957 Robert Guidi

Bite. A popular graphic device which is usually life-size and indicates consumption of food or its typographical equivalent.

Life-size slices of bread are eaten.
USA 1953 Robert Gage

The typographic version is eaten.
UK 1963 Sidney King

Black. See COLOUR SYMBOLISM.

Blackboard. A natural graphic field with its accompanying chalk marks giving a feeling of immediacy. It often has an educational reference and occasionally a 'spelling it out' connotation as in the presentation of facts of national importance.

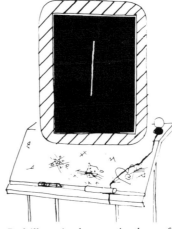

Book illustration demonstrating the use of graphic marks on graphic marks.
USA 1962 Paul Rand

Originally called 'Virgin Teacher' (symbolised by new white blackboard chalk).
UK 1974 Martin Causer

Blackmail Lettering. A COLLAGE of lettering where each character is cut from a different source and pasted down. It is invariably used (as in film credit titles) when the subject matter is appropriate. Quite often used purely as a stylistic device.

Record sleeve.
USA 1958 Ivan Chermayeff

Random forms gathered from random sources for an exhibition of 'Random Sculpture'.
USA 1965 Bob Gill

Bleed. Printed so as to run off one or more edges of the printed page after trimming. Bleeding off photographs in the 1960s was analogous to the use of wide screen imagery in the cinema and the blurring of reality and formal (artistic) constraints in painting and the theatre. (Paintings that became sculpture, performance events and audience participation.) Although bleed has always been a technical device, in the 1960s it was taken to its limits and could produce images close to the paintings of Rothko, Clifford Still et al.

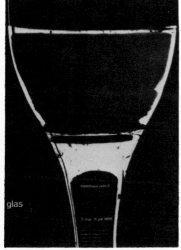

Dramatically bled poster for exhibition of glass. Image is cropped to show near-abstract space similar to the then contemporary American colour-field painters. Switzerland 1952 Carl B. Graf

Blind. A natural surface for typography and display as it can take up as much of the page as necessary, consistent with its habit of going up and down. The characteristic stitching and hand ring identify it. Obviously sexy (voyeuristic) overtones. See also VENETIAN BLIND.

Little blinds on eyes symbolise a blinkered attitude to life. An advertisement for an 'eye-opening' newspaper. USA 1954 Robert Osborn

Suitably provocative copy, '. . . if only you could be seen in lingerie by Ohrbach's'. USA 1946 Paul Rand

Visual euphemism for sexual activity. USA 1956 Saul Bass

Blindfold. A fascinating device, similar to the fancy-dress mask. Mixed associations, partly sinister (kidnapping and executions) and partly lighthearted (party games and conjurors). In advertising it is often associated with the senses other than sight (drinks and perfume). The implication is that the quality is self-evident, that there is no need to see the label. See also GUESS WHO?

Implication is that Le Rouge Baiser may be identified blindfolded. France 1951 René Gruau

Blindman. Represented by the visual shorthand of the dark glasses and white stick.

See also GLASSES (PAIR OF), HEART. UK 1962 Mel Calman

Block. The extreme enlargement of the halftone block. A favourite with Swiss designers for blockmaker or printer clients. Its symbolism is usually reserved for the print or newspaper industry.

Blood. Splashes, blots (see BLOT) and dribbles, particularly printed in red (see COLOUR SYMBOLISM) have an alarming similarity to the real thing. A useful euphemism.

Blot. The Stephens ink blot was a dynamic feature of pre-war advertising in British railway stations. The psychological effect is one of immediacy. See also BLOOD.

Advertisement for an advertising agency. Copy says 'CPV makes an art of blowing other people's trumpets' (see TRUMPET). The blots create a graphic dynamic. France 1956 André François

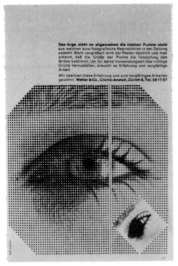

Stamp issued at the time of 'Enosis' in Cyprus registered a political protest against the British. 1954 Collection: Crosby/Fletcher/Forbes

Advertisement for a blockmaker. See also EYE. Switzerland 1936 Max Bill

Trademark for a process engraver. Switzerland 1960 Gerstner + Kutter

Trademark for a process engraver. Switzerland 1960 Hanscheini Pidoux

For an article on road deaths. UK 1964 Derek Birdsall

Spread from The Bald Prima Donna *by Eugene Ionesco. Use of blot to create new typographical dynamic. France 1965 Robert Massin*

Blue. See COLOUR SYMBOLISM.

Blueprint. Symbol of architecture and building generally. The word blueprint is often used in the more abstract sense of a plan for living.

War poster for use in factories to tell the workers the value of their labour. See also SCROLL. UK 1943 Pat Keely

Body. The ultimate graphic cliché. Due to the so-called permissiveness of the 1970s the gratuitous representation (photographic) of the body, especially the female form, has reached epidemic proportions. As with the BABY the body has been used to advertise everything, justified by the most tenuous copy lines. The graphic representation of the human body constitutes about 90 per cent of communication imagery from its iconic use (ROAD SIGN etc) to the expression of all human activities and emotions. See parts of body by name.

Early use of naked body in perfume advertisement.
Germany circa 1925 Errell

SEX *is taken out of the garage (traditional reserve of girlie calendars) and into the executive suite.*
UK 1964 Derek Birdsall

Body Language. The various attitudes of the face and body that are immediate visual signals for emotions, pain, requests, invitations and so on. They form an unspoken visual language and complex ideas can be expressed through them. See parts of body by name.

Characteristic attitudes of delivering a secret and listening. The typography is virtually a DOTTED LINE. *Hand gesture is identical in both.*
USA 1956 Herb Lubalin

Anti-noise poster.
Switzerland 1957 Müller-Brockmann

The typical gesture requesting silence.
USA 1959 Hal Davis

Immediate signal for supplication. A last resort 'divine-guidance' attitude.
USA 1965 George Lois

Body Painting. Body painting in graphic design in the 1960s echoed the current 'hippy' fad. See also PROJECTED IMAGE, TATTOO.

Daisy trademark (see DAISY) painted on model. Cosmetic advertisement.
UK 1964 Tom Wolsey

Poster for Penguin Books. See also STRIP-CARTOON STYLE.
UK 1965 Alan Aldridge

Life-size, full-colour mailing shot for the Art Director's Club, New York.
USA 1966 Tom Daly

Bolt. See NUT (AND BOLT).

Bondage. In general a symbol for captivity. The sexual fetish is permitted in fashion and advertising, though remaining socially unacceptable.

A visual realisation of the headline.
USA 1957 Norman Gollin

Advertisement for alligator shoes. Copy says, 'Andrew Geller captures an alligator – and unleashes a new shoe rarity . . .'
USA 1963 Gennaro Andreozzi

Fashion advertisement.
USA 1966 Henry Wolf

Book illustration, 'The parcel'.
Germany 1970 Hans Hillman

Book. The image of the book has strong elitist associations of learning, authority and high culture. Highly-wrought leather bindings emphasise these associations. The closed book has the same psychological effect as the closed BOX, hinting at unknown riches or surprises.

It's so hard to KNOW

Advertisement for Time *magazine. Copy says, 'It's so hard to know'. The image demonstrates the intensely concentrated character of the book.*
USA 1957 Jack Wolfgang Beck

Bookmark. Symbol for idea of selection or choice. A natural habit in book reader is given a visual significance.

 a Penguin Book 5/-

Chosen Words

Reality becomes the symbol. See also END VIEW.
UK 1960 Derek Birdsall

Book on Book. A sophisticated graphic joke, and an example of graphic tautology.

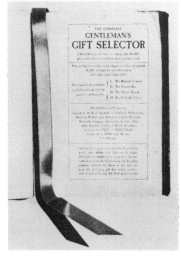

Page on a page.
USA 1956 Henry Wolf

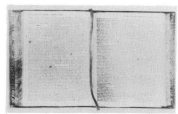

Advertisement for book.
USA 1961 Otto Storch

Double-spread on a double-spread.
UK 1964 Roy Carruthers

Boomerang. Apart from its use as a symbol for Australia, its springy shape made it a popular graphic device in the 1940s and 1950s, quite devoid of any literal meaning. Its shape was echoed in the painting of the period and the then popular Scandinavian furniture (kidney-shaped tables, etc).

Typical of the popular use of this graphic device.
Switzerland 1955 Fritz Bühler

The graphics reflect the formal obsession in the furniture of the 1950s.
USA 1955 Herbert Matter

Boot. Wide range of symbolic meaning according to type. For instance, military, sport, fashion or Christmas (Santa Claus) associations.

Poster promoting football pools. Switzerland 1959 Herbert Leupin

Jackboot as a symbol of repression. See also SWASTIKA. *UK 1969 David Pelham*

Border. An obsession shared with colour-field painters like Stamos, Yves Klein, Rothko. A device whereby the field of white paper is activated and accentuated.

Photographer's letterhead based on the characteristic notched border of sheet film. USA 1957 Robert Brownjohn

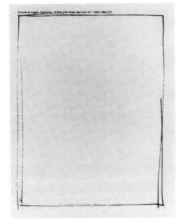

Letterhead with sketched border reflects one of the formal obsessions of the current fine art scene. USA 1965 William McCaffery

Bottle. Apart from its obvious use in advertising drink, it is often used to symbolise a particular life style. For instance a champagne bottle expresses the idea of affluence, milk bottle with a straw at one time in Britain would have expressed school, a coke bottle might symbolise youth or even US imperialism due to its universality. See also CORK.

Opening page in Esquire *for sophisticated (hence champagne) short story. See also* LABEL, SCRIPT. *USA 1956 Jerome Kuhl/Henry Wolf*

Bookjacket, 'Is there life after birth?'. UK 1963 Neil Godfrey

Champagne bottle as a launching symbol.
Copy says 'Europeans on the move'.
See also LOCOMOTIVE.
USA 1965 André François

Characteristic medicine bottle (tonic) with
surreal BOUQUET *as a symbol for euphoria.*
USA 1965 Arnold Varga

Bottle Top (Bottle Cap). The simplicity of its manufacture gives it the unmistakable characteristic look. This sort of functionalism in mundane objects endears them to designers. Naturally associated with the drink industry but also a compelling image in its own right, due partly to its high recognition value.

USA 1958 Brownjohn, Chermayeff &
Geismar

See also PARODY.
Poland 1969 Roman Cieslewicz

Bottom. The natural prurience of male designers in wishing to create images of the female bottom can only reasonably be contained within the constraints of trouser advertising. The ingenuity in breaking these boundaries is itself a cliché of modern advertising.

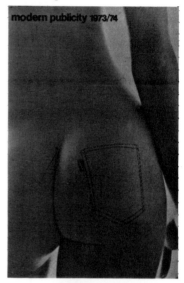

Advertisement for form-fitting Levis. See
also STITCHING.
Germany 1972 Designer unknown

Bouquet. A gift, a token of love, gratitude or success. See also FLOWERS.

Bouquet as a symbol of success. (Flowers
to the victor.)
Switzerland 1951 Herbert Leupin

'You will also love Dulaine.' Bouquet as a token of love.
France 1961 Savignac

Bow. Like the BOOMERANG, it had a fascination for designers in the 1940s and 1950s purely as a stylistic device (see also IMAGES OF MOVEMENT, with which it is closely associated). Used as a symbol for remembrance when tied around a finger. The lovers' knot association derives from the plaited girdles of Greek brides. (Plaited= interwoven= affection.)

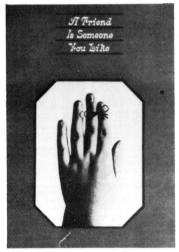

Page from an experimental magazine for children.
USA 1962 Henry Wolf

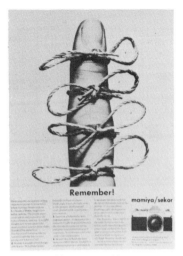

Bow around finger as an aid to memory. (Four bows equals four points to remember when buying a camera.)
USA 1965 Louis Danziger

Typewriter ribbon with third correction strip (typewriter called 'Editor') in obsessive bow shape.
Italy 1967 Giovanni Pintori

Bow as a moebius strip which forms a continuous surface for infinite walking.
USA 1976 Arnie Levin

Bow and Arrow. The bow and ARROW complement each other. Traditional symbol of the hunt. Apollo, Diana and Eros among other gods and goddesses are represented with bows and arrows. Strongest association today is with Eros and his human targets of love.

Bow and arrow as a symbol of penetration into countryside.
UK 1949 Hans Schleger

Bowler Hat. Sometimes a symbol for England or Great Britain, particularly in the fiscal or business area. It sometimes has a more general connotation of bureaucracy. See also CAP, HAT.

Stuffed bird as a symbol of extinction is an ironic comment on the title. The bowler hat and brief-case are symbols of officialdom. UK 1965 Mel Calman

Bow Tie. Indicative, when black or white, of extreme formality. When spotted they have avuncular overtones. Clowns when they use them as absurd props are turning the established order on its head. A strong formal device.

Wrapped lozenge (for sore throats) becomes a visual pun for bow-tie (which has happy jaunty associations). Switzerland 1966 Celestino Piatti

Box. The feminine principle of containing which can refer both to the unconscious and to the maternal body. A fundamental graphic device with strong psychological overtones (as in Pandora's box). See also BAG, BASKET, CASE, CUBE, DUSTBIN.

Virtually a kit of parts to grab the attention and titillate the senses. Basically a Jack-in-the-box with a SEAL substituted for Jack. See also JUGGLER. USA 1945 Paul Rand

A visual simile: the VW van is as capacious and as practical as a box. USA 1964 Bernie Rowe

Boxer. The lone aggressor or defender of mythic proportions. The defender represents and carries the aspirations and fears of the crowd. The essential one to one contest is analogous to other situations or states like electioneering or marriage.

Boxing as an analogy for the gentle art of marriage. See also BOW-TIE. UK 1962 Mel Calman

Boxing Glove. Often used as a surprise element. The word punch is commonly used in advertising and considered a desirable quality. Applied to things with power like petrol.

Aggressive communication symbol. Boxing glove symbolises hard-sell as opposed to the soft-sell of the blooming ROSE. Advertisement for an advertising agency. USA 1958 Norman Gollin/Tommy Mitchell

Bra. The design of bras and corsets strongly reflects the ethos of the particular period. They share common characteristics with car styling (fetish and fantasy masquerading as function). This is alluded to by painters like Richard Hamilton and picked up again by popular draughtsmen like Tomi Ungerer. Any article of female wear which is constraining is inevitably erotic.

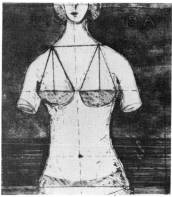

The Libra sign (see ZODIAC) as a visual pun for a bra. See also SCALES. UK 1975 Donna Muir

Braces (Suspenders). The associations are with hard work. One literally takes off the jacket and exposes the underpinnings, a strong signal for getting down to business. The stereotype workman is already wearing them. The formal interest lies in the crossing over at the back and the three inverted forked emblems which attach to the trousers.

Double agents. Braces as a joining device. Poster advertising artists' agents.
USA 1966 Tomi Ungerer

Image that demonstrates the fascination (shared by clowns and illustrators) for men wearing large trousers. See also RUSSIAN DOLL.

UK 1967 Angela Collins

Bracket. A typographic device which shares formal qualities with the hunter's bow but whose semantic significance is indeterminate.

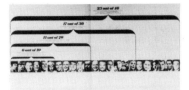

Brackets express groupings of popularity ratings.
USA 1961 Lou Dorfsman/Al Amato

Bracket as symbol for the family.
UK 1975 Philip Thompson

Brain. The characteristic side elevation popular as a symbol for whatever part of the brain is referred to: memory, reasoning, imagination, 'brain-washing', etc. See also CRANIUM.

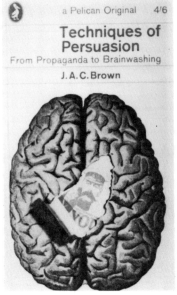

Brain and KITCHENER *image.*
UK 1963 Germano Facetti

Branding Marks. Proprietary marks by which movable property and livestock are distinguished.

Credit titles for the film Cowboy *consisting of branding marks.*
USA 1962 Saul Bass

Breasts. The life-giving milk of the human breast is one of the principal themes in the representation of woman in art from the caveman onwards. The concept of the eternal mother figure is conspicuous in pagan and Christian cultures from the Egyptian goddess Anouke to the Madonna and Child. The interest in the breast in our own time is largely erotic or aesthetic. The gratuitous representation of breasts to sell ideas and products unrelated to their prime significance (bra manufacturers excepted) is a contemporary phenomenon.

UK 1956 André François

A 'reductio ad absurdum' reminds us of the breasts' function.
UK 1956 André François

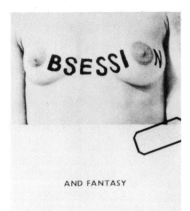

The obsession is made flesh. See also
SUBSTITUTION.
UK 1960 Robert Brownjohn

Brick. A basic building unit. The dimensional ratio of length to width to depth $(1, \frac{1}{2}, \frac{1}{3})$ is infinitely satisfying and accounts for its obsessional use by designers and by sculptors like Carl André. Any basic unit capable of infinite development is a natural symbol for man-made growth. As well as a symbol for building a real environment it is also applicable to abstract concepts like building a relationship.

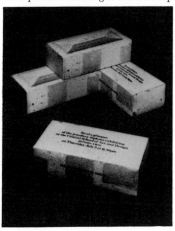

Three-dimensional bricks as an invitation to a jewellery exhibition.
UK 1974 Carole Ingham

Brick Wall. It is sometimes used as an impasse or an unyielding problem. It also suggests a denial of the senses (bricked-up eyes, ears, etc.). Used in the film *Walkabout* as a symbol of boredom. Its simple repetition and mathematically satisfying proportions partly account for its fascination.

Open your eyes and say "ah!"

Copy says 'Open your eyes' (to the advantages of advertising in Time *magazine). See also* CIGAR, GLASSES (PAIR OF).
USA 1964 Tomi Ungerer

A brick wall as a symbol for a non-communicating marriage.
UK 1972 Mel Calman

Record sleeve for Wonderwall.
UK 1970 Bob Gill

Brief as Image. The device of using a facsimile of the client's brief is one of the many such 'non design' solutions which were characteristic of the 1960s.

LETTER *from client to designer requesting an advertisement and explaining its purpose. Letter was marked-up and used as artwork.*
UK 1967 Derek Birdsall

Britannia. A symbol for Great Britain often nowadays used as a basis for parody.

Britannia. See also BOWLER HAT, TRIDENT.
UK 1972 Arthur Robbins

Brush. A Japanese symbol for purification. The idea of a fresh start is sometimes visually expressed through the image of the brush. The particular image of a paint brush is a hardy symbol for ART.

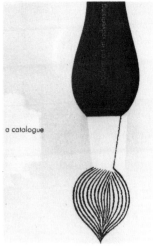

Brush as a symbol for art.
USA 1946 Paul Rand

Symbol for a summer sale. Copy reads 'Tomorrow is clean-up day . . .'
USA 1959 Arnold Varga

Building. The portrayal of a specific building can symbolise particular places, activities or ideas. Big Ben symbolises London; Le Moulin Rouge symbolises a whole epoch.

For an article on prohibition in America. See also DOME.
UK 1956 Mark Boxer

USA 1958 Ben Shahn

A building as a symbol of the de-humanising effect of office routine.
UK 1967 Frank Dickens

A drawing that literally describes McLuhan's concept of the tools of technology as physical extensions of man. Belgium 1968 Folon

A fusion of church and cinema. Cover copy says, 'The New Movies: Faith of Our Children'. USA 1970 George Lois/Carl Fischer

Bull. Symbol of strength and fertility. Associated with kingship in ancient Egypt. To some extent it still symbolises authority and power. The bull is sometimes used by heavy industry, such as construction companies, as a symbol of strength and reliability. Unofficial symbol for Spain.

Poster for beef cubes. France 1931 Leonetto Coppiello

For a film on the life of matador, Manolete. USA 1957 Ben Shahn

Bullet. As the nature of advertising is basically aggressive, the use of a bullet as a visual symbol is compulsive even when the context is not warlike. See also GUN.

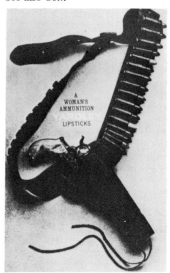

The copy uses phrases like 'A woman's ammunition' and 'sure-fire lipsticks' which underline the aggressive and hunting nature of courtship and sexual attraction. The lipstick and bullet is a visual pun. UK 1960 Angela Landels

Bullet Holes. When the subject matter is appropriate a spray of bullet holes is a convenient graphic device by virtue of its elementary form and its random disposition. The popular market sometimes demands frayed edges and in extreme cases real holes.

'Real' bullet holes for a novel. USA 1945 Paul Rand

Bullet Holes continued

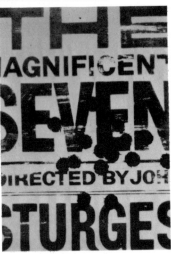

USA 1960 Saul Bass

Bullfighter. An exclusively Spanish image. Although a symbol of great complexity at the centre of a life and death struggle its associations are almost exclusively humorous or to do with tourism.

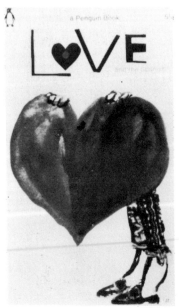

Loving HEART doubles as matador's (Spanish symbol) cape.
France 1964 André François

Bullhorn. See MEGAPHONE.

Burnt Paper. Disturbing because of its verisimilitude. See also TORN PAPER.

After printing and trimming the piles of various items of stationery were actually burnt with a blow torch.
UK 1967 Crosby/Fletcher/Forbes

Appropriately burnt poster for sculpture exhibition.
USA 1969 Sam Smidt

Bus. The Greyhound bus has strong associations with personal freedom. The British double decker has strange and mixed associations: it is partly a house on wheels; the passengers a self-contained community that temporarily submit to the conductor's authority. A favourite with children and designers.

Workers' bus as an early morning symbol.
France 1960 André François

Bust. A symbol of antiquity and therefore culture and ART. See also COLUMN.

Bust as a symbol of high art.
USA 1964 Milton Glaser

Butterfly. Because of its variegation a popular symbol for accuracy in blockmaking and dye transfers. Often used as a symbol of elusiveness (hence, cannot pin it down) or transience because of the creature's characteristics in the natural world.

Peripatetic butterfly as a symbol for travel.
Italy 1930 Augusto Giacometti

Poster for London Transport for summer travel.
UK 1940 Hans Schleger

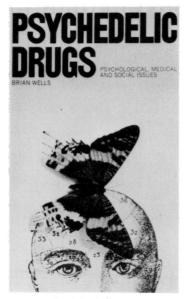

UK 1973 Derek Birdsall

Cover for a collection of French text books entitled Florilège.
France 1975 André François

Button. A general symbol for fashion. (See also BADGE.)

Poster for PKZ men's fashions.
Switzerland 1934 Peter Birkhauser

The new I. Miller Salon at Henri Bendel
invites you to tea and to see
the Spring Shoe Collection of David Evins,
our great American designer,
informally modeled with
American designer costumes from Henri Bendel
...this Tuesday afternoon,
April 9th,
from three to five ... Do come!
I. Miller at Henri Bendel,
10 West 57th Street

Invitation to a fashion show.
USA 1957 Andy Warhol

Cage. When occupied by a bird or similar caged animal it is sometimes an ANALOGY for man and his environment. A natural symbol for captivity or some such circumscribed activity. (See also PRISON CELL.)

An example of the popular use of the birdcage as a sophisticated domestic symbol in the 1940s and 1950s.
USA 1954 Andy Warhol

Bird bursting through restraining cage as a symbol for relief from pain.
Italy 1956 Franco Grignani

Cake. Symbol for celebration. See also CANDLE.

10th anniversary issue.
USA 1956 Paul Rand

20th anniversary poster for an airline. A fusion of celebration symbol with aeroplane runway.
UK 1967 Minale/Tattersfield

Cake Diagram (Pie Diagram). A useful 100 per cent device. More dynamic and self-contained than BAR DIAGRAM.

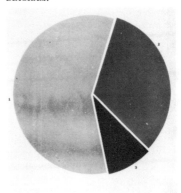

'Only Interiors reaches the Big Three in the Interior market : 1 Interior designers 2 Architects 3 Industrial designers.' An advertisement for selling space in Interiors magazine.
USA 1958 Designer unknown

Calendar. Popular image consistent with man's concern for temporal matters (see CLOCK/WATCH). The characteristic tear hole marks or the wooden version with side winders is often featured. See also DATE.

A January issue of Fortune magazine looking towards the year ahead.
USA 1959 Walter Allner

Mailing shot forecasting special issues of a magazine. *See also* TORN PAPER.
UK 1961 Colin Forbes

Calibrations. Superimposition of measurements or numbers on photograph.

FACE *divided into blockmaker's screens (55, 65, etc).*
USA 1957 Sylvester Brown

Calipers. Historically an emblem for builders and masons. Used symbolically for the concept of assessment in the general sense. Blake depicts God the Father drawing up his Divine Plan with a pair of calipers.

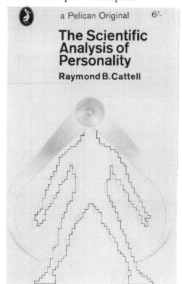

UK 1960 Frederick Price

Calligraphy. Literally, beautiful HANDWRITING. *See also* SCRIPT.

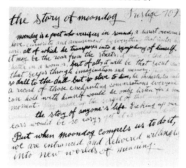

Elegant, informal handwriting by a non-professional.
USA 1957 Andy Warhol's Mother

Poster handwritten by artist.
Spain 1959 Picasso

Self-effacing pseudonym for designer.
UK 1960 Hans Schleger

Catalogue cover.
USA 1960 George Tscherny

Camel. A symbol for self-sufficiency. The cigarette pack is used as a basis for parody.

Camera. Sometimes used as an EYE substitute.

Trademark for Zeiss. Based on a side elevation of a standard lens.
1903 Designer unknown

Metamorphosis of CBS 'eye' into camera diaphragm demonstrating the morphological relationship. The diaphragm has since become a hardy symbol for photographers. See also TRADEMARK MANIPULATION.
USA 1952 William Golden

'I see Irving Penn as a Cyclops . . .' See also EYE, PHOTOGRAPHER.
USA 1962 Robert Osborn

Fusion of photographer's symbol (camera) and designer's symbol (BRUSH).
UK 1966 Alan Aldridge/Lou Klein

Camouflage. A characteristic graphic device (as in zebras and aeroplanes). It is part of the hiding, teasing and covering up obsession which habitually fascinates children, artists and designers. See also MASK, WRAPPING UP.

Copy says, 'Perfect dye transfers matching the original . . .' (Blue DOT background, one woman in blue dots, other in red dots.)
UK 1966 Bob Gill

USA 1974 Seymour Chwast

Can. A strong visual image with many of the qualities of the BOX. See also BAG, BASKET, CASE, DUSTBIN.

CBS 'eye' fused with film spool. The symbol becomes a film can.
USA 1958 William Golden

Our portfolio takes 18½ minutes.

The can containing film as a symbol for the industry. Advertisement for a film company.
UK 1961 Bob Gill

Promotional kit for NBC Television network. See also LABEL.
USA 1964 William Weinstein

Life-size bronze of can of brushes.
USA 1960 Jasper Johns

Silk screen print.
USA 1965 Andy Warhol

The heading, 'The final decline and total collapse of the American avant-garde' equates the avant-garde with Andy Warhol's paintings of Campbell's soupcans. A new symbol for modern art is thus minted. Meanwhile Warhol drowns (the final decline) in his own soupcan.
USA 1969 George Lois

Tin can as a general symbol for marketing. See also MAP.
UK 1969 Derek Birdsall

Cancellation Marks. The rubbing out, smudging or striking out of marks has a peculiar fascination for painters and designers. Instinctively understood.

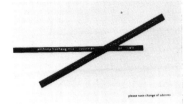

Change of address card. Design as an essential economy; cancelling out the old red heading with typographically dominant black.
UK 1952 Anthony Froshaug

Current obsession in graphics for vast areas of space that echoed the colour-field paintings of Yves Klein, Rothko, et al, of the period. See also CONSPICUOUS WASTE.
UK 1962 Tom Wolsey

Sigmund Freud is discredited with a SCRIBBLE.
UK 1973 John McConnell

ANTHONY ARBLASTER

ACADEMIC FREEDOM

The sociologist as ▮▮▮▮ in the employ of his employers is precisely a kind of ▮▮. The proper exercise of the profession is all too often ▮▮▮▮▮▮ from the proper ▮▮▮▮▮ of espionage only in the relatively greater electronic ▮▮▮▮▮▮ of the latter's techniques.

The sub-copy for the book was censored. The censored words appear on the back.
UK 1973 Philip Thompson

Universally accepted ROAD SIGN.
UK 1963 Jock Kinneir

Candle. Symbol for celebration, thanksgiving. Sometimes used as a symbol for the idea of time passing. See also CAKE.

Christmas card.
UK 1956 Tom Eckersley

Burning candle as a symbol for the passing of time.
UK 1973 Derek Birdsall

Cannon/Cannon Balls. A popular battle symbol. The pyramid of cannon balls is a characteristic image.

The cannon is implicit in the triangle of cannon balls. See also DOVE.
USA 1974 Ivan Chermayeff

Canvas. The image of canvas on a stretcher, preferably the back view, is a convenient field for messages. A symbol for ART.

Fusion of art symbol (canvas stretcher) with domestic symbol (HOUSE) for Domestic Arts Exhibition.
France 1954 Francis Bernard

Cap. Useful as a class-defining object from schoolboy to street musician. (PLAN VIEW of cap with coins.) See also HAT.

Cap as a condensed image symbolising a public servant (see SERVANT).
France 1963 Savignac

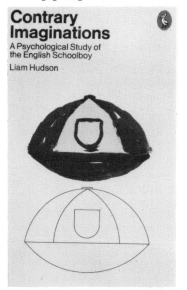

Symbol for school. The contrast in academic specialisations (arts versus science) is expressed in the graphic treatment.
UK 1974 Jones/Thompson/Ireland

Capital Out of Error. The use of obviously bad registration, camera shake, mis-spelling or any other 'error' to express an idea (sometimes verbal) connected with it.

Change of address card.
USA 1959 Gene Federico

Highlighting a detail (by keeping it in sharp focus) while the main image is blurred. See also KISS.
USA 1961 Art Kane

Car. The car has greatly influenced much that man is and does in the 20th century. Sometimes used to symbolise a particular life-style, for instance a Rolls Royce suggests affluence, a sports car feckless youth.

Logical link between two objects that travel. Copy says 'All goes well in Bata shoes'.
Switzerland 1951 Herbert Leupin

Artist's vision of man overtaken by the environment. See also EYE, FACE, HAT, TARGET.
Belgium 1965 Folon

Card Index. Symbol for classification, order and bureaucracy.

Cards. The language of playing cards is part of a universal culture with great symbolic meaning. The red suits represent the warmth and powers of light; the black the cold and powers of darkness. The four designs are life symbols: the spade is a leaf; the heart, the life force; the diamond, the feminine principle; the club, the masculine principle. The Ace is the single original unit, the King, Queen, Knave, among other things represent the Father, Mother and the Ego. The joker represents the spirit of the alchemists. Because of their complex symbolism and varied interpretations the graphic representation of cards has great power. See also GAMES.

Early use of sophisticated graphic imagery applied to mass-market books.
USA 1952 Jerome Kuhl

Playing card KING *as a symbol of the best. See also* CROWN.
Switzerland 1952 Herbert Leupin

The luck referred to in the copy is symbolised by the playing card motif.
USA 1954 Bradbury Thompson

A reminder of the club's origin. It immediately establishes the primitive relationship.
Italy 1954 Riccardo Manzi

The combination of the ace's formal and verbal meaning (excellence) is irresistible. As with other playing cards it is ideal for palindromic solutions (see PALINDROME). *Historically the ace of spades fills the entire space and is highly decorated. It is also a symbol of death. See* GRAFFITI, REBUS, SUBSTITUTION.
UK 1970 Robert Brownjohn

Marital Breakdown

J. Dominian

The archetypal mother and father figures
are torn apart.
UK 1973 Patrick McCreeth

Carousel. See ROUNDABOUT.

Carrot. A literary and visual symbol
for incentive, either with or without
the donkey.

Large carrot is an incentive to buy seed
packets. Typical attitude of prizewinner.
See also HYPERBOLE.
France 1958 Savignac

Poster.
USA 1967 Tomi Ungerer

UK 1974 Derek Birdsall

Case. The special significance of the
BOX and CAN is shared with the case.
An advantage of the case is that it
echoes the edges of the printed sheet
while leaving the inside free for
written messages. The case is very
closely associated with the owner; it
carries his clothes, documents, tools of
trade, secrets. The closed case is a
very potent image. The open case
symbolises the revealing of secrets or
the sharing of a confidence. See also
BAG, BASKET, DUSTBIN.

A primitive case; the knotted
handkerchief that holds the worldly goods
of the hopeful traveller.
UK 1898 John Hassall

Poster for cigarettes. The thing contained becomes the container.
France 1956 Savignac

Poster for a film festival. A fusion of suitcase and film sprocket image (see FILM*). See also* FLAG, LUGGAGE LABEL. *USA 1960 Saul Bass*

Cover for music book. See also KIT LAYOUT. *USA 1961 Seymour Chwast*

Poster for graphics exhibition. See also BORDER. *UK 1963 Fletcher/Forbes/Gill*

For IBM. An example of visual OXYMORON; *the juxtaposition of opposites, in this case the complexity of the type case with the simplicity of the 'golf ball' head. USA 1966 Bob Salpeter*

Shared marital suitcase torn apart. UK 1974 Mel Calman/Philip Thompson

Cash Register. A symbol for the retail trade.

See also FIST, STAR. *UK 1973 Mel Calman/Philip Thompson*

Castellation. The idea of a fortification is often used by firms concerned with impregnability and reliability like insurance companies and banks. Used too by the wine trade because of its chateau associations.

Cat. Symbol of independence, fashion, domesticity, etc according to the breed of cat depicted. Any characteristic can be referred to including the myths of seeing in the dark and having nine lives.

Poster for electric light bulbs. Based on the myth that a cat sees in the dark.
Holland 1920 L. Kalf

Advertisement to attract shoe advertisers. Cat as a substitute for elegant model.
USA 1957 Leobruno-Bodi/Richard Loew

Elegant cats are associated with the fashion world. Ohrbach's cat is a substitute for an elegant lady.
USA 1959 Bob Gage

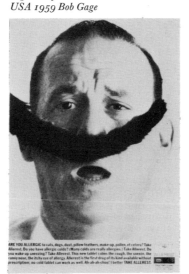

Part of cat (tail) to symbolise an allergy.
USA 1962 George Lois

Traditional night-locale for cats emphasised.
France 1963 André François

Characteristic cat's eye (lens) substituted for head.
France 1965 André François

Cats have an inevitable and logical association with windows. They are either looking into the house or looking out. See also ALBUM.
France 1966 André François

Cell. Biological structure. Transferred to the field of sociology it is an accepted symbol for the idea of community or socialisation. The HONEYCOMB structure supports the general idea of community.

A book about the socialisation of teaching.
UK 1974 Philip Thompson

Cellular structure makes up the city plan of Rotterdam.
Holland 1974 Total Design

Certificate. Symbol for authenticity. Most activities and institutions can be symbolised by using the relevant DOCUMENT as in the hotel industry (the bill) or education (the school report). See also RECEIPT.

Chad (Mr) A British graffiti character (see GRAFFITI) in World War II with the words 'Wot no . . . ?' followed by the item that was in short supply. A thinly veiled phallic drawing. The ubiquitous Kilroy was the American counterpart.

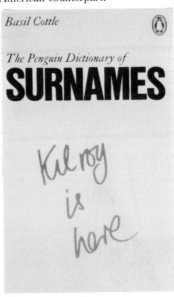

Kilroy crosses the Atlantic.
UK 1979 Penguin Books

Chain. Popular wartime symbol for friendship, solidarity and strength. Also its corollary; 'the weakest link'. Used a lot for heavy industry.

A post-war competition for the United Nations produced a crop of entries with chains, which was at the time a popular symbol for international solidarity.
Sweden 1947 Leif Paulson

TV personality is given a 'free rein'. Broken chain as a symbol of such freedom. See also BALL AND CHAIN.
USA 1948 Paul Rand

Chair. The empty chair is a symbol of great sentiment and power. Sometimes a euphemism for death. (See Luke Fildes' drawing of Dickens' chair after his death.) A symbol for a place; a park seat for a park, a director's chair for a film studio, four empty, anticipatory chairs for a string quartet in a concert hall.

Clothes on chair is a substitute for the person.
Italy 1911 Marcello Dudovich

Four chairs await their owners; the members of a string quartet.
USA 1955 Bob Gill/Tony Palladino

Poster for mineral water. Park chair is a summer symbol.
Switzerland 1956 Herbert Leupin

The film-director's chair is a substitution (metonymy) for Robert Aldrich.
USA 1957 Saul Bass

Kitten on chair establishes the clientèle of dress shop.
Switzerland 1957 Sandro Bocola

Four jazz interpretations symbolised by four chairs.
USA 1957 Herb Lubalin

Copy refers to '. . . the lady in the front row centre'. Coat on chair is a substitution (metonymy) for the person.
USA 1957 Edward Rostock

John F. Kennedy's chair as a EUPHEMISM *for the assassinated man.*
USA 1964 Lou Dorfsman

Characteristic Style. The use of other styles of essentially characteristic typography, etc (seed packets, small ads, telephone directory, soap flake packs, etc), to achieve a particular result.

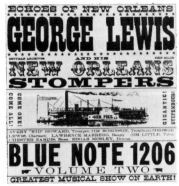

Early use of occulist's board typography.
USA 1953 Peter Adler/Harry Zelenko

Revival of playbill style.
USA 1956 Reid Miles

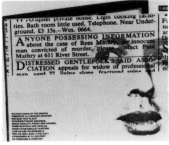

Small-ad style (missing person copy) made elegant.
USA 1957 Tom Courtos/Kurt Weihs

Copy reads, 'Wanted for holding captive a vast radio listening audience . . .' See also MUG SHOT.
USA 1959 Lou Dorfsman/Bert Newfeld/John Alcorn

The style of cinema fascia typography.
USA 1959 Henry Wolf

Small-ad style is used to advertise weekly publication specialising in small-ads.
UK 1965 Philip Meyer

Seed packet style is used to symbolise the allergy.
UK 1967 John Dodson

The style of soap flake packs for a serious book on housewives (see HOUSEWIFE*). UK 1974 Paul McAlinden*

Chess. As with many other board games (see GAMES), a well-established analogy for life, sometimes in its aggressive or even warlike form. The word pawn suggests manipulation but the image is not often visually realised.

Book jacket. UK 1960 Larry Carter

Chess as an analogy for marital strife. (Part of a three-frame strip.) UK 1972 Mel Calman

Children's Bricks (Children's Blocks). Popular as a symbol for primary education. A 1950s cliché for simplicity (literally, it's child's play). Sometimes a symbol for the elementary facts. Naturally used by the building trade but also by investment and money lending firms (building for the future, etc).

For a building corporation. Children's building bricks as a substitute for the real thing. USA 1962 George Tscherny

Children's Writing and Drawing. Sometimes infantilism is a solution especially when the subject matter is appropriate. The advantage of the child's drawing is its directness and lack of design niceties.

Poster for a cigar company. USA 1958 Paul Rand

Bookjacket. UK 1964 Derek Birdsall

Christmas Bauble (Christmas Ornament). Symbol for Christmas.

Fusion of end-sections (see END VIEW*) of* Charm *magazine with Christmas ball image.*
USA 1953 Tom Courtos

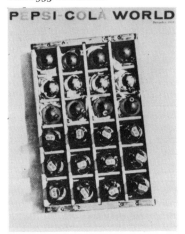

Christmas issue of Pepsi-Cola *magazine. See also* BOX.
USA 1959 Robert Brownjohn

Christmas Stocking. A coloured or decorated STOCKING is a suitable symbol for Christmas. An elegant SACK.

Christmas card. See also KNIGHT.
UK 1960 André François

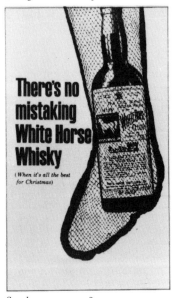

See also GUESS WHO ?
UK 1963 Bob Gill

Christmas Tree. Symbol for Christmas. See also TREE.

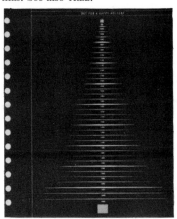

Page from a catalogue of swelled-rules (see RULES*) becomes a Christmas tree.*
USA 1952 Milton Glaser

The tree is also a visual pun for a second bearded SANTA CLAUS.
USA 1956 Paul Rand

Christmas card for a tobacco firm. See also MATCHSTICK, STAR.
USA 1956 Henry Wolf

Cigar. Symbol of affluence (tycoons and gangsters) and Christmas. Its proportions determine the format, the cigar band gives opportunity for decorative relief or message giving.

Card for a group of artists.
USA 1965 Tomi Ungerer

SANTA CLAUS *in international mood. See also* FLAG.
France 1967 Savignac

Cigar as a measurement of affluence.
UK 1975 Brian Delaney

Circle. See GENERAL SIGNS.

Circling Copy. An instinctively produced mark which has been adopted by designers. It attempts to be a perfect CIRCLE but the degree by which it falls short gives it its peculiar characteristic. A symbol for selection.

Advertisement stressing importance of low-priced cars.
USA 1952 Cal Anderson

Advertisement for two magazines. Contents list stressed to support headline, 'Women who want to get away from it all never come to us'.
USA 1963 A.Gargano

Circus. The circus is an enclosed world populated by people who perform precisely defined acts of skill. Because they command attention they are natural agents for the display and selling of merchandise. See circus performers by name.

The sword swallower is a character that belongs to the sideshows of both circus and fairground (see FAIRGROUND STYLE*). Here the inept performer turns the* SWORD *into an instrument of discomfort.*
Belgium 1969 Josse Goffin

Clapper Board. Symbol for the film industry.

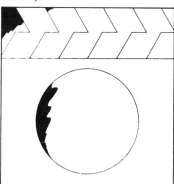

For Elecktra Films.
USA 1965 Milton Glaser/Vincent Ceci

Clock/Watch. For the Western world, since the invention of the first mechanical clock in the 13th century, a symbol of time. McLuhan says that the mechanical clock helps to create the image of a numerically quantified and mechanically powered universe. This obsession with time is reflected in the insistent graphic representation of the clock. As we allow all our activities to accommodate themselves to the clock, the image becomes as compelling and hypnotic as the real object.

Prospectus for an advertising agency.
Holland 1931 Piet Zwart

Poster for London Transport stressing importance of punctuality.
UK 1946 Tom Eckersley

TIME FLIES
WITH
BRITISH SOUTH AMERICAN AIRWAYS

A popular verbal cliché visually realised.
UK 1946 Pat Keely

USA 1956 Henry Wolf

Illustration. Subtle associations with
FATHER TIME, *the reaper.*
Germany 1963 Hans Hillman

IBM

The copy asks, 'How fast is a nano-second?' Presumably too fast for a normal pair of hands. See also HYPERBOLE.
UK 1963 Robert Brooks

School of Visual Arts

The copy begins with Delacroix's 'Art is a clock that moves too fast when measured by the public's sense of time', and literally illustrates it.
USA 1970 Ivan Chermayeff

Clockwork. Mechanically motivated. The childhood fascination of winding up clockwork toys with a KEY is shared by designers. Sometimes the symbolism is concerned with the manipulation of people.

Copy says, 'All wound up about what to give her?' A natural transference from verbal to visual field. See also SPIRAL.
USA 1958 Arnold Varga

Copy says, 'How to wind up a doll for Christmas'.
USA 1962 Onofrio Paccione

Poster for an exhibition of the work of Folon.
USA 1969 Folon

UK 1975 Jones/Thompson

Clothes Peg (Clothes Pin). The associations are varied. In one sense they are highly evocative of country-laundered freshness. The peg which is a mechanical clip is sometimes a symbol for classification. More imaginatively when attached to a person's nose reminds us of the sense of smell.

Cloud. Closely associated with the idea of freedom or creativity. The comic book convention of a cloud for thinking (see THINKS BUBBLE) supports this.

Clouds get a lift down.
USA 1970 André François

Cloud establishes the home of the Deity.
UK 1974 Mel Calman

Clown. The character that literally has a FACE drawn on it, thus capable of expressing the whole spectrum of emotions. Popular with poster artists and designers during the 1940s and 1950s both in the painted and photographic form. See also JUGGLER.

Light bulbs (like clowns) brighten life.
Switzerland 1955 Donald Brun

The clown here is doubling for a STRONG MAN under the influence of strong beer.
France 1958 André François

Coat-hanger. A symbol for fashion.

Coat-hanger as a symbol for fashion is also a visual pun for BIRD (Spring).
USA 1940 Paul Rand

Page from booklet describing the effective use of a process against moth damage.
UK 1956 Jan Le Witt

Coca Cola Bottle. Its unequivocal shape endears it to sculptors, painters and designers. Used widely as a metaphor (often ironic) for the United States of America, particularly in its imperialistic role.

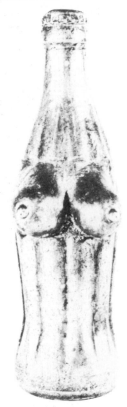

American Nude. *Bronze sculpture.*
See also BREASTS.
USA 1963 Charles Frazier

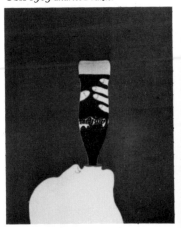

Paris Review *cover by sculptor.*
USA 1967 Marisol

Cock. A compelling symbol because of its configuration as well as its literal associations. Because of its 'cock of the walk' association it has been used commercially as a symbol of supremacy. More ingeniously used to promote newspapers and health salts because of its early morning associations. The advertising industry used to use it to symbolise itself – as in 'crowing'.

DON'T CROW ABOUT···THE THINGS YOU KNOW ABOUT

Wartime poster warning people against divulging secret information. Copy reads, 'Don't crow about the things you know about.' The verbal metaphor 'crow' is visually realised.
UK 1944 Abram Games

Poster for a newspaper. Again the early morning association is referred to.
Switzerland 1956 Herbert Leupin

Traditional French symbol lends itself to a national drink.
France 1920 Marcello Nizzoli

Here the early morning association is referred to.
UK 1925 McKnight Kauffer

Poster using cockerel as announcing agent.
USA 1953 Paul Rand

Poster for a printer specialising in full-colour posters. The multi-coloured and well-registered characteristic of the bird is referred to.
Switzerland 1956 Celestino Piatti

Code. The use of morse, deaf and dumb signs or any other sign system. Some code systems become absorbed into the general stream of communication, others (like tramps' marks or alchemists' signs) remain esoteric.

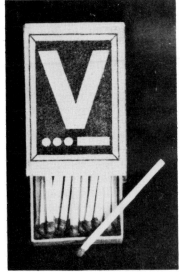

Wartime symbol for victory in letterform and morse code.
UK 1941 Designer unknown

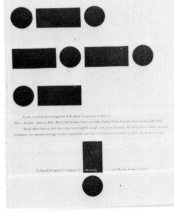

The morse spells out RCA (Radio Corporation of America). See also
EXCLAMATION MARK.
USA 1954 Paul Rand

FLAG *as a code medium. Flags spell out 'Operation peace'.*
USA 1958 Paul Rand

Symbol for nuclear disarmament campaign. The design represents the semaphore for initials N and D. The broken cross represents the death of man and the circle the unborn child.
UK 1956 Gerald Holtom

Beatles spell out Help *in semaphore.*
UK 1965 Robert Freeman

Coffee Pot. Sometimes a symbol for the early morning.

Coffee pot becomes a symbol for morning.
Switzerland 1960 Herbert Leupin

Uncaptioned poster for 'Chat Noir' (Black cat) brand of coffee.
Belgium 1966 Julian Key

Coffin. An unequivocal graphic shape and a compelling symbol for death. The photographic version is sometimes employed to give an added frisson to the sex scene.

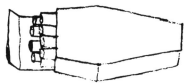

Coffin symbolises the ultimate deterrent.
UK 1968 Mel Calman

Cog. Popular symbol for industry or efficiency or de-humanising influence.

Currently popular industrial symbol becomes a visual pun for FLOWERS.
UK 1947 Tom Eckersley

Copy says, 'Wheels turn (medals are cogs) for the man who smokes Dutch Masters'. Complex fusion of visual/verbal language: wheels turning suggest influence, medals (see MEDAL*) suggest consequent rewards. France 1957 André François*

Collage. Assemblage technique.

Museum of Modern Art catalogue. The design naturally adopts the style it is advertising. See also BLACKMAIL LETTERING.
USA 1962 Ivan Chermayeff

Punch *cover made up of pages torn from the magazine.*
UK 1964 André François

Colour Correction. The techniques and methods of colour-correcting are sometimes applied to the idea of critical assessment of a person. ('Could be less complacent . . .' etc.)

'What Paris could do for the Queen.' Colour-correcting technique applied to beauty advice.
UK 1968 Derek Birdsall

Colouring In. The obsessive use in the last ten years or so of the colouring-in-book device or its derivative, the PAINTING BY NUMBERS device. Sometimes it refers to subject matter relating to childhood, but more usually it is used as a stylistic trick. See also SCRIBBLE.

The enlarged 't' (see INITIAL LETTER) contains a lipstick smear and refers to the copy line 'The language of praise belongs to the heart and the lips'.
USA 1956 Henry Wolf

USA 1960 Robert Brownjohn

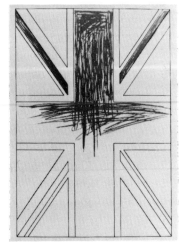

Poster for British Commonwealth artists.
See also UNION JACK.
UK 1962 Barry Bate

Duke Ellington
July 31 to September 2

Poster for the Rainbow Grill. RAINBOW coloured-in on stave lines (see MUSIC STAVE).
USA 1965 William McCaffery

Colour Symbolism.
Black. A symbol of mourning. The traditional graphic colour: graphite, black ink, lithographic chalk, etc. The essential colour of the printed page; the precise quality of black can be discussed in almost spiritual terms. Because of the advance in the last fifteen years of full-colour technology the peculiar qualities of black have not always been fully realised.

A plain black sleeve for a record called Blind Man's Movie. *Both examples recall the extreme paintings of Yves Klein of the 1950s.*
USA 1969 Murray Roman

Blue. Christian symbol of heaven. Symbol of prudence, peace, contemplation. Politically, it has associations with the status quo.

Gold. The ultimate symbol of preciousness, value, wealth and perfection. Curiously, the depiction of the actual colour graphically has little of the verbal associations and due to the ease with which it can be printed has even cheap and nasty connotations.

Green. In language, green is the colour of immaturity (greenhorn), jealousy (Shakespeare's green-eyed monster) and freshness. Graphically it is used to express the idea of natural purity. An ecological action group in America has designed a completely green American flag as a sort of symbol for the idea.

Red. The colour of love, danger, anarchy and the left wing politically. Part of its significance is derived from the colour of blood and fire.

'You're sure to tie him up with Red Tape ...' The name of a new lipstick.
See also BONDAGE.
USA circa 1960 Bob Gage

An example of latter-day Suprematism. Most of the advertisement is printed red. The copy mentions the 'red carpet' tradition of the store.
USA 1964 Arnold Varga

White. Symbol of innocence, chastity, purity and so on. It is also associated with peace, a white FLAG symbolising a truce or surrender.

Yellow. In symbolism it indicates jealousy, inconstancy, cowardice. In medieval painting Judas was depicted in yellow clothes as a symbol of betrayal.

Column. Visual symbol of great potency. To the primitive mind the column (like the TREE) supported the sky, and hence the sky god, Zeus. The idea naturally follows that representation of human beings on columns are godlike. Usually used nowadays (as with similar traditional symbols) in a spirit of parody.

In the history of industrial art (see ART) there is a special place of reverence for classical antiquity. It is loaded with prestigious associations. The Parthenon and not automobile engineering is responsible for the front elevation of the Rolls Royce. Antiquity is also useful as a basis for parody.

Poster for the Times. *A pun on the word column. See also* LAUREL, SMILE.
UK 1960 Abram Games

Rolls Royce in a financial crisis.
UK 1970 Mel Calman

Column (Broken). For the Renaissance the broken column symbolised the demise of civilisation. A symbol of death. Popular in graveyards.

Cigar on column (pedestal). The ultimate in perfection.
USA 1957 Paul Rand

Comb. An object anthropomorphised sufficiently to be deemed useless without 'teeth'. The act of combing in general is highly cultivating and refining (as in the raking of gardens and combing in the textile industry). Apart from its primary use as a tool for personal grooming it has a bonus use as a musical instrument and is indispensable in Hitler impersonations. A symbol for arranging and ordering.

Precise comb is a visual pun for neat hair.
USA 1963 Tomi Ungerer

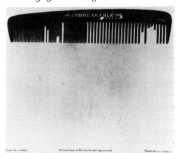

Unbreakable comb with broken teeth is an ironic illustration to the copy, 'Fifteen years of heartache and aggravation'.
USA 1969 Seymour Chwast/Milton Glaser

Compass. A symbol of travel or direction.

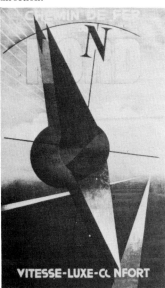

Poster for French Railways. *France 1930 Cassandre*

UK 1957 Ashley Havinden

Compass is simply reinstated as a symbol for geography. UK 1973 Derek Birdsall

Concertina (Musical). Associated with street musicians in general. Unofficially a symbol of French popular music and thus France. Highly evocative and hypnotic due to its undulating form.

Conductor. Tail-coated figure of authority and organisation. The characteristic view is from the back. Overtones of high culture.

Personal Christmas card. Santa Claus conducts dawn chorus from within reindeer's antlers. France 1957 André François

Conductor as a symbol for high culture. USA 1959 Lou Myers

Cone. Basic mathematical model. Symbol for dunce (fool's cap) or magician. See also GENERAL SIGNS.

Confinement. A visual HYPERBOLE. The figure (usually photographic) is put in an extreme environment to express an equivalent verbal hyperbole.

'Can't fit into your budget? Ohrbach will straighten you out.' USA 1960 Bob Gage

Advertisement to encourage expansion by getting a mortgage. USA 1964 Milton Wuilleumier

Conspicuous Economy. Design is an essential economy. Some graphics demonstrate the proposition 'Less is more'.

Typographic condensation. r and n share a common stem with i.
UK 1960 Robert Brownjohn

Conspicuous Waste. A technique which uses apparent waste to advantage. For example paying for a full colour printing on an advertisement or poster and only using it in one small area or a whole page advertisement with only one or two lines of copy.

Copy says 'Think small'. Advertisement for small cars.
USA 1959 Helmut Krone

USA 1960 Lou Dorfsman

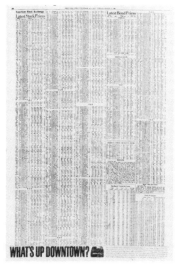

Booking the whole page of a newspaper and 'wasting' the space.
USA 1960 Herb Lubalin

Copy says, 'Our secret ingredient'. An orange honestly symbolises an orange juice drink.
USA 1962 Sidney Myers

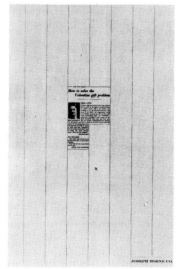

An agony column letter and reply to solving the Valentine gift problem.
USA 1963 Arnold Varga

Constellation. Outer space is a rewarding area for exploration. See also ZODIAC.

Copy says 'They go so fast you can spin off the earth'.
France 1896 Ferdinand Lunel

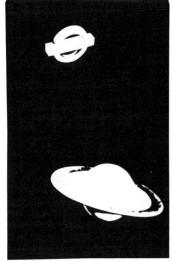

KEEPS LONDON GOING

Copy reads, 'London Transport in the future'. Outer space was almost the only symbol for future development in the 1930s.
UK 1935 Man Ray

Cork. A further condensing of the bottle image (see BOTTLE). For instance, the champagne cork has strong characteristics and can serve as a substitute symbol.

Champagne cork to symbolise affluence.
UK 1960 Larry Carter

Corkscrew. Usually represented with a cork on the end, its symbolism is invariably in the area of celebration (invitations to private views etc). See also SPIRAL.

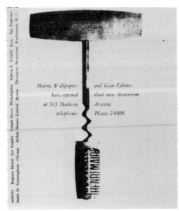

Announcement for convivial opening of new showroom.
USA 1959 Arnold Saks/James Ward

Cover for house organ of a temperance group. Corkscrew and cork, the normal symbol of conviviality is inverted: the reversal of the norm (see ACROBAT).
Finland 1968 Jukka Veistola

Corner. The folded-over corner revealing a glimpse of what lies beneath. Voyeuristic overtones. Much used by girlie magazines.

Film poster.
USSR 1926 Alexander Rodchenko

Advertisement for oriental carpets.
USA 1963 J.A.Parker

Logotype for American Institute of
Graphic Arts.
USA 1965 Herb Lubalin

Corners. Corners in photographic albums (see ALBUM). Used for nostalgic reasons or for personal biographies. Sometimes used to symbolise holidays, another reference to the family photograph album. See also SNAPSHOT.

Cornucopia. Horn of plenty. Symbol of fruitfulness. The horn belongs to the goat or bull which are themselves symbols of fertility. The graphic representation of the cornucopia these days has not much credence except as a basis for parody. A useful shorthand device for cartoonists. See also BASKET, ICE CREAM.

Cotton Reel (Spool). A symbol of fashion.

Fusion of spring FLOWERS symbol and
fashion symbol.
UK 1968 Holmes/Kitley

Couch. A useful shorthand for psychiatrist. Sometimes supported by a CERTIFICATE on the wall.

Psychiatric attitudes.
UK 1961 Bob Gill

UK 1972 Jones/Thompson/Ireland

Counterchange. One of the most elementary of graphic devices and usually discovered instinctively by children.

USSR 1922 El Lissitzky

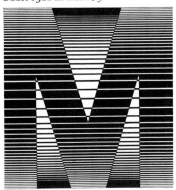

Trademark for firm dealing in high-fidelity recordings. See also INITIAL LETTER. *USA 1958 Brownjohn, Chermayeff & Geismar*

Counting Symbol. A universally accepted device. It derives from the convenience of counting in groups of five.

Art Director's Club of New York 38th Annual Exhibition symbol. USA 1958 Edward Rostock/ R.O.Blechman

Film trademark: The Magnificent Seven. *USA 1960 Saul Bass*

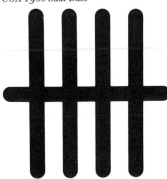

Symbol for a Singapore bank. An appropriate symbol for a bank with bonus associations of Chinese letterforms and security grille. UK 1969 Derek Birdsall

Coupon. As with the BEFORE AND AFTER device and the BANNER a rather unsophisticated one with bargain basement associations. In the 1960s it was revived in a spirit of parody. The SCISSORS and the DOTTED LINE are characteristic adjuncts.

Cradle. The cradle takes over where the LADDER leaves off and is thus associated with high rise buildings. There is usually a dramatic juxtaposition of SCALE (as in the case of painters working on a hoarding). An oddly favourite device which echoes the fascination of the real thing.

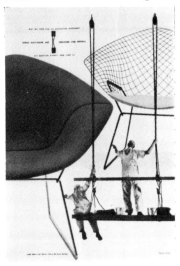

USA 1957 Herbert Matter

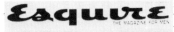

Record cleavage. USA 1963 George Lois

Cranium. The 19th century (now discredited) theory of craniology or phrenology that divided the SKULL into areas corresponding to the brain's capacities (see BRAIN) was responsible for the model and chart which delineated the supposed areas. The designer still makes use of both these forms as a basis for parody.

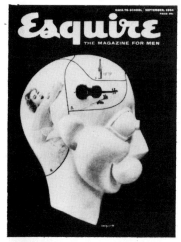

Contents of brain announce contents of magazine.
USA 1954 Henry Wolf

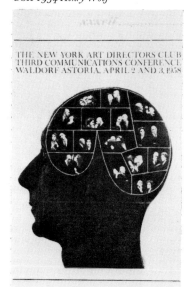

Announcement for communications conference.
USA 1958 Lou Dorfsman/Herb Lubalin

Crate. The rough wooden crate with STENCIL LETTERING is a strong symbol for industry.

See also HOOK.
USA 1953 Giovanni Pintori

See also ARROW.
USA 1959 Frank McCallum

Wooden construction.
USA 1962 Robert Rauschenberg

Creases. See FOLD MARKS.

Crescent. Ancient symbol of the MOON and later adopted by Ottoman Turks. Also a Moslem emblem. The basic shape is one that has great formal appeal. See also MELON.

Crest. A device above the shield on a coat of arms. Symbol of authority, power and excellence. Pseudo-crests are popular with industries where a superior appeal is considered important as in the cigarette and drink trade. Real royal warrants are jealously guarded and usually prominently featured.

Cripple. Archetypal cripples occur in drama and literature – Captain Hook, Captain Ahab, Long John Silver. Their infirmity symbolises their spiritual nature – they have yet to be redeemed. The word crutch in common usage implies an artificial device for support and aid to effectiveness.

Personification of strife-ridden country.
See also BANDAGE.
UK 1970 Mel Calman

Crocodile. Because of the idea that crocodiles cry while devouring their prey, the term 'crocodile tears' means hypocrisy. The cartoonist Low used the crocodile as a symbol for insincerity.

Crocodile's tears of insincerity.
UK 1941 David Low

A graffiti-like handle reminds us of the crocodile's destiny. A verbal/visual linkage. See also CASE.
USA 1963 Frank Kirk

Anthropomorphising the second time around.
UK 1977 Peter Brookes

Cross. Symbol of Christ's death and redemption of mankind, although the symbol is older than Christianity. The basic cruciform is a configuration which appeals to a deep rooted need in mankind. The cross has a multitude of variant forms: the Maltese cross, the double cross of Lorraine, the Egyptian ankh, the SWASTIKA and the ANCHOR being among them. As a pure form it is one of the strongest of compositional structures. It forms the basis of many authoritarian monograms, including the universally recognised Red Cross.

The perfect form of the cross (a union of male and female elements) is a structural basis for this advertisement. See also GENERAL SIGNS.
USA 1945 Paul Rand

Cross of St Andrews for MacFisheries Ltd.
UK 1954 Hans Schleger

Crossroad. Symbol for dilemma or the need for decision.

See also SIGNPOST.
UK 1962 Mel Calman

Crossword. PUZZLE in which words are made to run down and across the page. Sometimes a symbol for reasoning or thinking. Strongly characteristic image.

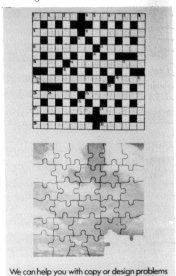

Crossword as a symbol for copy problem.
See also JIGSAW PUZZLE.
UK 1968 Bob Gill

Crowd. The photographic or naturalistically-drawn image of a crowd is as compelling and involving as the real thing. Sometimes allusions are made to the giant patterns composed of live people, popular at totalitarian-state rallies and seen in the choreography of Busby Berkeley.

The crowd as a substitute for the thing seen.
France 1892 Felix Valloton

Admiring crowd obscure the merchandise.
USA 1957 Bob Gage

Drawing of a crowd of art lovers (by Daumier) for an exhibition by Daumier.
UK 1960 Tom Wolsey

The crowd as image – in this case a celebratory BELL *to support the copy 'Happy Birthday USA'.*
USA 1975 George Tscherny

Crown. Symbol of victory and kingship (see KING). In Christian symbolism associated with martyrdom. In general communication the implication is supremacy. In general, headgear is a mark of status from the crown downwards. Laurel leaves are traditionally a victor's crown. Many firms, particularly in the cigarette and drink industry, award themselves crowns and use them as a MONOGRAM. See also CREST.

Crown defines bird.
USA 1958 Jack Wolfgang Beck

Crown establishes status of driver. Literally fit for a king (to drive). See also CARDS, PALINDROME.
Switzerland 1958 Herbert Leupin

INITIAL LETTER *becomes crown to imply the best.*
USA 1960 Paul Rand

Crystal Ball. Symbol for prediction.

UK 1970 Mel Calman

Cube. See GENERAL SIGNS.

Cup (Trophy). A natural prize symbol. It has strong association with the collector who makes gratuitous conquests.

Currency. The representation of coins or paper money is a symbol for private or public economics. A further condensing of information is achieved through the use of currency signs (see DOLLAR SIGN, POUND SIGN).

Small coin (dime or farthing) as letterform. See also SUBSTITUTION.
UK 1973 Derek Birdsall

Fusion of international paper currency with Buckminster Fuller map projection (see MAP).
UK 1973 Philip Thompson

Curtains. An old fashioned symbol for the theatre. Sometimes used to convey the idea of presentation to the public in a more general sense.

Copy says 'Eyes on Paris and America'. The EYE peers through a curtain of gloves.
USA 1959 Henry Wolf

Cut-out. A device derived from the language of children's annuals or magazines (like COLOURING-IN). This is the cutting out of the components of a person or object waiting to be assembled. Sometimes the inclusion of a DOTTED LINE around the object emphasises the device.

Personal Christmas card.
USA 1959 Brownjohn, Chermayeff & Geismar

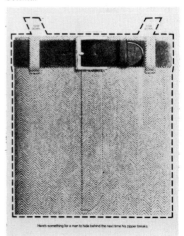

USA 1969 Arnold Varga

Cut-up. A technique where the image is fragmented and sometimes scattered around. As the technique is analogous to dismemberment, in the case of human imagery, the effect can be disturbing. Typographically it sometimes creates a new dynamic devoid of any symbolism.

Cover for Art Direction. The missing letters are the important ones. See also ALPHABET.
USA 1941 Paul Rand

Copy asks, 'Like a piece of Skelton?' to
attract advertisers.
USA 1951 Lou Dorfsman

The fragmented logotype was a
characteristic of the advertising on large
poster hoardings and advertisements.
France 1954 Atelier Charles Loupot

*Image reflects the technique of the film
which analysed and dissected the story.
USA 1959 Saul Bass*

Architectural Review *cover.
UK 1962 Philip Thompson*

Poster for Life *magazine.
USA 1963 Dennis Wheeler*

*Poster.
Italy 1965 Bruno Munari*

Dagger. Like the knife a symbol of
sacrifice, vengeance, death. Because
of its secret nature it has, unlike the
SWORD, associations of treachery.

Record sleeve : Romeo and Juliet,
Hamlet *soliloquies. See also* SKULL.
USA 1951 Erik Nitsche

*Aggressive dagger determines the
imagery. Book jacket for Edgar Allan Poe
stories. See also* SKULL.
Switzerland 1961 Heinz Stieger

Daisy. Symbol of infidelity. In popular usage a general symbol for simplicity, its configuration being the archetypal child's drawing of a flower. Chaucer refers to 'day's eye'.

Advertisement for a perfume. Symbol of indiscretion.
France 1940 Jean Colin

Poster for School of Visual Arts. The copy makes reference to the 'he loves me, he loves me not' theme.
USA 1961 George Tscherny

Dance. The stylised movements and gestures of dances in some cases are all that remain of rituals that once related to fertility, rain-making, crop-growing, etc. The gestures and attitudes of ballroom dancing (about 1920 onwards) although devoid of any precise meaning are very powerful signals. These are constantly referred to by illustrators when wishing to establish the idea of the dance in a normal social setting. The rhetorical gestures of classical ballet have strong associations of high culture.

Dancers symbolise the place and period.
France 1891 Toulouse Lautrec

The attitudes of a fisherman's free-dance movement expresses the idea of holiday happiness. See also BEACH.
UK 1908 John Hassall

See also COMPASS.
France 1952 André François

Dance Diagram. Typical example of functional graphics adopted by the designer. In this case an explanatory diagram is used as a symbol for the activity. See also ARROW.

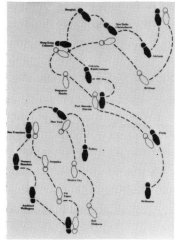

Copy says, 'Teach your manager the kangaroo hop'. An advertisement for Australian airlines.
UK 1970 Minale/Tattersfield

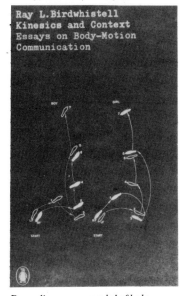

Dance diagram as a symbol of body reactions in social contexts. See also BODY LANGUAGE.
UK 1973 John McConnell

Date. Has many of the hypnotic qualities of the CALENDAR. The cliché usually dominates the particular design with emphasis on the characteristic full points or 'th' or 'nd' etc that follow the numerals (see NUMBER SYMBOLISM).

Whole year laid out with date stamp. See also KIT-LAYOUT.
USA 1960 Sheldon Streisland

Advertisement for a typesetter. Copy reference made to April Fool.
Canada 1961 John Evans

Poster for art museum.
USA 1968 Chermayeff & Geismar

Deckle-edge. The characteristic elaborately decorated edges of wedding stationery and photographs. Peculiarly redolent of suburban good taste in printed material, the designer uses the effect to evoke just such a feeling. See also CHARACTERISTIC STYLE, SNAPSHOT.

Deer. Appears regularly in civic heraldry to symbolise the forest areas. Used in the 1930s on posters exhorting town dwellers to visit the countryside. By implication a symbol for rustic open spaces and parkland.

Demotic Signs. The injection into the sophisticated designer's language of untutored marks and imagery, most notably the inscription of simple messages such as rooms to let or the private reminiscences committed to lavatory walls. In embracing this new language the designer invariably imbues it with a new elegance. See also CHILDREN'S WRITING AND DRAWING, GRAFFITI, HANDWRITING.

Desk (Child's). The characteristic desk and seat is one with sloped lid and inkwell. A natural symbol for school or elementary learning.

Field/figure 'painting' of child's desk reminiscent of the contemporary paintings of Franz Kline.
USA 1958 Ray Komai

Desk (Office). The office desk is a very subtle status symbol. Its size, position, and the way in which people are situated in relation to it are all part of a complex language of power and status struggles. In large corporations, hierarchies are established by them not only by size but by the degree to which they are left bare.

The desk as a status-defining-and-dividing object.
UK 1970 John Glashan

Detective. The Sherlock Holmes deerstalker, meerschaum pipe and MAGNIFYING GLASS are the stock-in-trade of comic book detectives.

Sherlock Holmes garb of deerstalker and pipe plus the characteristic attitude of detectives become a visual pun for QUESTION MARK.
France 1955 Savignac

Copy asks to 'Keep an eye on Cox's'.
USA 1955 Arnold Varga

Devil. Traditionally depicted with horns and tail and carrying a TRIDENT. Probably a Christian transference from pagan gods like Bacchus and Pan who were horned and cloven footed. The comic book version may well owe more to the creatures in the paintings of Hieronymus Bosch. See also WITCH.

Poster for cooling drink. Devil establishes idea of extreme heat.
USA 1958 Jack Wolfgang Beck

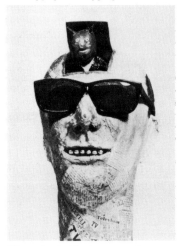

Illustration for Playboy magazine. Literally he was 'a devil' for women, drink, etc. See also RUSSIAN DOLL.
USA 1964 Paul Davis

Devil's appendages easily rendered.
UK 1970 Mel Calman

Diagonal. The use of lines of type at an angle to the page (by the Futurist, Dadaist and Bauhaus artist/typographers from roughly World War I to the 1930s) was a revolutionary gesture by which the tyranny of the vertical/horizontal page was broken. In so doing a new typographic dynamic was created. This device filtered down to the commercial design of the 1930s and 1940s (particularly in posters) and became one of its main characteristics. With the development of photosetting this device has become less typographically defiant and has become absorbed into the common currency of design.

Poster.
Germany 1926 Herbert Bayer

Poster.
Switzerland 1961 Müller-Brockmann

Dial. The depiction of dials is a general symbol for technological complexity. The more dials the more complex the technology. It is also a sort of status symbol in domestic or semi-domestic hardware: cookers, timepieces and the dashboards of cars. See also CLOCK/WATCH, SUNDIAL.

Diary. Strongly characteristic typography of large numerals and light and heavy rules. The appointments' book has strong associations of big business and private secretaries while the record-of-private-thoughts diary has strong literary allusions, used for political and literary biographies. The main visual characteristic is the contrast of casual HANDWRITING with the strict typography. See also CHARACTERISTIC STYLE.

A version of the diary theme: the office notebook as a symbol for business projects.
USA 1962 Tony Palladino

A version of the diary theme. Cover of booklet introducing nine new Pirelli slipper models. Name (address) equals name (style). A transference of meaning.
UK 1966 Crosby/Fletcher/Forbes/Gill

Dice. The cube with dots for numerals on its six faces is a powerful visual signal. The association is exclusively gambling as opposed to skill; often reckless and sometimes reprehensible. This is underlined in such expressions as 'dicing with death'.

Advertisement for store. The copy makes reference to a 'lucky experience'.
USA 1947 Paul Rand

Austria 1953 Hans Wagula

Advertisement for Merchandiser's Mart (taking a chance).
USA 1955 Morton Goldsholl

Dictionary. One of the hardy clichés of the 1960s. First recorded use in late 1950s. The use of a dictionary quote (usually a straight photographic print from Webster's or The Oxford) was a natural reaction to the use of visual imagery which had reached saturation point by the early 1960s. In a sense it was getting back to first principles, returning to a bland, objective statement of fact. Ironically, the dictionary, by the necessary economics of its typographical format – tight setting, use of small caps, italics, parentheses and the characteristic method of emboldening and throwing out the first word into the margin (as opposed to the more usual method of indenting) – itself became a very strong visual signal. See also CHARACTERISTIC STYLE.

Joan Lĕ-wän-dŏẃ-skä representing Carl Fischer, photographer; Edward Sorel, illustrator; 421 east 54 street, New York City, N.Y., telephone MU 8-2828

The phonetic breakdown characteristic of dictionary setting is used for a client with a difficult name.
USA 1959 George Lois

Omnific (ǫmni·fik), *a*. 1667.
[f. med. or mod. L. *omnificus*,
f. OMNI- + -*ficus* making.]
All-creating.

Stationery design.
UK 1964 Derek Birdsall

Webster's Dictionary. *Pencil and ink on canvas. (30 × 40 ins.)*
USA 1965 Arakawa

Dimensions. The dimensions of inches or millimetres with the lines and arrows (see ARROW) as on architects' drawings are very evocative of precise activities such as engineering, etc. Used to symbolise the whole area but also more imaginatively used to symbolise the abstract concept of assessment when applied to imprecise subjects.

Industrial dimensions for an industrial designer's letterhead.
USA 1959 Franz Altschuler

Fingernails as substitute for dimensional arrows. See also FIST.
USA 1959 Onofrio Paccione

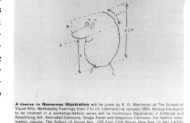

Analysing (i.e. measuring) the problems of the humorist.
USA 1960 R.O.Blechman

Audience reaction is interpreted as measuring the word 'ha-ha'. See EXPRESSIONISTIC TYPOGRAPHY.
USA 1960 Lou Dorfsman/Al Amato

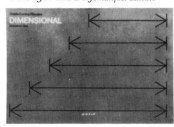

Dimensional marks related to sound control products.
USA 1966 George Tscherny

Dinosaur. Highly recognisable animal both in its normal and skeletal form. Has strong visual associations of pre-history. In verbal terms (like the word DODO) symbolises the idea of obsolescence although this is not often transferred to the visual field. Much loved by cartoonists.

Distortion. Any departure from the norm in human life (the dwarf, the hunchback) is a visual shock to some degree. This partly accounts for the peculiar visual qualities of children's drawings and faux-naif drawings. The photographic distortion (the controlled use of double exposure for instance or technical tricks in the dark room) adds a further dimension. Typography, also, is a natural subject for distortion by means of blurring or being projected onto undulating surfaces or through frosted glass. See also MAGNIFYING GLASS, PROJECTED IMAGE.

Poster for Pelikan ink. Classic distortion.
See also FOUNTAIN PEN.
USSR 1924 El Lissitzky

The distortion is consistent with the
flexibility of fabrics. Advertisement for
textile exhibition.
Italy 1960 Franco Grignani

Domus *cover.*
Italy 1960 William Klein

Advertisement for a new lipstick. The
headline says 'see'. The EYE *looks through*
the lipstick which is actually translucent.
USA 1962 George Lois

Poster for School of Visual Arts.
USA 1964 George Tscherny

Catalogue cover for The American
Federation of Arts.
USA 1964 George Tscherny

Diver (**Deep Sea**). A strongly characteristic shape viewed with a combination of awe, affection and humour. Unequivocally symbolic of the deep uncharted ocean. Sometimes used more imaginatively for the idea of depth as in a deep pile carpet.

Verbal association of ideas: deep-sea with
deep-pile (carpets).
USA 1959 Gene Federico

Document. The document or pseudo-document has strong associations with the idea of authorisation, legality, excellence, etc. The typographical style is necessarily dense with a partiality for unreadable type sizes. The red seal is a sometime appendage to the document. See also CHARACTERISTIC STYLE, SEAL (NOTARY).

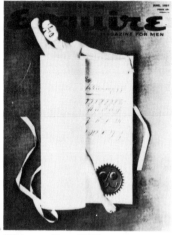

USA 1957 Henry Wolf

Dodo. A symbol for obsolescence. Probably not characteristic enough visually to be significant without typographical support. See also DINOSAUR.

Dog. A universal symbol of fidelity to man. In many ancient cultures dogs were guardians of and carriers of the dead. The peculiar forms of devotion the dog shows to his master are subject of legend. One such is the life-saving qualities of the St Bernard with the barrel of brandy around its neck. This has become a visual cliché in its own right although the medical authenticity is doubtful. Nowadays the symbolism of the dog is almost exclusively in the general area of domesticity – a necessary adjunct to the home.

St Bernard dog rescues in the nick of time. USA 1954 Roy McKie

Display card for Pirelli slippers. Canine penchant for carrying slippers referred to. UK 1966 Bob Gill

Pass along?
Who'd borrow it?

Dog's ears used as a visual pun for 'dog-eared' magazine. 'Dog-eared' becomes a symbol for popularity. USA 1963 Henry Sandbank

Do-it-yourself. A last resort solution which invites the reader to participate in the design. This includes techniques like COLOURING IN, JOINED-UP NUMBERS, CUT-OUT, etc.

How to do a
Volkswagen ad.

Advertisement inviting the reader to design his own VW advertisement. USA 1962 Helmut Krone

Doll. Not much symbolic significance although a feature of all cultures predating history. Associations however are strong and various as a victim substitute (witchcraft), wife or girl friend substitute (Kokoshka) or as a companion for an only child. It also has somewhat disturbing and sinister attributes and is a cliché in horror films. A natural EUPHEMISM for a child in any picture showing the death of a child. See also PUPPET, RUSSIAN DOLL, TOY, VENTRILOQUIST'S DUMMY.

Dollar Sign. Unmistakable graphic symbol for American currency and (by implication) for America itself. It has high recognition value and therefore withstands distortion. See also CURRENCY, POUND SIGN.

Dollar sign made up from initial letters of Sudler & Hennessy. See also INITIAL LETTER.
USA 1959 Herb Lubalin/George Lois

Sick currency. See also CRIPPLE.
UK 1970 Mel Calman

Dome. Unofficially a symbol of authority and power (as in St Paul's, St Peter's Rome, etc). See also BUILDING.

Don Quixote. See under **Q.**

Donkey. Although the donkey is at one and the same time a symbol for stupidity, humility, lowliness and stubbornness it is still regarded generally with affection. A low-technology method of transport.

Doodle. Similar in spirit to DEMOTIC SIGNS and GRAFFITI, it is more specific-ally associated with blotting pads or the walls of telephone booths. It is therefore closely connected with the idea of waiting or boredom. See also SCRIBBLE.

Doodling as a symbol of meditation. Poster for an exhibition of meditative images.
Austria 1960 Winfred Gaul

Book jacket. The doodle expresses the title.
USA 1960 Stanley Eisenman

Door. Part of the BODY, HOUSE analogy. Although historically the door has no particular symbolic significance it is quite often used as a general symbol for acquiring know-ledge (the doors of a university). The front door to a man's house is a symbol of inviolability. The sexual parallel to this has been symbolically realised by many artists in recent years. See also VAGINA.

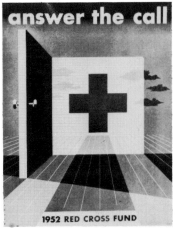

Copy implies: 'Answer the door'.
USA 1952 Joseph Binder

Door as an opportunity symbol. Poster announcing art scholarships.
USA 1966 Bob Gill

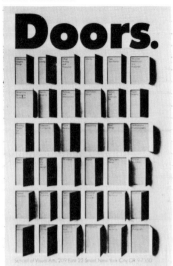

The doors of an art school with the names of the various departments on them becomes a symbol for an art school.
USA 1967 Milton Glaser

An adjunct to the door.
UK 1975 Jones/Thompson

Dot. According to Rudolph Kock the dot is the origin from which all signs start and is their innermost essence.

*Copy refers to creativity, sensations, etc. One of a series of 'poetic' advertisements for a printer stressing intangible qualities.
Italy 1958 Franco Grignani*

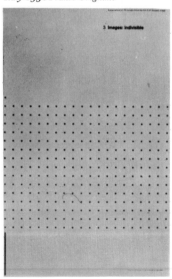

*Copy, '3 images: indivisible'.
USA 1960 Rudolph de Harak*

Dotted Line. Part of the drawing language of diagrams enabling one to see what lies beyond an opaque surface without changing the viewpoint. Also used to show where an object has been in a kinetic image (see KINETICS), as in someone in a rocking chair. This useful and universally understood device is an indispensable part of the illustrator's or designer's equipment. See also COUPON, CUT OUT, DANCE DIAGRAM, DIMENSIONS, GAMES AND BATTLES, PERFORATION.

*Book jacket. Dotted line shows earlier shape of mountains.
Switzerland 1954 Hans Thoni*

*Technical drawing convention applied to photograph to suggest hopeful new shape. Copy says 'Wishful thinning?'
USA 1967 Henry Wolf*

Dove. Symbol of peace.

Personal Christmas card.
USA 1960 Ben Shahn

Peace poster.
USA 1970 Ivan Chermayeff

Dovetail. The characteristic configuration of the dovetail in joinery sometimes symbolises the ultimate in craftsmanship. In language it implies a successful conjunction of responsibilities.

Full-colour photograph for an article on apples and pears.
UK 1966 Lester Bookbinder

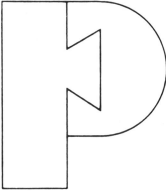

Trademark for F.W.Purser, builder.
UK 1966 Crosby/Fletcher/Forbes/Gill

Dragon. Apart from its heraldic use it is mainly depicted nowadays in a spirit of parody by cartoonists to suggest something undesirable (bureaucracy for instance). Its evil associations have got entangled with the SNAKE image. Popular with designers of tea packaging because of its Oriental associations. A strong exotic image.

World War I poster. Early use of dragon as war symbol.
Austria 1918 Julius Klinger

Drawing Board. Symbol for the design and architectural profession.

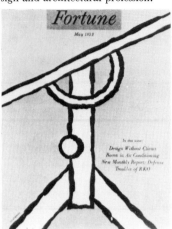

For an issue on 'Design without Clients'.
USA 1953 Leo Lionni

Dream. The paintings of the Surrealists had their effect on the designers and poster artists of the 1930s and 1940s. The dream image was a popular feature of SURREALISM. One such dream device was the use of lines of PERSPECTIVE converging to the horizon with object placed at random on this dream landscape. Cotton wool clouds completed the cliché. The use of Victorian engravings mixed with photographs has strong dream associations.

Dressmaker's Dummy. A popular symbol for fashion. Beloved by cartoonists in mistaken identity situations.

Poster for clothing firm.
Switzerland 1934 H. Mahler

Driving Mirror (Rear-view Mirror). A symbol for motoring. As with other reflecting objects it is much used as it allows a multiplicity of viewpoints and visual ambiguities. See also MIRROR, REFLECTION.

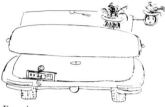

Drawing.
France 1952 André François

USA 1954 George Giusti

See also ANALOGY.
UK 1955 Gerard Hoffnung

Drop. It is immediately evocative of drops of oil, water and the TEARDROP. An image of tension. See also BLOOD, BLOT.

KIA-ORA the fruit squash
UK 1952 Dawson Thompson

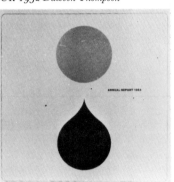

Symbol for Sunset Petroleum.
USA 1965 Jerome Gould

Although the same formal configuration as the teardrop, the brain immediately accepts the viscosity on sight of the word 'oil'.
Trademark for Ocean Oil. See also INITIAL LETTER.
UK 1967 Minale/Tattersfield

Drum. The drum has been important in dances and ritual worship in many cultures. It has strong associations with the human heart beat. Its visual symbolism is common in the general area of soldiering and warfare and army recruiting through the ages. Because of this persuasive aspect it was borrowed as a symbol by the advertising industry for its own activity; 'beating the big drum' is a verbal equivalent. Although technically a musical instrument it 'stirs the heart' in nationalistic rather than musical terms. It is also a general symbol for announcement in the form of the drummer boy who warns or precedes a proclamation. The surface presents a large area for message carrying.

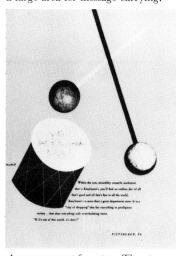

An announcement for a store. The copy reads: 'If it's out of this world it's here'. The drum-stick end is a GLOBE.
USA 1947 Paul Rand

Duck. Its symbolism is usually in the farmyard or urban parks area. The ceramic flying duck on the living room wall is a symbol for extreme suburban taste.

Duck as a symbol of the town-dweller's 'countryside'.
UK 1931 Charles Paine

Record sleeve for Art Ducko. Suburban symbol of bad taste pushed to extreme limits as real, bleeding ducks replace the ceramic kind.
UK 1970 Hipgnosis

Duel. An example of a situation cliché. The choreography and manners are precisely observed.

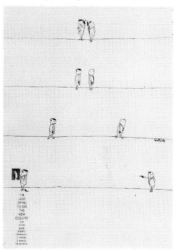

Copy says 'I'm just dying to see the new Esquire' (said by duellist reading Esquire).
USA 1956 Robert Benton

Duelling as an ANALOGY for marital arguments.
UK 1972 Mel Calman

Dunce. The coned cap with the letter D is the characteristic symbol.

Dustbin (Garbage Can, Trash-can). The galvanised iron model with the corrugated strips is the most characteristic one. Used to suggest a run-down urban area but often used symbolically to suggest the idea of excessive consumer spending, obsolescence and subjects pertaining to ecology.

Dustbin as a symbol of built-in obsolescence in consumer goods.
UK 1967 Larry Carter

Obsolescent people. 'The new American woman: through at 21.'
USA 1967 George Lois

Eagle. Symbol of power and glory. The American eagle came from the Romans who in turn took the symbol from Egypt and Greece. National emblem of Poland. The double headed eagle came from the time of the Crusades, has strong military associations and was later adopted as the national emblem of Germany, Russia and Austria. In Christianity the symbol of St John the Evangelist.

Eagle as a symbol of German air power.
Germany 1917 Julius Gipkens

Ear. Many ancient cultures regarded the ear as a symbol of wisdom and as a recipient of the word of God. Enlarging the ear by the use of heavy JEWELLERY was to many people a way of increasing such wisdom. As the ear continues to grow into old age, long ears are visually characteristic of old age. We identify very closely with images of sensitive areas of the human head, the more so when the image is fragmented or torn apart.

Booklet for CBS Radio Network. Ear as REBUS figure. See also SUBSTITUTION.
USA 1953 Louis Dorfsman

Book jacket for The Open Mind.
USA 1959 Chermayeff & Geismar

Advertisement for an advertising agency. Copy says, 'If advertising isn't memorable, it doesn't sell'.
USA 1960 Herb Lubalin

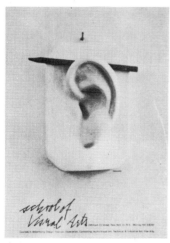

The plaster cast ear from the antique room as a symbol for art. An advertisement for School of Visual Arts, New York. See also PENCIL, HANDWRITING.
USA 1960 George Tscherny

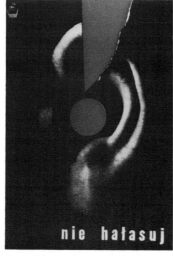

Poster for noise abatement in factories. See also EXCLAMATION MARK.
Poland 1964 Wladislaw Przystanski-Zdzislaw

Poster for the Zurich police. See also TORN PAPER.
Switzerland 1977 Olivier Delacrétaz

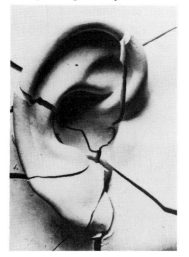

Chrysler Corporation's war against noise. 'Noise is a challenge wherever we find it.' USA 1963 Harold Becker

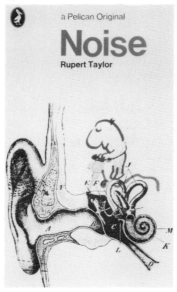

UK 1970 Mel Calman/Philip Thompson

Polish state anti-noise poster. Poland 1977 Danuta Zukowska

Easel. Symbol for fine art.

France 1961 André François

Egg. Universal symbol of creation. A symbol for Easter. In commercial art the qualities usually referred to are its fragility and paradoxically its structural strength and its preciousness (in the life-containing sense). It has a unique and unmistakable silhouette and a high recognition value in its pristine, sliced or fried form. At one time a popular symbol for the idea of packaging. The broken egg is an immediate symbol for an accident. See also NEST.

The copy refers to 'the light touch' in advertising. Here the egg is a symbol of fragility.
USA 1957 Louis Danziger

Egg used as a symbol of Easter. (Easter issue of Esquire.*) See also* LADDER, SCALE.
USA 1956 Henry Wolf/Ben Somoroff

Egg as a symbol of vulnerability. See also FRANKING, PARCEL, STAMP.
UK 1972 Shirt-Sleeve Studio

The quote is from Emerson, 'Every wall is a door'. The apparently impenetrable wall of the egg becomes a door for the emerging chick.
USA 1964 George Tscherny

Electrical Symbols. The plus and minus symbols are always used in conjunction. See also ARITHMETICAL SIGNS.

Symbol for electrical products manufacturer. UK 1960 Henrion

Trademark for batteries (lead=pb). UK 1971 Fletcher/Forbes/Gill

Elephant. A general symbol for Africa. An animal regarded with great affection by designers and illustrators. Naturally its strength is referred to but also humorously other attributes like its good memory. Sometimes the verbal aspects of white elephant and pink elephant are transferred to the visual field.

Copy says, 'Repetition means remembrance' and supports the myth that elephants never forget. BLACKBOARD supports the idea of repetition. (In the sense of an often-repeated lesson.) USA 1946 Paul Rand

Rubber elephant as a safety symbol; the ultimate in road holding. A new cliché is minted for the future. France 1961 André François

Alcoholism
Neil Kessel and Henry Walton

Pink elephant. UK 1975 Michael Morris

Embossing. Mark of quality and good taste in stationery. The technique is often used to simulate the characteristic surface of the product.

The graphic technique of embossing used to simulate the real indenting and riveting in motor vehicles. USA 1942 Paul Rand

PLASTICS TODAY 28

Embossed bootprints. UK 1966 Crosby/Fletcher/Forbes

End View. Similar to WORM'S EYE VIEW and PLAN VIEW in the sense of attempting to see common objects freshly. The end view of logs is one of the most characteristic because of the ring SECTION.

See also BODY LANGUAGE, GUN.
USSR 1925 A.Lawinski

Face peers through rolled-up copies of Vogue.
USA 1957 Richard Loew

The end view of a pile of magazines indicates the sheer quantity of content.
USA 1961 Gilbert Lesser

End view of a roll of corrugated paper for a packaging firm. See also SPIRAL.
Switzerland 1963 Siegfried Odermatt/ Rosemary Tissi

Cover for an annual publication containing articles from the pages of Fortune.
USA 1966 Gilbert Lesser

End view of toothpaste tube for record: Keep your hand on it.
UK 1975 Hipgnosis

Envelope. An obsessive graphic image (whichever side is represented). Similar to the closed BOX or CASE in its psychological effect. The particular configuration on the reverse side (due to its manufacture), has a high recognition value. The envelope is rich in association and ritual. The idea of security and secrecy is strong (the interference pattern inside is a strong visual characteristic) as is the idea of an official declaration (of love or of a debt). The envelope features considerably in drama, film and opera. In its journey from sender to recipient the envelope picks up a good deal of ACCUMULATED GRAPHICS.

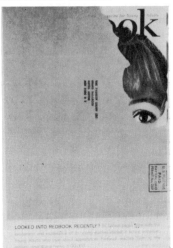

Magazine advertisement. See also EYE, TORN PAPER.
USA 1960 Michael Pennette

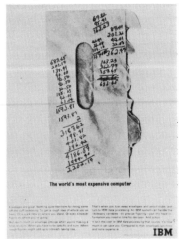

Envelope as a humanistic symbol for off the cuff calculations. Advertisement for IBM computers.
USA 1963 Gerald Weinstein

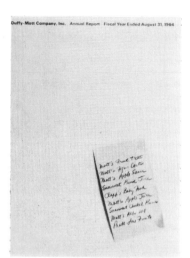

Characteristic medium (back of envelope) for shopping list of company's products.
USA 1964 Roger Cook

Epic Lettering. A form of lettering peculiar to film posters of epic religious and western block-busters. It consists of lettering apparently made out of stone monuments seen from a low eye level with a pronounced PERSPECTIVE. It is a tradition which dies hard.

Illustration to a political parable.
UK 1962 Brian Haynes/Bill James

Euphemism. A rhetorical figure of speech where an acceptable word or phrase is substituted for an unacceptable one. This is frequently transferred to the visual field. For example, a broken DOLL may be substituted for a dead child.

Widow substituted for victim.
UK 1946 W.Little

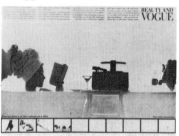

Naked body in bath suggested by other clues : hair in towel, book for reading, drink and so on.
USA 1957 Richard Loew/Irving Penn

Exclamation Mark. A typographic sign of great emotive power.

Poster.
Germany 1924 Walter Dexel

Magazine cover. See also DANCE.
USA 1940 Paul Rand

Visual pun for glass of beer.
UK 1951 Abram Games

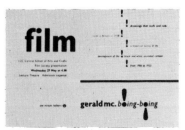

The exclamation mark is a visual pun for a footprint (films that walk and talk) and a visual equivalent for sound. (Gerald McBoing-Boing could imitate the sound of an orchestra.)
UK 1952 Derek Birdsall

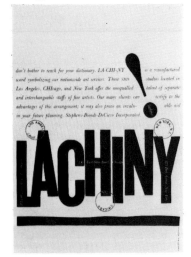

The exclamation mark creates the necessary dynamic to accompany the FRANKING *of Los Angeles, Chicago and New York (whose initials make up the name LACHINY).*
USA 1956 Charles MacMurray

Advertisement to attract advertisers.
USA 1957 Irving Miller/William Weinstein

Expletive. The comic book convention of asterisks as an expletive substitute and a typographical mix of exclamation marks (see EXCLAMATION MARK), dashes, commas, etc. Both forms firmly in the common currency and occasionally given a refined typographical treatment.

Exploded Drawing. Part of the language of diagrams where an object is fragmented in order to see the SECTION as well as the side view.

Explosion. A comic book convention of a freely drawn multi-pointed STAR is part of the common language of communication. Beloved by designers of advertisements for cut price stores but also used by sophisticated designers.

The comic book explosion device is used in a fine-art context.
USA 1961 Roy Lichtenstein

Expressionistic Typography. Concrete poetry was a movement developed in the 1940s (and flourishing today) by groups of painters, typographers and poets interested in the audio/semantic/syntactic relationships in words and ideas. Although a relatively esoteric interest their influence has gradually seeped into commercial typography.

Logotype for Pirelli. An expression of elasticity.
Italy 1908 Designer unknown

Logotype for an adding machine.
Sweden 1957 Ladislav Sutnar

John. is that Billy coughing? Get up and give him some Coldene.

Night dialogue.
USA 1958 George Lois

ha — lf   addding
            subtrcting
            multimultiplying
            div id ing

aboutɘɔɒf   ɒeaning

      st len
o
ver   o   deaᴅ

UK 1959 Robert Brownjohn

Advertisement for an electronics firm. USA 1959 Brownjohn, Chermayeff & Geismar

Advertisement for advertising agency. Copy refers to advertising 'tonnage'. USA 1960 Donald Egensteiner

Trademark for Canadian National Railways. The lettering is made from a railway track layout. Canada, 1960 Allan Fleming

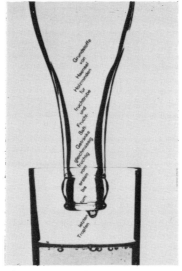

Typography flows like wine. Advertisement for a drinks company. Switzerland 1962 Gerstner + Kutter

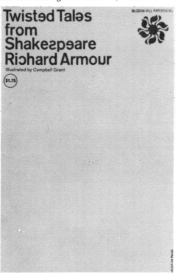

The use of REVERSE type left to right to express literally the word 'twisted' in the title. USA 1965 Rudolph de Harak

Cinema commercial for bank. USA 1967 Robert Brownjohn

Trademark for textile firm. Flexible motif capable of graphic and three-dimensional treatment. See INITIAL LETTER. Switzerland 1969 Siegfried Odermatt/ Rosemary Tissi

Free-painted lettering for painting exhibition poster. UK 1974 Alan Fletcher

Eye. An Egyptian symbol of deity and providence. Also a Christian symbol in church ornament and architecture. One of the most obsessive of devices used by religious and secular designers, primitive and sophisticated alike.

Film poster. Withdrawn from British hoardings for being too sophisticated for the market. See also ARROW.
USA 1952 Paul Rand

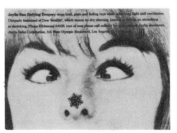

Advertisement for non-fade drapery. Early example of cross-eyes which for some reason started a vogue. See also SNOWFLAKE.
USA 1960 Louis Danziger

The eye patch is a strong indication of eye loss or injury.
UK 1938 Tom Eckersley

Trademark for CBS TV.
USA circa 1951 William Golden

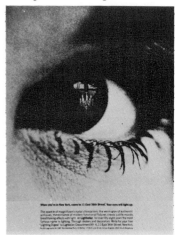

'Your eyes will light up.' Reflected image of a lightfitting in the eye. See also REFLECTION.
USA 1962 Herb Lubalin

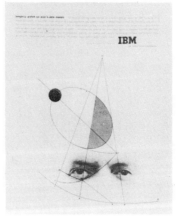

Advertisement for computers. Comparison made between computers' and human brain capabilities.
USA 1959 Matthew Liebowitz

Film poster.
USA 1952 Eric Nitsche

See also MAP.
UK 1979 Peter Davenport

Eye Substitute. The use of a peacock FEATHER or FLOWER as an eye substitute (a visual pun). Usually a photographic interpretation.

Cover for Harper's Bazaar. *See also* BUTTERFLY.
USA 1939 Herbert Matter

Peacock's eye substitutes for model's.
USA 1959 Henry Wolf

A ROSE *is a poetic eye substitute.*
Switzerland 1966 Sandro Bocola

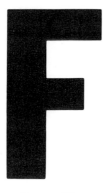

Fabulous Beasts. The portrayal of compilation ANIMALS such as the DRAGON, SPHINX or UNICORN. They figure in the legends of most countries and probably fulfil a need in man to imagine animals which combine all the desirable qualities of other selected animals. The animals are represented in numerous symbols and trademarks.

Copy refers to the Greek experiment of horsepower. Illustration for Standard Oil. See also HORSE.
USA 1965 André François

Face. One of the most compelling of visual objects from the primitive configurations consisting of circles and dots to the portraits of Rembrandt. Most of the information about a person is contained in the face and our own mental image of ourselves is derived largely from the mirror REFLECTION of our own face. There is a strong guilt-inducing factor in the image as in the watchful representation of deities and the Orwellian concept of 'big brother'. One of the hardiest clichés of the advertising industry is merchandise held at face level. See also PROFILE, SMILE.

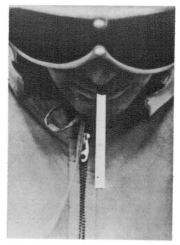

Advertisement for cigarette.
USA circa 1960 Art Kane

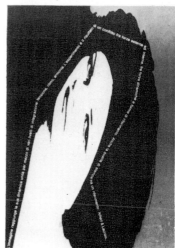

Advertisement for Italian typefounders. Copy says, 'The image reaches its dynamic unity by various degrees of integration, tension, rhythm and harmony'.
Italy 1963 Franco Grignani

Face Substitute. A fairly common graphic cliché where a FACE from a different field of visual reference is superimposed on a photograph or drawing. The real life equivalent occurs from time to time when people read a magazine which has a life size face on the cover.

Magritte-like technique where the real image and the photographic image visually correspond. Advertisement for photographic film.
Belgium circa 1940 Jacques Richez

For an exhibition of work by André François. See also CLOCK/WATCH.
France 1977 André François

Factory. The smoking chimney and the raked roofs of the factory are essential images, unmistakable and indispensable in spite of the architectural advance in factory design.
A symbol for heavy industry.

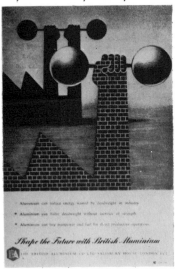

Advertisement promoting aluminium as an energy saver in industry. See also STRONG MAN.
UK 1947 Henrion

Students' poster at the time of the 1968 rebellion in Paris. See also ARM.
France 1968 Atelier Populaire

Fairground. Like the circus, the fairground is a microcosm. The artefacts of the fairground provide a symbolic language of luck, achievement, fantasy, frustration, etc. Because of the personal involvement in the fairground, the situation closely parallels real life.

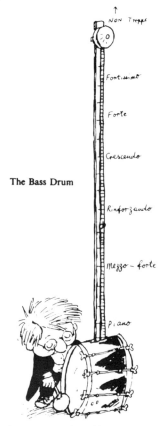

The Bass Drum

Test-your-strength machine measures musical dynamics. See also ANALOGY.
UK 1955 Gerard Hoffnung

Funny fairground mirror image (see MIRROR*) for a funny man.*
USA 1959 Burt Goldblatt

One of the characteristic fairground GAMES; here symbolic of romantic achievement. See also HEART.
UK 1962 Mel Calman

Lollobrigida behind a painted fish. Quick fancy-dress device and persona change. See also HEADS/MIDDLES/TAILS.
USA 1963 Paul Davis

Fairy. Primitive cultures have always tried to interpret the forces of nature in terms of malevolent or benign spirits in more or less human form. The continuing insistence on fairies, elves, pixies, etc in entertainment, books and ornamental gardens suggests a timeless appeal. The fairy godmother figure is a powerful symbol for benevolent expectations.

Family Tree. Part of the repertoire of diagrams.

Family tree of various alphabets showing derivations.
UK 1965 B.Kapadia

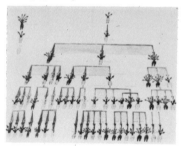

Pictorial rendering of the family tree of the Bach family.
Belgium 1966 Folon

Fan (Hand Held). A symbol of concealment with genteel and coquettish associations. The stage MAGICIAN uses it as a visual metaphor in sleight-of-hand tricks with CARDS.

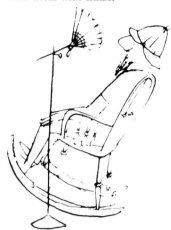

UK 1952 André François

Fan (Mechanical). The large ceiling fan immediately creates the ambience of tropical or sub-tropical climate. A useful shorthand for illustrators.

Fan establishes the sweaty ambience.
USA 1964 Milton Glaser

Fan as a substitute for sun-drenched photographic location.
UK 1965 Helmut Newton

Fan Dancer. Because of the low premium on nudity today the fan dancer is a somewhat nostalgic figure. Associated with a period of entertainment from Art Deco (Josephine Baker, et al) to the end of World War II. Strongly evocative in America of vaudeville. A useful symbol for the idea of concealment.

Father Time. Symbol of approaching death. A more benevolent figure than the medieval image of the Dance of Death from which it probably derives. Father Time is usually depicted carrying a scythe and an HOURGLASS and at the end of the calendar year introduces the new year in the shape of a new-born babe. An indispensable PERSONIFICATION.

UK 1970 Mel Calman

Feather. In every age and culture bird feathers have decorated man's head. The wearers were usually kings, chieftains (see RED INDIAN), rulers and lords of the sun. Ostrich feathers formed the emblem of the badge of the Prince of Wales. A single white feather is a symbol for cowardice. A general symbol for lightness.

Feather as a symbol of lightness and thus portability.
UK 1952 Henrion

Fence. A symbol for the demarcation of territory or GARDEN. Strong associations of neighbourly rights and responsibilities. The literary figure of 'sitting on the fence' (referring to an equivocating person) is sometimes given a visual form, particularly by political cartoonists.

Fence as barrier symbol. Copy asks, 'Prevented from using full colour?' Full colour halftone screen appears as background.
USA 1958 Bob Gill

The garden fence as a symbol of suburbia. Reference is made to a competition for best lawns.
USA 1975 R.O. Blechman

Fig Leaf. An often-used symbol for prudery. A fashion trade symbol. See also ADAM AND EVE.

Universally acceptable style of artist, used to illustrate sexually delicate subject. Illustration for pharmaceutical firm. See also EUPHEMISM.
France 1954 Raymond Peynet

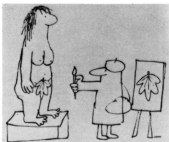

USA 1957 Ed Renfro

Figurehead. Strong maritime associations. The figure (usually female with bared BREASTS) serves no function on a ship apart from decoration. This accounts for the expression used for nominal heads of organisations. Curiously this is rarely given a visual form.

File. Symbol of classification. Overtones of espionage.

Letterhead becomes the file.
USA 1955 Herb Lubalin

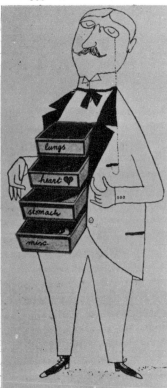

'To the organised man.' A drawing of classified parts of the body. The artist shares the same obsession with Dali and other surreal artists of the 1930s.
USA 1959 Tomi Ungerer

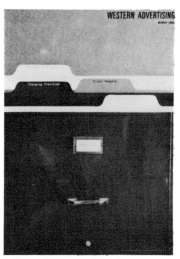

Filing cabinet as a symbol of management.
USA 1964 Carl Freedman

Filing cabinet as a symbol for information. Folder that gives information on season tickets for Swiss Railways.
Switzerland 1966 Donald Brun

Film. The strip of film with sprockets and sound track is a strong symbol for the cinema or the cinema industry. It is a perfect equivalent for the idea of moving film. Sometimes it is used as an added dynamic simply to revive rather indifferent photographs. Film strip with sprockets is also a symbol for still photography.

Editorial page in Russian magazine.
See also EXCLAMATION MARK, KINETICS.
USSR 1923 Alexei Gan

Everything left on negative as a stylistic device.
USA 1962 Herb Lubalin

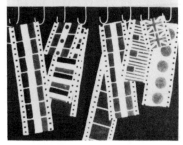

Poster for 8th International Film Festival.
See also FLAG.
USA 1964 Saul Bass/Art Goodman

Trademark for American Film Institute.
American STAR *becomes a kinetic image.*
See also STARS AND STRIPES.
USA 1968 Chermayeff & Geismar

Letterhead for a photographer based on the frame-guide. Letterhead is yellow, the characteristic colour. Dots form a TROMPE L'OEIL *effect.*
UK 1968 Robert Celiz

Poster for film festival.
USA 1970 Arnold Saks

Finger. The finger isolated from the rest of the HAND is a very hypnotic image. The finger-nail characterises it unmistakably. The SCALE is often established by showing the particular item between the finger-tips. The finger-nail thus establishes the scale. See also FIST, KITCHENER.

Fingers in characteristic selecting gesture. Literally selecting the best.
France 1954 Jacques Nathan

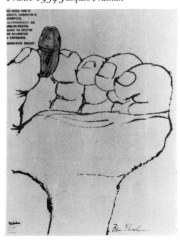

Finger establishes scale of pill. Advertisement for veterinary division of Upjohn Company.
USA 1958 Ben Shahn

Personal greetings card. The text is a quote from Blake, 'To see a world in a grain of sand . . .' The finger-nail is crucial to the contrast in scale.
USA 1959 Norman Gorbaty

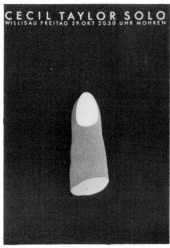

Poster for jazz concert by classically-trained jazz pianist. Single finger is a symbol of dexterity as well as supporting the word 'solo'. Colours red, green and black underline the surreal image (see SURREALISM).
Switzerland 1977 Niklaus Troxler

Fingerprint. Extremely expressive image. A prime symbol for crime because of its proof of identification. Because of the physiological uniqueness of the fingerprint it is also a symbol for uniqueness or subjects related to the idea of the personal, individual touch. See also FOOTPRINT, HANDPRINT.

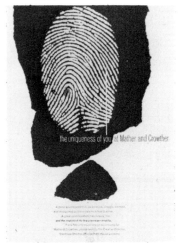

Advertisement to attract designers to an advertising agency. Copy refers to 'the uniqueness of you'. See also EXCLAMATION MARK.
UK 1959 Hans Schleger

Fire. One of the basic elements. Seemingly conjured out of thin air, fire had strong magical qualities for primitive man. It formed a focal point in his social and economic life and his family while retaining a strong element of mystery and danger. Civilisation has not changed our attitudes in our symbolic use of fire, such as the Olympic flame. See also TORCH.

Fire as a symbol of destruction.
USA 1957 George Olden

Fire as a symbol of pain.
France 1957 Savignac

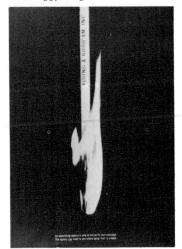

Fire as a symbol of creativity.
Advertisement for advertising agency.
See also PENCIL.
USA 1963 Vincent Salmieri

Fireman. A strongly visual occupation characterised by the AXE, boots and top-heavy helmet (either USA or British variation). Smokey Stover is a well known American cartoon figure. See also OCCUPATIONS.

Association of putting-out-the-fire idea with thirst.
France 1953 Jean Carlu

Fireman supports headline, 'Incendiary' and copy which refers to 'kindling' the male interest.
USA 1957 Gene Federico

More putting out of fire.
Switzerland 1964 Herbert Leupin

Fireplace. The primeval significance of FIRE is embodied in the modern fireplace (where it still exists). Strong symbol of domesticity and a primitive focal point.

Fireworks. A box of fireworks or a firework display is a general symbol for celebration. Individual fireworks have specific associations; a rocket is a distress signal, a catherine wheel has martyrdom connotations. Figuratively to put a squib (or firecracker) under somebody is to galvanise them into action. In that sense it becomes a symbol for motivation.

Fireworks as a symbol of festivity.
Italy 1959 Dante Vernice

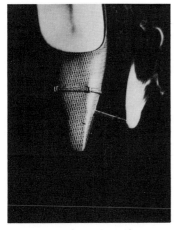

Advertisement. Copy refers to 'fiery footwork' to promote new shoe range.
USA 1962 Gennaro Andreozzi

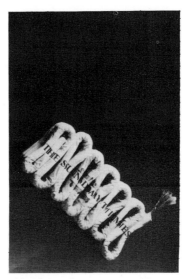

Advertisement for newspaper equating fireworks with stimulating reading.
UK 1966 Designer unknown

Book jacket.
UK 1973 Nigel Thompson

Fish. One of the earliest Christian symbols of Christ, faith and baptism. A MONOGRAM for Christ forms the Greek word for fish. More generally the fish is a symbol of abundance, providence and fertility. A strong phallic object it figures prominently in many cultures and religions. The scale pattern is a universal one and expresses the idea of fecundity.

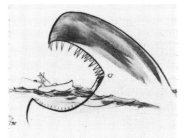

USA 1954 Robert Osborn

International poster theme: 'Water is life'.
See also SKELETON, WATER.
East Germany 1973 Dietrich Schade/
Jurgen Stock

Fist. The printer's fist is the precursor of the printer's ARROW (SQUARE and TRIANGLE) and an intensely expressive graphic device. It is used continually and without apparent abatement. See also FINGER, HAND, KITCHENER.

Typical of the formalism of the period. Mundane imagery and jobbing printers' sorts were rediscovered and put together in new relationships. Symbolism is subjective but certain elements like the EGG shape and printer's fist merge as part of the designer's new-found vocabulary. See also JUGGLER.
USSR 1919 El Lissitzky

The characteristic stylised printer's fist is rendered photographically.
Holland 1932 Piet Zwart

'Someone talked.'
USA 1943 Henry Koerner

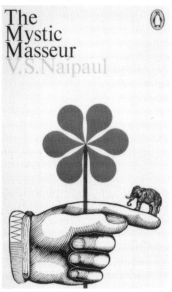

Enlarged engraving of printer's fist reverses SCALE of ELEPHANT. See also FLOWERS.
UK 1970 Derek Birdsall

Fist (Comic Book). The foreshortened fist beloved of comic book artists (usually SMASHING THROUGH PAPER) is a cliché which is often used with affection by designers.

Flag. One of the most fundamental of graphic clichés and one of the most specific and unique national identifications. The idea of the flag as being the possession of the people rather than the sovereign is a republican idea originating in the Italian maritime republics. The revolutionary nature of flags partly accounts for the preponderance of flags bearing red, white and blue, the colours of freedom. The powerful effect of the symbolism of flags and the fierce loyalties they arouse invest some flags with an almost sacred quality; the flag actually becoming the people as if by an act of transubstantiation. See also STARS AND STRIPES, UNION JACK.

The flag shown to represent the people as opposed to the establishment.
USSR 1919 Designer unknown

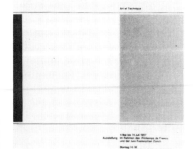

A precisely cropped graphic interpretation of the French flag.
Switzerland 1957 Gottlieb Soland

American store advertisement appears in Japan. Red CIRCLE *indicates Japanese flag.*
USA 1963 Arnold Varga

Tricolour painted on cobblestones in shoe advertisement.
UK 1964 Ric Harle

Flasher. A relatively recent phenomenon. The shock tactics are directed to displaying the merchandise. Closely related to the sudden revelations of the inside pockets. See also INSIDE LINING.

SANTA CLAUS *exposes the cigars (see* CIGAR*).*
USA 1959 André François

Flasher reveals inside lining full of BREASTS.
Poland 1975 Marck Goebel

Poster for exhibition of posters. Association of words 'exhibition' and 'exhibitionist'. See also SANDWICH BOARD.
France 1977 Alan Le Quernec

Flask. A symbol of chemico/industrial research. See also TEST TUBE.

Poster for General Dynamics.
USA 1955 Erik Nitsche

Flattened-out Perspective. The dispensing with converging lines of PERSPECTIVE in order to show objects or people in the background with as much detail as those in the foreground. In photography the use of a telephoto lens tends to have this effect but with a flattening of the image.

'Broad spectrum' mentioned in copy produces flattened-out comprehensive view of city square.
USA 1964 Seymour Chwast

Flowers. In general flowers are indicative of creativity (as in the colloquial expression 'flowering of ideas'). Plant and TREE forms are analogous to creative thought processes and the flower is the ultimate (and short-lived) expression of that process. See also BOUQUET, GARDEN and flowers by name.

Flowers as a symbol of creativity.
Advertisement for an advertising agency.
See also DRAWING BOARD.
UK 1956 André François

Flower bulb as a symbol for spring.
Advertisement for a department store.
USA 1965 Arnold Varga

Fly. A much maligned INSECT. Used to arouse feelings of disgust, particularly in relation to food. Reference is sometimes made to its typical habit of crawling on the ceiling.

Obsessive Kafkaesque image beloved by illustrators and makers of horror films.
USA 1963 Milton Glaser

Foetus. A symbol of developing life. Sometimes used to convey more generally the notion of new ideas or creativity.

Foetus as a symbol of creativity in the artistic and philosophical sense. See also THINKS BUBBLE.
UK 1973 Philip Thompson

Fold Marks (Creases). A naturally graphic albeit random mark. The associations are with old documents or love letters that have been folded and stored for years. Sometimes they are used as a dynamic without having a specific meaning.

Magazine cover. Hand-fold marks add an extra dynamic. See also FACTORY.
USA 1941 Paul Rand

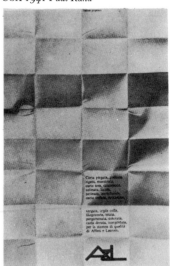

The fold mark is the invisible typographic grid. Advertisement for a printer.
Italy 1963 Franco Grignani

Foot. According to Jung, it confirms man's direct relationship to the earth's reality. Like other parts of the body its historical significance is complex and profound (as in the vulnerability of the heel in the Achilles legend).

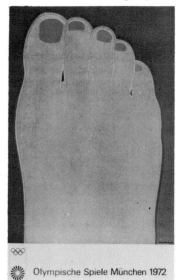

Poster for the Munich Olympic Games. USA 1972 Tom Wesselmann

Footprint. The footprint has somewhat sinister overtones due to the element of mystery. A symbol of life and human endeavour. A record of a visitation. See also MARKS AND TRACKS.

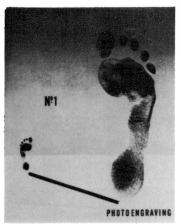

A formal composition demonstrating lessons recently learned from the Bauhaus. Symbolism is uncertain but there is a relationship between the first issue and the first step. This example of graphic design was influental in the handling of graphic elements and photo-montage techniques. See also NUMBER SYMBOLISM. USA 1938 Lester Beall

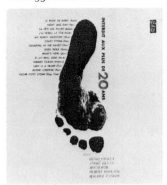

Record sleeve for dance music. Uncharacteristic view of footprint. Usually they are going away from the viewer, except when facing a dancing partner. See also DANCE DIAGRAM. Japan 1959 Hiroshi Kusaka

Fork. The four-pronged fork used for eating has not much significance outside of restaurants. The three-pronged fork (the TRIDENT) when held by the Hindu god Siva, Poseidon or Neptune or more recently BRITANNIA symbolises dominion over the sea. See also PLACE SETTING.

Poster for food client. Switzerland 1945 Herbert Leupin

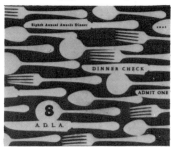

Dominant feature in a luncheon symbol. USA 1952 Louis Danziger

Further luncheon invitation. Fork makes characteristic marks on tablecloth. See also MARKS AND TRACKS, NUMBER SYMBOLISM. UK 1966 Minale/Tattersfield

Forked Emblem. See GENERAL SIGNS.

Fountain. The typical configuration of the fountain with its showering arcs of WATER is a strong formalisation of RAIN. Historically, a symbol of eternal life.

Poster for mineral water.
France 1924 Jean d'Ylen

Fountain reference emphasises life-giving qualities of mineral water.
France 1950 Savignac

Fountain Pen. Although the ballpoint and its derivatives have made the fountain pen almost obsolete, the image of the rather bulbous fountain pen has a great hold on the designer. It has now acquired some of the feeling of an heirloom and is a popular symbol for the idea of authorship and even literature where its slightly old fashioned look is an advantage. A regular visitor on letter pages of women's magazines.

Frame. The highly decorated picture frame has been a strong symbol of fine art for most of this century. Still used by cartoonists because the information it carries about the nature of ART is powerful.

Poster for walls and floors.
France 1954 Savignac

Franking. It has all the elements that make for compulsive graphics. Predesigned and having originally a precise function, its positioning is almost random and may become part of an accumulation of overprintings in a time period. See also ACCUMULATED GRAPHICS, STAMP.

Book cover.
UK 1952 André François

Letterhead for an advertiser's mailing service.
USA 1954 Lou Dorfsman

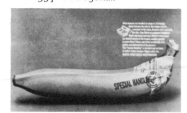

Copy says that bananas are handled (franked) only three times, unlike some other bananas. See also BANANA.
USA 1962 Bill Petti

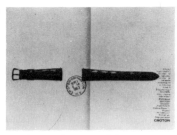

Franking mark as a watch face substitute and a symbol of address change. See also CLOCK/WATCH.
USA 1963 Len Bauman

We can't mail you
a color chemist.

Advertisement for colour laboratory. Problems claimed to be solved by return mail.
USA 1964 Carl Stewart

They are still two of the cheapest ways
of crossing the country.

Volkswagen symbol is a franking mark implying that the mail and the VW are two cheap methods of travel.
UK 1973 Derrick Hass

Frog. A favourite character in children's books although the real creature is not particularly cherished except by small boys. In general a symbol of transformation; tadpole into frog (water to land), frog into prince.

Front View/Back View. A device on book jackets where the back cover shows the rear view of the front cover. The thickness of the spine enhances the illusion. See also REAR VIEW, REVERSE.

UK 1964 Derek Birdsall

France 1964 Robert Massin

Fruit. Literally one of nature's gifts. A natural symbol of plenty. There is often an analogy between fruit and human flesh, particularly female, with a common terminology (peach complexion, etc). See fruit by name.

Fruit Machine. A natural and highly decorative symbol for gambling in general and winning the jackpot in particular. Such GAMES of chance are popular as analogies for life itself.

Sale advertisement for store: 'Put a little money in and get a lot of value out . . .'
USA 1957 Arnold Varga

Funnel. A symbol for the idea of filtering – as a mass of facts and figures might be sorted and channelled for easy comprehension. Sometimes used as a symbol of congestion, as in bottleneck. See also FORKED EMBLEM.

Funnel as a symbol of concentration. The device maximises the marksman's efforts. See also TARGET. *UK 1950 André François*

Fur/Fur Coat. A fur coat is one of the foremost badges of wealth.

Gallows. Simple and unmistakable graphic sign symbolising death and capital punishment. Suggestive of the official death penalty as opposed to the tree which suggests lynch law. See also GUILLOTINE, NOOSE.

UK 1952 André François

Games. Board games, especially those with a reasonable mix of skill and luck, are an ANALOGY for life and designers and illustrators use the metaphor constantly. The one to one game (like CHESS) has more than an element of personal aggression in it and is a natural war analogy. This applies to games like tennis where the area of aggression can open out to include matrimony. It is generally supposed that football (both American and English) is a thinly disguised war game.

Tennis as a matrimonial contest. See also HEART. *UK 1962 Mel Calman*

Deliberately archaic found-image of golfers for a forward-looking film-commercial company. The associates are their own models, their poses based on an Edwardian drawing. UK 1967 Bob Gill

Election crosses in the appropriate political colour. Noughts and crosses as an ANALOGY *for the blocking tactics of politics. See also* X.
UK 1970 Laurence Bradbury

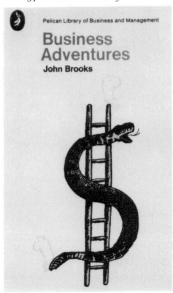

Book on American business. Fusion of Snakes and Ladders and DOLLAR SIGN.
See also LADDER, SNAKE.

UK 1970 Mel Calman/Philip Thompson

Games and Battles. A form of diagram which takes its name from graphic renderings of both activities.

Political poster, 'Beat the Whites with the Red Wedge'. See also TRIANGLE.
USSR 1918 El Lissitzky

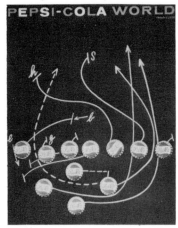

Cover for Pepsi-Cola World. *Bottle tops substitute for footballers in a tactical diagram. See also* ARROW, DOTTED LINE.
USA 1958 Brownjohn, Chermayeff & Geismar

Tactical diagrams as a substitute for letterform in a TV advertisement for American football.
USA 1961 Lou Dorfsman

Garbage Can. See DUSTBIN.

Garden (Yard). The garden represents the cultivation of civilised values against the surrounding forest of dangers, fears and doubts. In psychological terms the garden is the intellect and the surrounding forest the unconscious. The walled garden which is a graphic device used a great deal in literary areas is a reinforcement of these symbolic ideas. See also FENCE.

Book illustration.
UK 1938 Eric Gill

Garden Gnome. In Britain a symbol of suburban taste.

Garter. A highly erotic symbol, associated with chorus girls.

Article on SEX *and the* CAR.
USA 1973 Bob Post

Gate. The gate as a portcullis of a fortified town is a general symbol for security. Used on the reverse side of some coins. A whole range of status and social aspirations may be suggested from the wrought iron gates of the mansion to the suburban gate with its sun ray motif.

General Signs. The circle, square, triangle, CROSS, forked emblem. These are signs which together form the basic plastic language. The circle is the traditional symbol of eternity and the heavens. The square represents the world and denotes order. The triangle is a symbol of generative power and spiritual unity. The CROSS is a combination of active and passive elements. The forked emblem (Y), a medieval symbol for the trinity, is also an emblem for the paths of life. Although these broad interpretations occur in many religions and cultures throughout history, because of their formal simplicity they can be invested with infinite subjective meanings.

Three-dimensional versions of general signs. Cube, cone and sphere as elementary symbols of design. Cover for Bauhaus. *See also* TOOLS.
Germany 1928 Herbert Bayer

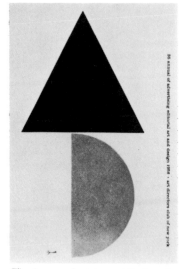

The viewer grafts on known letterforms to basic forms. Cover for art director's club.
USA 1956 George Giusti

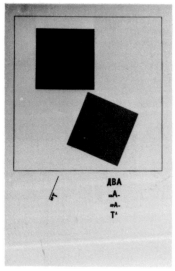

Stability of the square disturbed. See also NUMBER SYMBOLISM Four.
USSR 1920 El Lissitzky

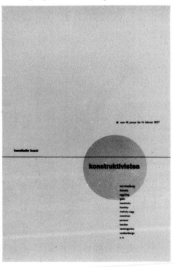

Poster.
Germany 1937 Jan Tschichold

Trademark for BECH. Equal tension between bled letterforms and dynamic square.
Switzerland 1957 Gerstner + Kutter

Kieler Woche   21.-28. Juni 1964

Triangle becomes a yacht when headline (Kiel Week) is read.
Germany 1964 Hans Hillman

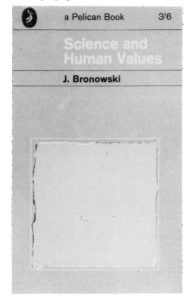

a Pelican Book   3/6

Science and
Human Values

J. Bronowski

Square representing human values falls short of perfection.
UK 1968 Fletcher/Forbes/Gill

Giant. Like the FAIRY and the elf it carries associations, half benign, half malevolent. American advertisers in the popular advertising market occasionally use the giant as a benevolent figure providing for all. See also MAGICIAN.

'China awakes.' Personification of country as Gulliver. See also BONDAGE. Germany John Heartfield

'Consultant designer to giant industry.' Designer's own publicity. See also FOOT. USA 1954 Jack Wolfgang Beck

Giraffe. No particular historical significance. An animal regarded with affection, its long neck is usually the characteristic referred to (as in the drink industry – long cool drink, etc).

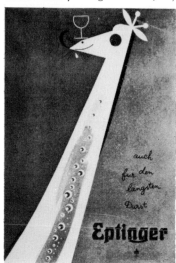

auch
für den
längsten
Durst

Eptinger

Giraffe's neck establishes the long drink.
Switzerland 1954 Herbert Leupin

Girder. The characteristic H section of a girder has been a symbol for heavy industry for many years. A natural format-filling image with high formal and recognition value, it is sometimes used to suggest the idea of extreme weight as in the Guinness advertisements of the 1930s and 1940s.

GUINNESS
FOR STRENGTH

Poster for a strength-giving drink. See also STRONG MAN.
UK 1934 John Gilroy

ZN

ZAHN-NOPPER...

Typical SECTION of RSJ girder is a symbol for iron works.
Germany 1964 Anton Stankowski

Glass. The profile of the typical wine glass is a very strong signal. The necessary agent of wine. A constituent of many still-life groups where it symbolises worldly pleasures. A popular symbol for festivities or the general idea of conviviality. It is used on packing crates as an indication of fragility because of its unmistakable form. Like a great many common objects its many forms carry with them precise information about class, ambience and life styles (beer glasses, champagne glasses, etc).

Glass as a symbol of Christmas festivity. Olive is CBS symbol plus Christmas tree sprig. See also CHRISTMAS TREE, EYE. *USA 1954 Rudi Bass*

For an article on the 'wonders of water'. A further opportunity for refracted and ambiguous images. See also DISTORTION. *USA 1959 Henry Wolf*

Glass (Pane). Visually non-existent it is naturally a favourite with mime performers. The cartoonist's convention of two or three diagonal lines to suggest reflected light is universally acceptable. The shattered pane is a stronger and popular image.

Glasses (Pair of). The compulsion by graffiti artists (see GRAFFITI) and others to draw glasses and MOUSTACHE on every face is held by Freudians to be an unconscious wish to make a phallic drawing (see CHAD). Besides this, glasses have an immediate disguising effect; the joke shop version with nose attached being a possible symbol for espionage. See also MIRROR, REFLECTION, SUNGLASSES.

Influential piece of photo-type synthesis. USSR 1924 Alexander Rodchenko

The compulsive eye/roundels parallel the copy. See also EYE SUBSTITUTE, TARGET. *USA 1960 Milton Glaser*

Prime function of spectacles (magnification) refers to the clarity of printing. See also MAGNIFYING GLASS. *Italy 1966 Franco Grignani*

Poster in honour of the 80th birthday of Berthold Brecht. Glasses symbolise the man. See also INITIAL LETTER. *East Germany 1978 Marita Herold*

Globe. In the cinema a popular prop in romantic period dramas. Strong maritime and exploration associations. Quite often cross-referenced with other spherical objects like the BALL or FRUIT (where the segments may echo the lines of latitude). See also ATLAS, MAP.

Circular cheese pack already bears the map of the world. Pushed further to become a globe.
France 1958 Savignac

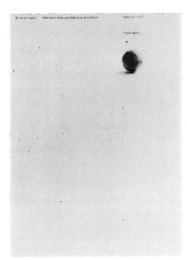

Symbol for a travel agent.
USA 1959 Louis Danziger

BOTTLE TOP *and globe support says 'world-wide'.*
USA 1963 Eugene Sercander

Glove. There is a great deal of medieval symbolism associated with the glove; the KNIGHT wore the glove of his lady in his helmet and defended her to the death. Not much of this symbolism is left except in language; expressions like 'hand in glove' or 'the iron fist in the velvet glove' persist. Often a fashion symbol and a natural occupation-defining object.

Characteristic glove as a symbol for winter sports resort.
Switzerland 1939 Herbert Matter

Destroyed knitting is an immediate signal for 'moth-eaten'. For an anti-moth preparation. See also FINGER.
Switzerland 1951 Herbert Leupin

Glove continued

Glove as an occupation-determining object.
Advertisement for a bank attracting
workmen.
USA 1960 Saul Bass

God/Goddess. Many Gods and Goddesses are used as symbols of qualities and emotions associated with them. The ones with any meaning for western civilisation are Greek or Roman. Typical examples are Neptune, Roman god of the sea, Hercules, symbol of strength, Minerva, Eros, Jupiter and many others. They frequently occur in trademarks, where as well as having a tenuous link with the product give a certain prestige. The French car, the Citroen DS, is a typographic condensation of 'déesse' (goddess).

Mercury, god of science and patron of travellers, is borrowed by motor fuel company to represent them.
UK 1959 Henrion

Gold. See COLOUR SYMBOLISM.

Graffiti. The scribblings on walls consisting of drawings and writings of a scatalogical, erotic or sometimes political nature. In 1837 a Bishop Wordsworth made a collection of the graffiti of Pompeii which has been of great use to scholars. The revival of interest in graffiti began about the late 1940s and early 1950s with artists such as Dubuffet. The 'art' of children, idiots, criminals and the like has always had an enthusiastic following by minorities. The general idea of adding a casual comment in a graffiti-like manner as part of a design is a fairly popular one. See also CHAD (MR), DEMOTIC SIGNS, DOODLE, GLASSES (PAIR OF), HANDWRITING, MOUSTACHE, WOMEN WITH MOUSTACHES.

Early use of graffiti in advertising.
France 1902 Bouisset

Revival of graffiti as an advertising medium.
UK 1939 Designer unknown

USA 1949 Milton Ackoff

Female partner in a comedy duo added as an afterthought. See also FILE.
USA 1953 George Olden

The copy refers to aggressive, protesting typography. Advertisement for a printer.
Italy 1960 Franco Grignani

USA *1960 Robert Brownjohn/Tony Palladino*

End titles for West Side Story.
USA 1961 Saul Bass

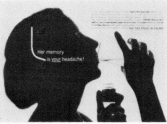

Scribbling-on principle which radically alters consecutive numbers. Magazine cover. See also NUMBER SYMBOLISM.
UK 1965 Crosby/Fletcher/Forbes

Grapes. The tangible form that expresses wine. The configuration is as simple as it is unmistakable. Bacchus pressing grapes was a popular medieval sign for wine producers and innkeepers.

Graph. The line graph and the compound line graph are diagrammatic devices.

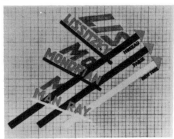

Exhibition advertisement.
See also ARROW, SHADOW.
USSR 1922 El Lissitzky

Memory. Graph superimposed on head. 'Her memory is your *headache.' An advertisement telling advertisers that consumers have short memories. See also* PROFILE.
USA 1957 Lou Dorfsman

Graph Paper. (*$87\frac{5}{8} \times 68$ ins.*)
USA 1967 Alex Hay

Book jacket. See also STARS AND STRIPES.
UK 1963 Bob Gill

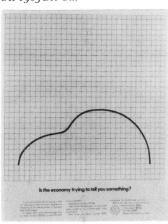

Is the economy trying to tell you something?

The copy asks, 'Is the economy trying to tell you something?'
USA 1970 Ted Shaine

Graph 115

Grass. An elemental material. Ancient symbol of victory, grass representing the vanquished land. Crown of grass was thus the highest award in the Roman army. The graphic rendering of grass can amount to obsessive doodling. The result is deeply satisfying.

Cover for architectural magazine.
USA 1961 Ray Komai

Magazine cover.
USA 1963 Paul Hogarth

Gravestone. A characteristic outline. A natural symbol for death. 18th century gravestones were decorated with engravings of the scythe and HOURGLASS (reminders of the limited span of man's life). The characteristic engraved lettering frequently used for rubbings. See also CHARACTERISTIC STYLE.

Green. See COLOUR SYMBOLISM.

Group Photograph. The group photograph (such as the school class or football team) is a ritualistic record with a strict iconography rigorously observed. This gives it a timeless, classical appearance and makes it a popular subject for affectionate parody and pastiches. See also KEYLINE DRAWING.

Record sleeve. See also DRUM.
UK 1967 Peter Blake/Jan Haworth

Drawing of a school photograph.
Advertisement for the children's department of a store.
USA 1968 Arnold Varga

Guardsman. Although guardsmen are combatant troops the popular image remains that of custodians of royalty. It therefore remains a symbol for the capital city of those countries (like England and Denmark) who still have a monarchy. It has strong associations of tourism. Occasionally the image is condensed to the head and busby which carry enough information.

Characteristic guardsman's drill put to good use.
UK 1952 André François

Guess Who? A traditional advertising technique that invites the reader to join in a guessing game before the brand name is divulged. Part of the WRAPPING-UP, teasing and disguising obsession.

See also MONKEY.
USA 1955 Savignac

Guess who:

Will out-advertise any other bourbon in Washington?
Will have all Washington talking about its unique ads?
Is the finest Kentucky bourbon...literally born with the Republic 175 years ago?
Is the brand could better start stocking right now?
It's James E. Pepper.

Guessing who visually makes reference to guessing by taste. Advertisement for a distillery.
USA 1956 Helmut Krone

There's no mistaking White Horse Whisky

(the mellowness gives it away)

Advertisement for a distillery.
UK 1962 Bob Gill

Guillotine. Named after the 18th century doctor J. Guillotin who first proposed its use, its association is in the area of the French Revolution. In general a symbol for a precise and definitive cut. See also GALLOWS, NOOSE.

Our Friends, the French

It's difficult to keep a level head about the French when your oldest ally has become one of your severest critics. Tonight producer-writer Perry Wolff and CBS News Correspondent Eric Sevareid take a provocative look at the differences which have made anti-Americanism the semi-official policy of France. This witty and incisive special broadcast also examines differences Frenchmen are having among themselves. Differences which find the French heart in the eighteenth century and the French mind in the twentieth.

Tonight 10-11 In Color CBS News ⊚2

Guillotine as symbol of criticism. Advertisement for news programme examining the anti-American attitude of the French. See also UNCLE SAM.
USA 1958 Lou Dorfsman

Guitar. A natural symbol for music in general and Spanish music in particular. Since the invention of the LP they have been much in evidence advertising blues and folk music (acoustic) and rock music (electric), the multifarious designs of which enter the realms of surrealist fantasy. One of the popular condensed images for the guitar is the representation of the tuning mechanism at the top of the guitar. See also MUSICAL INSTRUMENTS.

Gun. One of the most popular of clichés. Most publicity for books or films of violence and war use the gun as an important element in design. Overt reference is usually made to its phallic symbolism and it is often seen being manipulated by nubile females. A potent and aggressive object even in humorous contexts. See also BULLET.

See also DIAGONAL, X.
USSR 1929 Alexander Rodchenko

Wifely concern for suicidal husband.
France 1950 André François

Gun continued

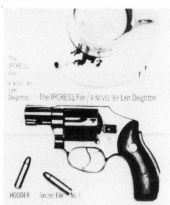

Gun as an espionage symbol. See also
PLAN VIEW.
UK 1962 Raymond Hawkey

*Implication of suicide gesture is that fuel
consumption is excessive. Copy suggests
alternative to suicide '. . . or buy a
Volkswagen' (low fuel consumption).
USA 1979 Charles Piccirillo*

Gyroscope. An industrial and aero-
nautical tool which is usually seen in
the form of a child's toy. A natural
symbol for the idea of equilibrium,
sometimes used as an ANALOGY for
physical and mental well-being in
human beings.

Hair. Primary female characteristic.
Despite the fashion for longer hair in
the male the idea still remains. In
women, pinning back the hair is
associated with order, even primness –
literally being in subjection. Con-
versely letting down the hair is a
symbol of freedom or perhaps aban-
don. In early Christianity long hair in
women signified virginity, in men,
virility. Hair has strong associations
of authority and rebellion against it;
cutting it suggests submitting to a
higher order. The serpent hair of
MEDUSA signifies the evil female
principle.

*Copy says, 'Does today's teenager
influence the adult world? "Ridiculous"
says Ed Sullivan'. Beatles haircut became
an early 1960s symbol for emerging
rebellious youth.
USA 1965 George Lois*

*Poster for Bob Dylan concert. The hair is
picked out in bright colours and represents
the life force, thought, creative energy.
USA 1966 Milton Glaser*

*Loose flowing hair signifies the nubile state.
Wet hair as a strong erotic signal.
UK 1968 Hans Feurer*

Halo. A symbol of the sun in pre-Christian religions. It is now most commonly associated with Christian saints. In popular graphics it is an immediately understood symbol for saintliness or mock innocence. See also SAINTS' SYMBOLISM.

Halo establishes angelic herald. See also ANGEL, TRUMPET.
USA 1957 George D'Amato

Senator Joe McCarthy's hatchet man Roy Cohn maintains his innocence.
USA 1968 George Lois

Hammer. Part of the emblem of the USSR (hammer and sickle) since 1923. The original blacksmith's symbol of a brawny ARM with up-raised hammer became a more general symbol for productive work in factories and then by implication assumed a certain militancy. Unofficially adopted by trade unions. The wooden hammer or gavel is also a symbol for auctioneers. See also ANVIL/HAMMER.

Trade advertisement (for selling carpets). Carpet hammer as a symbol for hard-hitting advertising techniques.
USA 1952 Gene Federico

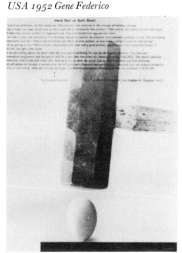

Symbol of hard-sell advertising. Copy says, 'You can't smash your egg and eat it too'. See also EGG.
USA 1957 Louis Danziger

Book jacket. Symbol of trade unionism. See also ARM.
UK 1970 Derek Birdsall

Hammock. A symbol of carefree relaxation, which also has strong maritime associations.

Hammock as a symbol of contentment.
USA 1954 Roy McKie

Hand. In early Christian art a symbol of the Deity. In secular use the disembodied hand is a popular and powerful symbol. Used widely in the 1940s and 1950s where its sense of urgency was used in graphics for safety in factories and road traffic situations. It also had a vogue in the 1950s as a symbol for the human element at the heart of a technological revolution. See also FINGER, FIST, HANDSHAKE, KITCHENER, PALMIST'S HAND.

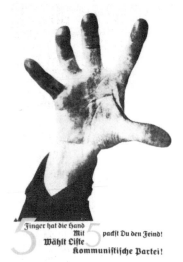

Germany 1928 John Heartfield

Political poster. The hand gesture symbolises the pledge contained in the copy 'We shall fulfil the plan of great works'.
USSR 1930 Gustav Klutsis

The open hand of Chandigarh, a symbol of gathering, giving and taking that preoccupied Le Corbusier for over thirty years.
France 1955 Le Corbusier

Handcuffs. Symbol for crime. The two horse-shoe shapes with link are a strong gestalt.

Advertisement for a CBS TV programme.
USA 1952 William Golden/Yudel Kyler

Handprint. A record of man's creative endeavour. See also FINGERPRINT, FOOTPRINT.

For a 10th Graphic Arts Yearbook.
USA 1950 Bradbury Thompson

See also SKULL.
USA 1952 George Giusti

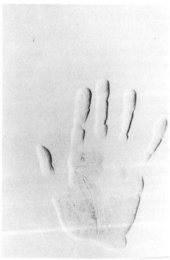

Embossed hand (see EMBOSSING) for cement company. The reference is to Graumann's Chinese Theatre where celebrities leave their prints in wet cement.
USA 1963 Vance Johnson

Handshake. A common symbol of friendship or concord. The ancient Greeks used it on their tombs as a symbol of life after death. Extremely popular in wartime as a rhetorical device for solidarity between nations fighting a common foe.

Painting.
USA 1962 Roy Lichtenstein

Brewery sign. Handshake as symbol of hospitality.
USA 1964 Paul Davis

Handshake becomes a symbol for a new working relationship. Designer appointed as consultant.
UK 1968 Bob Gill

Handwriting. Handwriting has a great sense of urgency and immediacy. A handwritten menu suggests freshness, a handwritten message suggests an up-to-dateness that is unique. Because fishmongers have to identify daily a great variety of catch, the chalk marks on BLACKBOARD have become associated with their trade. See also CALLIGRAPHY, DEMOTIC SIGNS, GRAFFITI.

The demotic style of the café owner becomes a trademark.
UK 1965 Bob Gill

Newsagent's board as a direct-mailing shot.
UK 1972 Alan Fletcher

Harp. Symbol of Ireland. A comic book shorthand for the after-life where the inhabitants play harps among the clouds. Although angels playing lutes in medieval painting outnumber harps by four to one, the harp persists in popular imagination as the heavenly instrument. See also MUSICAL INSTRUMENTS.

Harp as a lovers' symbol. Harp strings are a visual pun for RAIN.
UK 1964 Raymond Peynet

Hat. In Freudian psychology the hat is a sexual symbol. It can stand for rank, authority, position in life and dignity. See also CAP.

Nationality and thereby brand of cigarette defined by fez.
Austria 1920 Joseph Binder

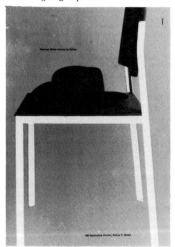

Hat on CHAIR *establishes that store is open.*
Advertisement announcing opening of new store.
USA 1955 George Tscherny

Record sleeve. BOWLER HAT *as substitute for the band leader.*
UK 1960 Ian Bradbery

Country and occupation defined by hat.
See also PROFILE.
USA 1961 Saul Bass

Hatstand. A record of attendance. A primitive and effective means of communicating such information.

Clothes Tree. *Life-size construction.*
USA 1961 George Brecht

Heads/Middles/Tails. The children's book device which is given fresh life from time to time.

A version of the heads/middles/tails principle showing incongruity of image.
See also SANDWICH BOARD.
France 1940 Henz Morran

Merger of three designers.
UK 1960 Fletcher/Forbes/Gill

The incongruity principle applied to an
ever-changing real-life situation on a BUS.
UK 1960 Alan Fletcher

The same principle of incongruity but
using a single fold.
USA 1960 Irving Miller

Heart. Symbol of love and affection.
In many cultures of many periods the
heart has been treated with reverence
and the idea that it is the essence or
soul of the human being is strong. The
graphic representation of the heart
appears inexhaustable.

The SUBSTITUTION of heart for head makes
a subtle link with the word 'wisdom'.
See also FACE SUBSTITUTE.
USA 1958 Chermayeff & Geismar

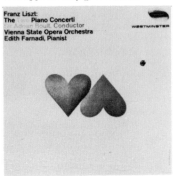

Liszt: high priest of the Romantic period.
Two hearts become the PLAN VIEW of two
pianos (the two Liszt concertos). See also
PIANO.
USA 1960 Rudolph de Harak

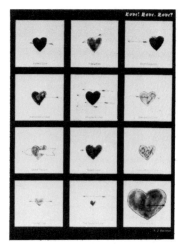

Description of character according to size,
disposition, etc of heart and ARROW. For
instance, a large heart with many arrows
embedded: 'easy to love'.
USA 1961 R.O.Blechman/Tony
Palladino

Heart as treble pun: FLAG, FACE, heart.
France 1964 André François

Heart continued

ALBERTINE MANEVAL
LE CŒUR
ET LA GÉOMÉTRIE

PROMOTION ET EDITION

The heart repositioned is associated with the BRAIN. *See also* CRANIUM, WINDOW.
France 1966 Savignac

Blood donation campaign. See also BLOOD, DROP.
Japan 1966 Hiroshi Tanaka

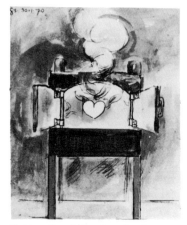

'Cupboard love.' One of a series of illustrations for a desk DIARY.
UK 1970 Graham Sutherland

Feb. 12, 1979   THE   One Dollar
NEW YORKER

Ironic comment for St Valentine issue: rose-tinted, heart-shaped SPECTACLES.
USA 1979 André François

Helicopter. There is a close connection with ascension mythology where the revered one is taken from the crowd into the clouds. See also AEROPLANE.

Hidden Element (Seek and Find). The device used in children's books where a drawn illustration contains elements foreign to the illustration which are cunningly disguised as other objects. (For instance, leaves or clouds containing faces.) An artistic joke which artists like Holbein used.

Find the . . . A children's book of hidden shoes.
USA 1964 Tomi Ungerer

Holes in Books. Modern fine art typographers like Massin, Munari and Dieter Rot have experimented with defining the three-dimensional aspect of books by cutting, sewing, tearing and boring holes in book pages. This exploration has sometimes been picked up by designers or book illustrators working in a more commercial area. See HOLES IN PAPER.

From Libri Illegible.
Italy 1959 Bruno Munari

Holes in Paper. The punching of holes in flat surfaces to reveal vistas and to create new spatial relationships is a feature of much architecture and sculpture. The same process is available to designers with two-dimensional structures. For instance, holes in posters may reveal parts of other posters underneath. Sometimes the semi-cut portions may be folded to take advantage of light and shadows. See also HOLES IN BOOKS, SMASHING THROUGH PAPER, PAPER SCULPTURE.

Ticker-tape holes. Trademark for news agency. See also PERFORATION.
UK 1965 Crosby/Fletcher/Forbes

Holes as a symbol for electronic music.
USA 1966 Milton Glaser

Poster for exhibition, Magic of Paper. *The colours of the previous posters on the hoarding show through the perforations.*
Switzerland 1969 René Gauch

Honeycomb. Easily formalised as a series of circles or hexagons. The symbolism is usually that of industry or socialisation. See also BEE, CELL.

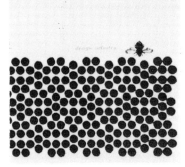

The copy reads, 'Design/industry'. A direct visual metaphor.
USA 1957 Jack Wolfgang Beck

Honeycomb structure as a symbol for busyness. See also AMPERSAND, REBUS.
UK 1960 Gene Federico

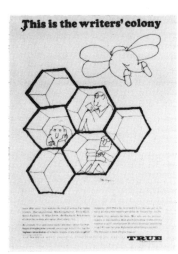

Honeycomb structure used as a symbol for social community (of writers).
USA 1966 Tomi Ungerer

Hood. The FACE being the most expressive part of the body any covering of it is anxiety making. In masked benevolent figures like Batman their whole attitude is outgoing and counteracts such anxiety, but be-stockinged gunmen, Ku-Klux-Klansmen and hooded executioners symbolise the ultimate in anonymous terror. See also MASK.

Hook. The hook on the end of a crane was a popular symbol for heavy industry during the 1940s and 1950s.

Crane-hook as a symbol of reconstruction.
France 1947 Jacques Nathan

Hook continued

France 1956 Raymond Peynet

Symbol for construction division of a corporation.
USA 1958 George Giusti

Hoop. The act of jumping through hoops is a symbol for coping with tasks proposed by others.

Hopscotch. A children's game and therefore a symbol of childhood. It hovers between a game (see GAMES) and real life; the paving stones are the board, the children are the pieces. An economy that appeals to designers. See also NUMBER SYMBOLISM.

Editorial photograph for Look *magazine.*
USA 1962 Art Kane

Horn. Musical symbol. In general the brass instruments serve as announcing symbols. The French horn's configuration falls into a square making it a natural symbol for record sleeves. See also MUSICAL INSTRUMENTS.

Political poster.
USSR 1918 Designer unknown

Poster for an exhibition of musical instruments.
Switzerland 1962 Richard Lohse

Poster for a music festival.
Switzerland 1966 Celestino Piatti

Horns. Symbol of strength and power. Appear on the helmets of mythological figures and real warriors who 'borrowed' their strength from the BULL whence they came. A cartoonist's shorthand for 'Viking' and also the DEVIL who is often represented throughout ART as having horns and tail.

Horse. Symbol of strength and courage, the horse represents energy at the disposal of man. In antiquity a horse was often represented as carrying the souls of the dead from one life to the next. In ancient mythology the horse features considerably; the winged horse signifies poetic imagination. This still holds good in modern thinking. Romantic ideas of freedom probably date from the time of Delacroix. The motor car absorbed some of the romance, mythology and terminology of the horse.

Mechanised horse in transition.
1930 Jean d'Ylen

Visual and literal meaning of 'horse-power' are fused.
Switzerland 1940 Hugo Läubi

Poster for a brand of CIGAR *called 'Little Horse'. See also* REBUS.
Switzerland 1954 Herbert Leupin

HYPERBOLE: *a poetic exaggeration;* CLOWN *sleeps even on galloping horse. For a sedative.*
France 1957 André François

Horse (Panto). Its essentially schizoid nature endears it to surreal cartoonists. A Christmas symbol.

For a Christmas issue of Punch.
UK 1954 Lewitt-Him

Poster for 50th anniversary of American Institute of Graphic Arts.
USA 1965 Paul Rand

Horseshoe. Symbol of protection and good luck. The multiplicity of explanations from various sources throughout history partly accounts for its persistance as a universally accepted good luck sign.

Christmas card.
USA 1957 Onofrio Paccione

Hourglass. Symbol of time running out and thus a symbol of death. Much seen in graveyards. The configuration symbolises the upper and lower worlds and is echoed in the mathematical symbol for INFINITY.

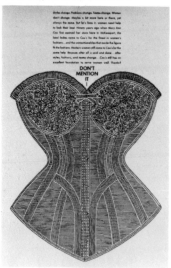

A visual ANALOGY*; the 'hourglass' figure is a universal cliché for the feminine ideal despite the advance in fashion. An advertisement for a department store. See also* BRA.
USA 1962 Arnold Varga

The hourglass as a symbol for old age.
UK 1969 Mel Calman

House. The house is an essentially female symbol; enclosing, maternal, womb-like. It is also a metaphor for the human BODY in a more general sense, in regard to its rooms, various openings and functions. Like other fundamental necessities the house can be unequivocally expressed in graphic terms. The typical child's drawing of a house with a pitched ROOF, windows (see WINDOW), central DOOR and smoking chimney (see SMOKE) is an archetypal image and immediately expresses ideas of protection and comfort. See also TENT.

*Advertisement to encourage the home fashions trade to take space in a magazine. The advertising is designed to 'attack' (*ARROW*) the home dweller. The childlike drawing (see* CHILDREN'S WRITING AND DRAWING*) reinforces the idea of the home as a shelter. See also* DOT.
USA 1957 Bill Sokol

Condensation of house to pitched ROOF.
See also FIRE.
USA 1958 Tony Palladino

Fusion of house sign with present (buying) sign. See also BOW, PARCEL.
UK 1970 Penny Abrahams

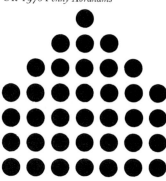

Trademark for Halftone House. See also BLOCK.
USA 1970 Tom Woodward

House of Cards. A metaphor for an insecure scheme or operation likely to collapse. See also CARDS.

Ironic comment on 'The thousand-year Reich'.
Germany 1932 John Heartfield

Book jacket. House of cards as a symbol for a shaky romance.
UK 1965 Feiffer/Brian Haynes

Housewife. According to advertisers of soap flakes and junk food a youthful person always smiling and invariably holding the merchandise at eye level. This idealised portrait is a useful basis for parody.

Poster. See also PLUG.
France 1952 Savignac

Magazine illustration. Variation on an archetypal theme.
UK 1971 Hans Feurer

Humanised Alphabets. As alphabets are based on the human form humanised alphabets are simply echoing their origins.

CLOWN *becomes* INITIAL LETTER.
Switzerland 1952 Herbert Leupin

Alliterative product and GLASS. *Poster for Guinness.*
UK 1958 Abram Games

Hyperbole. The literary figure of 'poetic exaggeration' is easily transferred to the visual field.

Exaggerated image reflects copy 'This is the size of it: strawberries are never out of season at Hornes'. See also GLASS.
USA 1963 Arnold Varga

An excessively exaggerated way to spell the word 'inflation'.
UK 1973 Derek Birdsall

Ice Cream. The ice cream cornet (literally horn), is visually an amalgam of the CORNUCOPIA and the Greek TORCH of immortality (its whirl of ice cream a visual pun for the flames). An icon of mythic proportions it is a fitting symbol for childhood and seaside holidays.

The copy mentions '. . . the benefits of freedom (American) for yourself and your children . . .' Advertisement for Campaign for a Union. Ice cream used as symbol of childhood. See also ANALOGY.
USA 1959 George Lois

Ice Skater. Symbol of confidence and nonchalance. Sometimes the expression 'skating on thin ice' is given a visual form with the addition of a star-shaped hole in the ice (overconfidence). See also MARKS AND TRACKS.

Ice skater here symbolises winter. A visual OXYMORON *(contrast of opposites): retreating skater (winter) and emerging cotton-sheer-dressed girl (summer).*
USA 1957 Gene Federico

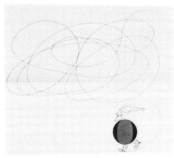

Christmas card for Show *magazine. See also* MARKS AND TRACKS, SANTA CLAUS, SUBSTITUTION.
USA 1964 Henry Wolf

Ice skating waiter serves dinner from the deep-freeze. A symbol for frozen foods. See also SERVANT.
USA 1967 Otto Storch

Ice Tongs. A highly characteristic and evocative image that is deeply rooted in the American psyche. (*The Iceman Cometh*, etc.)

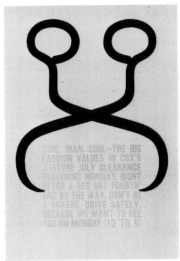

Copy says, 'Cool, man, cool'. Advertisement for fashion store referring to clothes to wear in a hot summer. USA 1956 Arnold Varga

Copy says, 'Frozen assets'. For an article on freezer foods. USA 1961 Otto Storch

Identikit. FACE assembled from component features to aid criminal identification and detection. First used in Los Angeles in 1957. See also MUG SHOT.

TV title sequence. UK 1963 Bernard Lodge

Igloo. An Eskimo version of the basic HOUSE. Its characteristics are the half sphere and entrance tunnel and blocks of ice. Strong symbol for cold climate.

'Gentleman with cold feet . . .' UK 1962 Mel Calman

Image on Image on Image. The device where for instance a character on the book cover is reading the same BOOK ad infinitum.

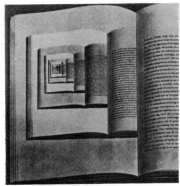

Poster for a book fair. Holland 1960 Total Design

Cover of Show *magazine. USA 1962 Henry Wolf/Ben Somoroff*

Images of Movement. The graphic recording of vibration figures on a pendulum machine was rediscovered by designers in the 1940s and 1950s and added to the current repertoire of formal designs in the same way as were images of ATOMIC STRUCTURE.

Magazine cover.
Italy 1955 Bruno Munari

Infinity. The abstract shape (roughly of the mathematical figure infinity) that had a strong hold on the imagination of designers in the 1940s and early 1950s purely as a formal device devoid of any literal meaning. See also BOOMERANG, BOW.

Initial Letter. The use of an initial letter as the main element in a design. See also MONOGRAM.

Alliterative use of initial letter.
USA 1949 Paul Rand

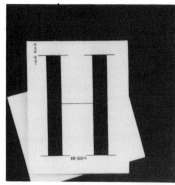

For Hurd's 'suede finish' stationery.
USA 1951 Erik Nitsche

Gordon and Gill join forces. See also CHAIN.
USA 1954 Bob Gill

Trademark for W. Raven & Co. See also REBUS.
UK 1954 Hans Schleger

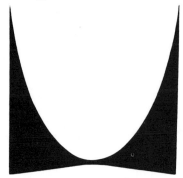

USA 1956 Paul Rand

Letter M for Herman Miller Furniture.
USA 1957 Irving Harper

Trademark for Artone, makers of inks and poster colours. The letter has a flowing quality suggestive of ink and paint.
USA 1961 Seymour Chwast

An example of an acronym. Logotype based on the sound of the initial letters of Standard Oil.
USA Designer unknown

Ink Pot. A strongly humanistic and personal image, the more so since the decline of letter writing and the use of PEN and ink. The elaborately carved inkstand with its many inkwells and QUILL pens has strong literary associations. It also has connections with the idea of authority, power and order (as in the signing of wills, charters and similar documents).

A further example of the obsession with 'taking the lid off' buildings. See also BUILDING, CALLIGRAPHY, DESK, DOME, QUILL, SANTA CLAUS.
France 1954 André François

Ink pot as a symbol for literature. See also CREST.
USA 1956 Paul Rand

Advertisement for artists' agent. See also LABEL.
UK 1956 Len Deighton

Insect. Modern taste regards insects without enthusiasm (except for the BUTTERFLY, BEE and LADYBIRD).

Man with a roving eye.
Germany 1969 Hans Hillman

Inside Lining. There is a psychological fascination in seeing both sides of the same garment at once. The turned-back CORNER of a piece of paper has the same effect. In fashion drawing this is a useful expedient as it is required sometimes to show the quality of a lining of a coat. See also FLASHER.

Copy says 'Psst funny peectures' which is a reference to the cliché 'Psst dirty peectures'. Although the use of the device is symbolically gratuitous, the attention is held. See also SPY.
USA 1957 Bob Curtis

Inside Space. Defining lettering by use of the inside space.

Cover of booklet for The Composing Room.
USA 1959 Brownjohn, Chermayeff & Geismar

Symbol for Friedericks Heyking (steel).
Germany 1960 Anton Stankowski

J

Jack-in-the-Box. Symbol of surprise, repetitiveness, indestructibility.

One of a series of posters for a newspaper.
UK 1960 Patrick Tilley

Janus. The two-faced Roman god. Used by designers in specialised contexts and by cartoonists in a spirit of parody. See also GOD/GODDESS.

Two-headed man indicative of speed. Classic poster.
UK 1930 John Reynolds

UK 1970 Mel Calman

'Shell' man image applied to HMV dog to become a symbol for stereo.
UK 1976 Jones/Thompson

Jester. The opposite to the KING, the idealist, the lofty KNIGHT. Sometimes the coarse and aggressive pragmatist, at other times the court comedian. In graphics his complex role is not much referred to. Rather he is a general symbol for fun and frivolity. His visual characteristics are the caps and bells.

Advertisement for artists' agent, Stephan Lion. Fusion of LION and jester (copy refers to 'serious and gay') he is also a REBUS figure.
USA 1954 Herbert Leupin/Henry Wolf

Jewellery. Precious stones although rich in symbolism are nowadays regarded only as symbols of wealth or as part of body adornment.

Jewellery as a shoe substitute. See also FOOT.
UK 1962 Philip Thompson

Jigsaw Puzzle. Any cut or torn shape has a natural 'graphic' quality. The male and female pattern made up by the jigsaw is one such. Its fascination lies in its obvious analogy with problem-solving. See also PUZZLE.

Jigsaw piece as a selecting symbol. (Rotterdam picked out of Europe.) See also MAP.
UK 1963 Colin Forbes

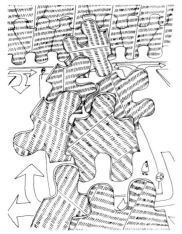

Man as a piece in an overall social system.
USA 1965 Folon

Joined-up Numbers. A device derived from comic books and children's annuals.

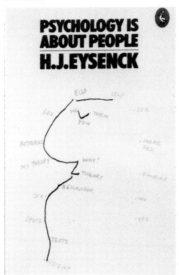

Psychological phrases join up to make a person.
UK 1978 Mel Calman

Juggler. The characteristic design of the 1940s and 1950s was a precarious balance of formal elements. Sometimes the pictorial elements consisted of the CLOWN, SEAL, juggler, etc, which underlined this formal preoccupation. In advertising, the juggler can play as easily with the merchandise achieving the same hypnotic effect.

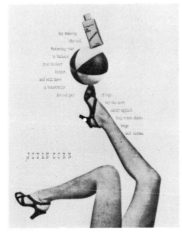

Copy refers to 'Balancing hosiery budget'.
USA 1944 Paul Rand

Self-promotional advertisement for designer.
USA 1947 Matthew Leibowitz

Copy says, 'Anything you ever wanted to do . . .' Juggling equated with the impossible.
USA 1957 Lester Bookbinder/Gene Federico

K

Kangaroo. Symbol of Australia.

'Gauloises . . . in every pocket' (see
POCKET).
Switzerland 1959 Donald Brun

Advertisement for a non-stretch jumper
with reinforced pockets (see POCKET).
USA 1970 Arnold Varga

Key. In metaphorical language the
key suggests the explanation or the
way in to a particular problem. It is
this figurative aspect which is of most
use to designers. Because of the male/
female aspect of the key and KEYHOLE
together with the meaning of un-
locking and having knowledge there
is a strong sexual connotation. It is
also a symbol for saving in the sense
of something of value being locked.
Keys play a large part in many rituals
of state and church.

Invitation permitting one to 'view the
House of Simplex'. Access symbol. See also
HOUSE.
UK 1951 George Mayhew

Hotel key with tag, 'Be our guest' becomes
an invitation to a showroom (room 603).
USA 1959 Hal Davis

A wide variety of car keys (see CAR)
becomes a symbol of free choice.
Advertisement for advertising association.
USA 1963 George Rappaport

Symbol for Antiques & Things.
See AMPERSAND, CLOCKWORK, INITIAL
LETTER.
USA 1965 Arnaud Benvenuti Maggs

Keyhole. Has all the connotations of a KEY but because of its compelling shape and the fact that it pierces the picture plane it is a much used device. The meaning is usually associated with spying or voyeurism. See also PRISON CELL.

Keyline Drawing. The necessary device whereby a complex photograph is copied in line and numbers added for purposes of identification. This unconscious piece of design has instant recognition value and is sometimes used to express as yet unidentified groups of people.

Kinetics. The use of real kinetics such as flick books or the simulated kinetics of a sequence of photographs on a page taken perhaps with a motor-driven camera.

The figure moves and is filled up cinematically. The EYE also moves independently. Originally brought out as single posters in sequence.
France 1934 Cassandre

Copy says, 'What the Duchess saw'.
SERVANT *imitates master. Voyeuristic reference.*
UK 1964 Colin Millward

Keyline treatment for specific group. (Staff of advertising agency.) See also GROUP PHOTOGRAPH.
UK 1966 KMP Ltd

Typography expresses the movement of FILM.
USA 1958 Brownjohn, Chermayeff & Geismar

For a boutique entitled 'Way in'.
UK 1967 Paul Posnick

Keyline treatment for unspecific group.
See also CIRCLING COPY.
UK 1973 Philip Thompson

Book jacket.
Switzerland 1960 Müller-Brockmann

An advertisement for football on CBS TV.
A stop-frame technique simulating
continuous motion.
USA 1963 Lou Dorfsman

King. The paraphernalia of a king that establish his rank are the ceremonial robes of coronation (CROWN, ermine, cloak, orb, sceptre). This is the immediately understood stuff of comic books, and illustrators and designers use the convention. As a metaphor a king usually means 'the best', literally 'fit for a king'.

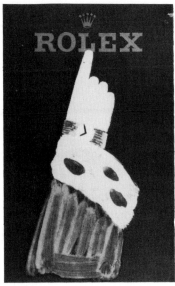

Condensed image (ermine) of king
implying 'the best'. See also CARDS, FIST.
Switzerland 1958 Herbert Leupin

King Kong. The 1933 giant ape from the cinema which has become a metaphor for our ambivalent attitude towards animals. See also MONKEY.

Characteristic Kong gesture transferred
ironically to Norman Mailer (in his
treatment of women's liberationist,
Germaine Greer). See also PIETA.
USA 1971 George Lois

Kiss. Ancient and popular expression of friendship, salutation, farewell, reverence, sexual love, adoration, servility (in the sense of kissing the feet) and in the case of Judas, treachery.

Comment on the artifices of film world.
France 1952 Savignac

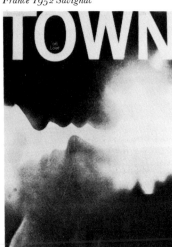

The full romantic treatment for an article
on love.
UK 1963 Art Kane/Tom Wolsey

Kitchener. The compelling, guilt inducing image of Kitchener with the accusing FINGER has become an icon of mythic proportions on a par with the MONA LISA and Michelangelo's *Creation of Man* and forms part of the heroic sacrifice myth. See also FIST.

Comic book kiss for an article on love comics.
UK 1967 Richard Hollis

UK 1914 Alfred Leete

Exhibition poster.
USA 1966 Roy Lichtenstein

Kiss Imprint. A perfect and inevitable piece of graphic printing first established as an icon by the students of the Bauhaus and used repeatedly ever since. See also LIPS, MARKS AND TRACKS.

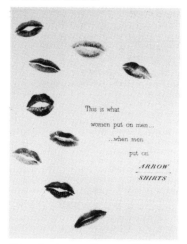

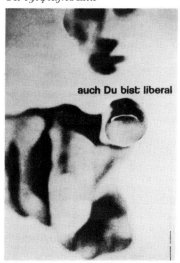

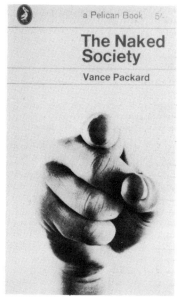

Poster. 'You are too liberal.'
Switzerland 1959 Karl Gerstner

A non-fiction book about 'You are being watched' revelations.
UK 1968 Derek Birdsall

Shirt advertisement. Copy says, 'This is what women put on men . . . when men put on Arrow shirts'.
USA 1952 Jack Anthony

Kite. An airborne graphic device. Strong associations of childhood.

Kit-layout. The taking apart of a product and systematic laying out of its components. In effect a statement of honesty – literally not having anything to hide. A favourite device in the 1960s when it was used as an antidote to the gratuitous image making of the time. See also CUT-OUT, CUT-UP.

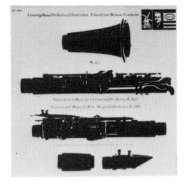

The obsession for laying out the components of an object is justified in the case of the clarinet.
USA 1957 S.Neil Fujita

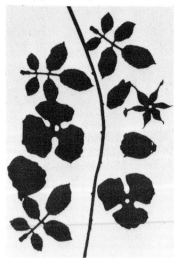

Plastic FLOWERS for a plastics firm.
UK 1960 Colin Forbes

Flat BOX before folding.
Switzerland 1960 Heiniger/Müller-Brockmann

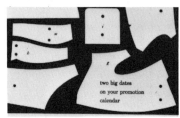

Dress pattern to advertise fashion pages of New York Times.
USA 1960 Louis Silverstein

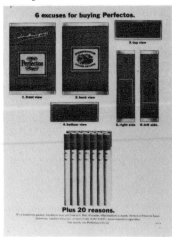

Advertisement. 'Honest' laying out of the pack to promote a new brand of cigarette.
UK 1960 Tony Palladino

Knight. The knight represents the struggle of the spirit over the material aspects of life. Honour, chivalry and high ideals eventually lead to his 'winning the spurs' which even in today's language suggests lofty endeavour. See also ARMOUR, SWORD.

Traditional symbol of sword (for protection) in pharmaceutical trade is here developed into the complete person (knight) who protects. Lance flies FLAG with temperature declining. For an antibiotic.
See also BANNER, GRAPH.
Belgium 1958 André François

Punning knight.
UK 1958 André François

Copy says, 'Jack Kennedy was a prince among men. How do you feel about Lyndon Johnson?' Traditional knightly qualities tentatively applied to LBJ. USA 1965 George Lois

Associations of knightly qualities including chivalry towards damsels in distress. UK 1972 Mel Calman

Knitting. It shares certain visual characteristics with the KNOT. Humorously, reference is made to its time-consuming aspect and the sedentary nature of knitters. More fundamentally knitting involves creating a 'soft' structure (home, nest, etc) and is sometimes a female home-building symbol.

Knitting pushed to tubular limits. UK 1954 Gerard Hoffnung

Knitting as a symbol for marital harmony. UK 1972 Mel Calman

Pregnant sheep knits for a spring season television programme about having a BABY. UK 1977 Peter Brookes

Knot. Knots have strong nautical and boy scout associations. As a visual metaphor the knot represents a difficult problem. A fascinating configuration as the pattern is determined by necessity. See also BONDAGE, BOW.

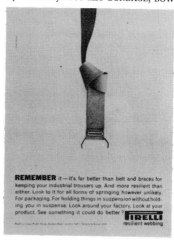

Knotted webbing as a reminder symbol. UK 1963 Derek Birdsall

The knot used as a prime attention-getter as part of a contortionist. See also CLOWN. France 1967 Savignac

Knot 141

Label. The characteristic appearance of a label that bears a message of warning or urgency has ruled borders which vibrate because of their colour or proximity. Sometimes the message is applied in a semi-formal HAND-WRITING. The label thus commands attention. See also LUGGAGE LABEL.

Poster advertising newspaper small-ad space.
UK 1963 Bob Gill

Book jacket.
UK 1974 Philip Thompson

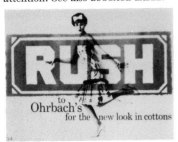

Poster.
USA 1959 Bob Gage/Wingate Paine

Large painting. Mundane object transformed into art by dramatic change of scale.
USA 1967 Alex Hay

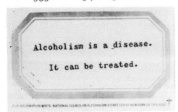

Medicine bottle label for an advertisement against alcoholism. See also TYPEWRITER TYPE.
USA 1961 R.O. Blechman/Tony Palladino

Commercially produced all-purpose label.
UK 1972 Philip Thompson

Ladder. Symbol of ambition and aspiration.

Ambition's ladder supports the copy, 'Fifty-one per cent of Punch *readers hold top jobs'.* CIGAR *symbolises the managerial class.*
UK 1964 Lindsay Gutteridge

EQUAL OPPORTUNITIES
A Careers Guide for Women and Men
Ruth Miller

Book jacket.
UK 1977 Carole Ingham

Ladybird (Ladybug). No historical significance but regarded with affection and thought vaguely to symbolise good luck.

Landscape. The landscape as an analogy for life is supported in dreams, psychology and literature (Bunyan's *Pilgrim's Progress*) and is one frequently used by illustrators. The CROSSROAD (decision), SIGNPOST (spiritual and philosophical guidance), RIVER (barrier), MOUNTAIN (problem), and beautiful secret places (childhood memories) are some of the natural symbols. The configuration of landscape too is an inevitable ANALOGY for the human BODY. See also GARDEN.

Laurel. In ancient Greece the victor's CROWN was made of laurels. Today it is still a symbol of honour, peace and victory and of excellence in general.

Autumn leaves from a laureate's crown fall as his creative powers wane.
France 1975 André François

Lay Figure. Symbol of art schools and artists in the Beaux-Arts tradition. As a substitute for the human body its symbolism is varied.

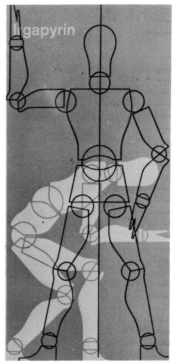

Chief characteristic of lay figure is the joint articulation. A natural symbol therefore for rheumatic references. The lay figure became a popular EUPHEMISM *in medical advertising, representations of the real thing being unacceptable.*
Switzerland 1956 Geigy Design Team

Leaf. A popular symbol in the 1940s and 1950s for the countryside. At that time there was a vogue for making direct printed impressions of leaves. Often adopted as emblems for companies and countries. See also TREE.

Trademark for National Film Board. See also FILM.
Canada 1963 Derek Rabinovitch

Letter. The formal address and signing off is a strong visual signal for the idea of personalised information. A device much favoured by direct mail advertisers.

Handwritten copy in the form of letter from the countryside.
UK 1934 Gregory Brown

Advertisement for restaurant in the form of a personal letter to restaurant critic (after savage review in magazine).
USA 1970 George Lois

License Plate. See NUMBER PLATE.

Lifebelt. Symbol for survival. The real object carries lettering and therefore lends itself to a typographic treatment.

The navy has traditionally strong links with tobacco.
UK Designer unknown

Light Beam. The revealing wedge of light that cuts through the dark is a graphic device beloved of children and designers.

The light beam from flashlight is echoed in the SPEECH BALLOON image.
France 1966 Savignac

Light Bulb. A light bulb is a popular symbol for an idea or creativity.

Object associated with the inventor (Thomas Edison) is itself a symbol for creativity.
USA 1963 Ernie Smith

Brilliant ideas change according to the status of the thinker.
USA 1970 R.O.Blechman

Lighthouse. The actual lighthouse shape with its characteristic LIGHT BEAM is a strong gestalt image. Associations of permanence and reliability.

View from PORTHOLE. *Symbol for reliable (tough) glass.*
UK 1946 Tom Eckersley

Reliability symbol. Poster for electric batteries.
France 1954 Jean Colin

Lightning Flash. Forked lightning formalised as a Z shape. A universally understood dynamic form.

Advertisement for BP petrol. See also
DIAGONAL, HORSE.
UK 1936 McKnight Kauffer

INITIAL LETTER. *Trademark for Quebec Hydro-Electric.*
Canada 1960 Gagnon/Valkus Inc

Line/Lines. The use of lines to denote smell, heat, steam, etc. are a reminder of the essentially graphic nature of drawing and its conventions. See also DOTTED LINE, MARKS AND TRACKS, WAVY LINE.

Line as an indication of heat.
France 1929 Charles Loupot

Line as an indication of smell.
UK 1934 Will Owen

Lines of Motion. Probably established by the Italian Futurists as part of their research into the visual rendering of movement. Later adopted by comic book artists. It is now an indispensable part of the language of drawing.

Advertisement.
UK 1952 Hans Schleger

Advertisement. See also TYPEWRITER.
Italy 1953 Giovanni Pintori

Lion. A general symbol of strength, courage and kingship. Known as a symbol for Britain although slightly fallen into disuse since the loss of empire.

HEART *doubles as lion's face (English symbol).* FLAG *and* ROSE *support the national symbolism.*
France 1964 André François

Lips. A favourite photographic subject. A cliché of the 1960s was the full-colour image of the lips blown up as large as possible in magazine spreads. See also KISS IMPRINT, MOUTH.

Lips (over a foot across) from an article on female emancipation. See also SCALE.
USA 1959 Irving Penn

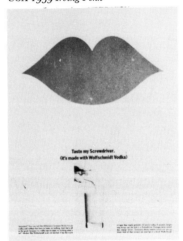

Copy says, '. . . All that remains on your lips is a word. Wolfschmidt'.
USA 1961 George Lois/John Alcorn

Poster for exhibition of artist's own work.
USA 1966 Man Ray

Lipstick. Formally aggressive and phallic. The symbolism is complex. The structure is almost identical in size and shape to a BULLET.

Lipstick as a prime female symbol. For an article on draft dodgers.
USA 1966 George Lois

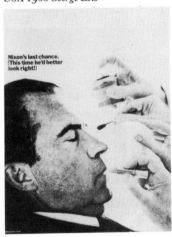

Lipstick as an aid to political image-making. See also COLOUR CORRECTION.
USA 1968 George Lois

Loaf. Similar to cake and biscuit design. As the basic technology does not change the designs have remained the same for centuries, encouraging feelings of nostalgia and stability. See also WHEAT.

Locomotive. Fundamental part of the romantic Victorian idea of freedom. The image of the great iron HORSE belching FIRE and SMOKE and roaring across the country remains in the popular imagination as the archetypal and only form that a locomotive should take. Freedom symbol. As with other vehicular developments such as the BICYCLE and the AEROPLANE it represents freedom and independence and ultimately restlessness.

Engine (puffer) copies smoking driver (puffer).
Switzerland 1955 Donald Brun

Luggage Label. A strong gestalt, its characteristic shape is determined by its function. A symbol for travel. See also LABEL.

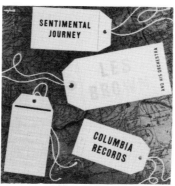

Seminal record sleeve. Early use of travel label as symbolic motif.
USA 1949 Robert Jones

Label as a symbol for a travel agent.
USA 1959 Robert Brownjohn.

Magician. The benevolent magician is a recurring figure in mythology, fiction, advertising and real life, personified in rainmakers, Christ figures, SUPERMAN, Robin Hood, etc as well as in selfless scientists and inventors. He frequently appears in downmarket advertising as a benefactor in mythological dress or as a pseudo-scientific adviser. The stage magician uses his skill in harmless deception. Part of his stock-in-trade is the RABBIT and playing CARDS. A strict ritual of dress and manner is observed. There is an obvious connection between magical transformations and the buying of goods. The deception connection is unconscious.

The image of the conjuror/magician to suggest that women who shop at Ohrbach's are 'wizards' at saving. See also WOMEN WITH MOUSTACHES.
USA 1958 Bob Gage

Magnet. The characteristic horse-shoe shaped magnet can symbolise the general idea of attraction.

The copy begins, 'If bargains attract you . . .'
USA 1958 Michael Wollman

Magnifying Glass. Strong associations with detection. More generally used to express the idea of looking at some subject in detail, in other words a 'close-up'. The view from behind the glass showing the viewer's enlarged EYE is an obsessive image devoid of any specific meaning but having the same fascination as DISTORTION.

Quality printing bears scrutiny.
USA 1952 Saul Bass

Painting as a joke on the artist's use of mechanical screens. See also BLOCK, DOT.
USA 1963 Roy Lichtenstein

Manhole. Somewhere in the 1950s manholes were discovered as being worthy of aesthetic interest. Steinberg has always emphasised the manhole covers in his street drawings, sometimes using engraved collage. Manhole covers have a perennial fascination as they are a link between the world we know and a subterranean world of service conduits and fantasy. Strong mythological associations with the underworld.

Map. Originally the map was a guide to travellers and a means of education – a representation of the earth's surface and an indication of its physical and political characteristics. Maps have developed as a basis for giving information of a statistical kind like population mobility or the location of industry. The straightforward representation of a country's outline is a natural symbol for that country. The strong visual characteristics of the map allows it to withstand considerable distortion without loss of identity. The map projection is a 'peeled' GLOBE laid flat to show selective information.

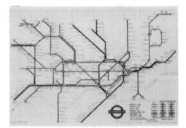

London Transport map. Information is sequential and not strictly geographical. This map has been vastly influential in design thinking ever since its inception.
UK 1933 Henry C.Beck

Poster for airline. Copy says, 'Shrinking travel time'.
UK 1948 Lewitt-Him

Poster for British Rail.
UK 1952 Abram Games

Map of New York with names of songs on
the appropriate streets.
USA 1959 Charles Goslin

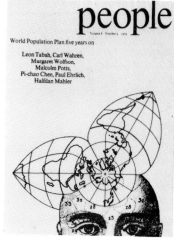

'The great divide'. A pun that refers to the
split between viewers watching different
channels.
USA 1961 Lou Dorfsman/Joseph
Schindelman

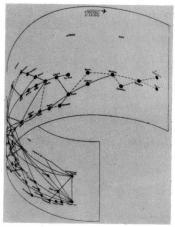

Computerised airline network.
Switzerland 1965 Siegfried Odermatt/
Rosemary Tissi

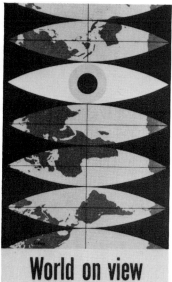

Poster showing world as series of gores
which make a globe. See also EYE.
USA 1952 Leo Lionni

Distorted projection for an article
emphasising Scotland.
UK 1964 Anthony Froshaug

Cover for magazine using tetrahedral
projection for an issue on world population.
UK 1979 Philip Thompson

Map 149

Marks and Tracks. The marks and tracks left by sticks dragged in the sand, the FOOTPRINT, ICE SKATER, skywriter, SMOKE, SNAIL, etc, which leave their own idiosyncratic record of a journey through time. See also KISS IMPRINT, LINE/LINES.

Magazine cover. A visual ANALOGY: pen lines are like SMOKE from a factory chimney (see FACTORY).
USA 1943 Paul Rand

Book jacket. Lorca's name is given an idiosyncratic treatment in the sand.
USA 1955 Alvin Lustig

Perfume advertisement. Perfume distracts signwriter. See also HEART.
USA 1959 R.O. Blechman

Emphasis by absence. Change of address card. See also BORDER.
USA 1959 Robert Brownjohn

Pencil drawing. 37 minutes. 3879 strokes. ($24\frac{3}{8} \times 19\frac{1}{2}$ ins.)
USA 1961 Robert Morris

Perfume advertisement. Having one's name written in the sky is a symbol of the ultimate, fabulous life-style.
USA 1963 Bert Steinhauser

Coffee cup stain as a symbol for creativity. Designer's own letterhead.
UK 1973 Bobby Gill

Mask. Identity is mysteriously hidden or transformed by the wearing of a mask. The mask is a recurring theme in the history of drama and literature and in social and religious ritual. The actual object or the representation of one has an equal hold on the ingenuous and sophisticated imagination. In our time in the light of Freudian or Jungian psychology the idea of crises of identity and the conflict between our private and public personae ensure that the mask is an immediately understood symbol. See also HOOD.

The Greek masks of tragedy and comedy are fused with the MAP of America to symbolise the American theatre.
USA 1962 R.O.Blechman

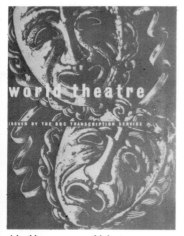

A booklet cover on world theatre.
UK 1948 Cecil Keeling

UK 1965 Mel Calman

An utterly meaningless symbol for a non-existent product. Part of a World Publicity Week event to excite public curiosity for its own sake. A poster which is virtually a KIT-LAYOUT of attention-getting qualities: HAND, top hat, CIGAR, logotype and mask.
France 1962 Savignac

HOUSEWIFE *assumes a fixed expression for breakfast.*
UK 1960 André François

Advertisement for the Ogden Corporation aimed at recruiting graduates. The student/Einstein METAMORPHOSIS *is hinted at optimistically.*
USA 1970 Henry Wolf

Matchstick. A potent image in its own right, it also carries with it all the primitive and historical association of FIRE symbolism. The different feelings evoked in the image of the unused and used match correspond to the potential and then released energy. Apart from fire symbolism matches are also used as substitute currency (in CARD games) and are components in children's PUZZLE games.

Fusion of match and HOUSE. *Fire prevention poster.*
Switzerland 1956 Fischer Corso

Proffered lighted match as a symbol for smoking.
USA 1963 Matthew Leibowitz

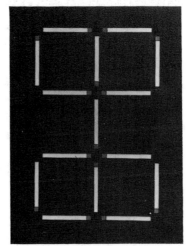

A Christmas mailing; a book of match puzzles. The matchstick is a traditional puzzle and game-playing element.
UK 1975 John McConnell

Poster for Uncle Vanya *by Chekhov. Although a strong image the symbolism is a little ambiguous. Uncle Vanya thinks he has wasted his life (a burnt-out match?). At the same time, as a landowner he has chopped down his forests and burnt them.*
Germany 1977 Holga Matthies

Maze. In modern thinking the legend of the Minotaur and labyrinth persists, but in general the symbolism of the maze refers to a PUZZLE or problem. Sometimes they are incorporated into a larger LANDSCAPE of life. In recent years there has been a revival of interest in creating mazes as a fine art activity.

HEART *becomes maze (snare).*
UK 1962 Mel Calman

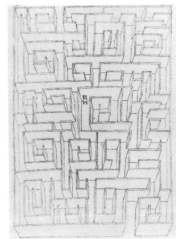

Invitation to an exhibition of drawings by Folon. In the centre of the maze is a solitary CHAIR.
Belgium 1966 Folon

Medal. A reward symbol.

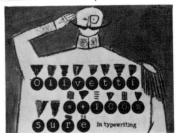

Medals substitute for TYPEWRITER *keys on a uniform.*
UK 1956 André François

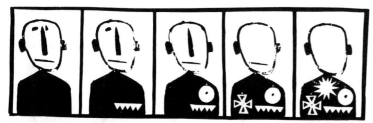

The rewards of a bureaucratic state at the expense of the humanity of the individual. Poland 1960 Jan Lenica

The reward refers to awards won for creative advertising. USA 1956 Herb Lubalin

The DCB award: Distinguished Crawford Biscuit. UK 1963 Blackburn & Gardner

Medusa. Chief Gorgon and one-time beauty who was transformed by Minerva into a snake-haired monster. Useful for symbolising unattractive females. See also HAIR.

Coy Gorgon. See also SNAKE. UK 1970 Mel Calman

Megaphone (Bullhorn). A strong visual object. The shape says unmistakably 'sound'. The hand-held version has associations with the sport of rowing and the FILM industry (assistant film-director's equipment). A natural symbol for advertising and amplification in its widest sense.

Editorial photomontage. USSR 1930 Gustav Klutsis

Copy says, 'The whisper that becomes a shout'. Advertisement for store expansion. See also SUBSTITUTION. USA 1953 Bob Gage

Melon. No particular symbolic meaning but being a basic CRESCENT shape it occurs frequently as a design element.

The crescent shape and triangular BITE are obsessive formal devices which at times satisfy the designer's plastic needs before any other consideration. See also GENERAL SIGNS.
USA 1957 Arnold Varga

A slice of life. See also TRADEMARK MANIPULATION.
USA 1964 Hugh White

Mermaid. One of the vast family of FABULOUS BEASTS with indeterminate tops and bottoms. Illustrators enjoy confusing things further. The mermaid is a hardy standby for seaside holiday brochures.

Tenuous copy link with word 'twist' justifies mermaid image. See also WAVE.
USA 1957 Saul Mandel

Metamorphosis. A natural phenomenon. It features in mythology, literature and popular imagination (HAIR into SNAKE, pumpkin into coach, FROG into prince).

A record sleeve 'On the way to war'. Civilian into soldier.
Sweden 1966 Bergentz/Falk/Lenskog/Roos

Mickey Mouse. Arguably the most potent symbol/sign/icon of the 20th century. Oldenburg has shown Mickey Mouse to be part of an iconography of interchangeable elements. In some senses Mickey Mouse is an adjectival abuse. Steinberg uses the image as a symbol of tawdry values.

Micrometer. Symbol for accuracy.

Poster. Micrometer as a symbol of accuracy in news reporting. Copy says, 'To a hair's breadth'.
USA circa 1932 Paul Smith

Microphone. A strong symbol for the idea of world-wide communication. The barrage of microphones is a powerful image and has associations with oligarchies and dictatorships signifying world domination.

Booklet for lighting firm that specialises in precision work. Fusion with INITIAL LETTER of client.
USA 1951 Ray Komai/Andrew Morimoto

Advertisement for CBS Radio to attract advertisers. Battery of microphones implies large audiences.
USA 1953 Lou Dorfsman

Microscope. Symbol for the pursuit of knowledge.

Microscope as a symbol of curiosity (a high-risk instinct for a CAT).
USA 1965 Saul Mandel

Minus Sign. See ARITHMETICAL SIGNS.

Millstone. A millstone round the neck can be a strong image of somebody burdened with a heavy responsibility.

Mirror. Mirrors play an important symbolic role in folk-lore, legend, fairy tales, painting and films of many periods. The hand mirror is a very feminine symbol being associated with Venus and Aphrodite. The cliché in films or TV plays where the action is seen to have taken place in a mirror intrigues us as we readjust to the new reality. Vampires who don't reflect and filmed sequences in halls of mirrors are two more examples. The REFLECTION in a pair of GLASSES (first established in a painting by Ben Shahn in 1944) is one of the most common images in advertising.

A Magritte-like device. The mirror is a simple symbol for fashion. See also GLOBE. USA 1952 Bradbury Thompson

Illustration for Seventeen *magazine demonstrating the spatial ambiguity that is a timeless obsession for painters, illustrators and film-makers. USA 1958 Ben Shahn*

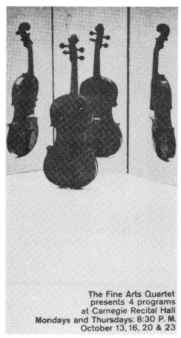

Three mirror images of a single VIOLIN for four concerts of a quartet. USA 1957 Bob Gill

Theatrical mirror with characteristic greasepaint HANDWRITING. See also LIGHT BULB. USA 1961 George Tscherny

Model (Shop Window). A symbol of fashion.

Copy says, 'Where we are bound – the new Jo Collins showrooms'. USA 1957 Gene Federico

Lots of legs for lots of nylons. USA 1959 William Taubin

Mona Lisa. A sort of unofficial symbol of high ART and culture. There are thousands of products that use the Mona Lisa as their trademark to suggest excellence. Duchamp when he drew a MOUSTACHE on the Mona Lisa in 1919 was questioning the whole basis of art values and attitudes. See also WOMEN WITH MOUSTACHES.

Monk. Although the subject matter is pious the associations are invariably humorous. The characteristics are the tonsure and long habit. Sometimes used to recommend wine.

Association of cleanliness and Godliness. UK 1880 Henry Stacy

Monkey. Historically, a symbol of the baser instincts. In Picasso's later erotic engravings the artist depicts himself in the posture of a crouching monkey who observes the erotic action. He is regarded with a mixture of amusement and embarrassment as we see in him a distorted mirror-image of ourselves. Monkeys are often used in situations required to show mischievous, inquisitive or imitative behaviour. See also KING KONG.

Advertisement for toothpaste. Monkey's imitative behaviour extends to hygiene. Italy 1920 Terzi

Syntactic and semantic associations. CHAIR for children. USA 1955 Herbert Matter

Commercial for Xerox copier. Literally '. . . it's so simple even a monkey could do it'. USA 1962 Sam Scali (Papert, Koenig & Lois)

Monogram. Two of the most celebrated monograms in history are those belonging to Jesus Christ: XP (from the Greek) and IHS (various explanations but 'In hoc signo' – in this sign – is one of them). It is thought by some that monograms – either personal or belonging to a famous fashion house – on silk shirts and other garments confer status on the wearer. Monograms are a suitable symbol for ideas of personalisation and ownership. See also INITIAL LETTER.

Painter's personal monogram. France 1892 Henri de Toulousse Lautrec

Reversed f turns into right-way-round b for a monogram for furrier. Switzerland 1958 Marcel Wyss

Monopoly. Board GAMES can be analogous to the journey through life. Monopoly maintains its popularity because it is about money, an abiding preoccupation. In communications its symbolism is usually in the area of fiscal or property dealing.

Monopoly HOUSE *as a symbol for environmental disorder.*
UK 1970 Pentagram

Monument. A monument such as the Statue of Liberty is a symbol for the ideas and country associated with it. There may be a nobler BUILDING in Paris than the Eiffel Tower but none expresses the city so forcibly.

Travel poster. Although its original significance is lost, it is borrowed as a symbol for Britain.
UK 1932 McKnight Kauffer

The statue of Liberty as a symbol of oppression and imperialism.
USA 1967 Tomi Ungerer

Comment after New York's bad press on account of violence and bankruptcy. See also TORCH.
UK 1970 Mel Calman

Moon. There is much legend and mythology surrounding the moon. It has obsessed poets, myth-makers and lovers from the beginning of time. The American landing on the moon has not dispelled any of the romantic allusions. The symbolism in modern thought is fairly unspecific although ideas of love and romance feature largely.

Illustration for children's book I know a lot of things.
USA 1960 Paul Rand

Mortar Board. A symbol for teaching or higher education although the object is rarely seen except in comic books and films.

Mosaic. Associations of Greek, Cretan and Roman antiquity.

TV credit titles for a classical subject.
UK 1960 Bernard Lodge

Mosaic (Photographic). As a last resort the use of many small photographs when the subject matter is diffuse. (For example on the cover of an encyclopaedia.)

Cover for magazine showing a thousand famous people of the 20th century. See also BANNER.
UK 1969 Michael Rand

A Nation of Nations

Poster for The National Museum of History and Technology. Each 'dot' is a complete photographic head shot.
USA 1977 Chermayeff & Geismar

Mother and Child. The Madonna and child of Christian art and the pagan version of Venus and Cupid are recurring themes in the history of ART. This profound relationship stays in the popular imagination as some sort of timeless ideal. It is the very stuff of advertising aimed at mother and BABY. See also BREASTS.

American enlistment poster showing emotive image of mother and child drowning (in Lusitania).
USA 1917 Fred Spear

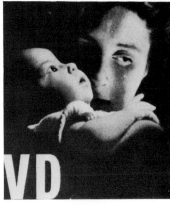

Poster.
UK 1946 Henrion

Archetypal pose of mother and child in 'tasteful' out of focus to avoid offending 1956 readers. See also CAPITAL OUT OF ERROR.
USA 1956 Irving Penn

Mountain. In modern thinking its symbolism lies in the area of a 'problem' (a mountain of work, etc) or as the ultimate in excellence, as in reaching the summit. See also PYRAMID, ZIGGURAT.

Combination of the idea of the best (the top) with ideas of good suspension.
France 1963 Savignac

Trademark for a PR organisation, Mountain & Molehill. The symbol simply returns the name of the firm (which means large or small problems) to its visual source. See also TRIANGLE.
UK 1966 George Mayhew

Mouse. The graphic rendering is beloved by children and illustrators even though the real creature is persecuted.

Extreme situation supports myth that women climb onto a CHAIR in presence of mice. See also GUITAR, MUSIC STAND.
UK 1952 Gerard Hoffnung

Mousetrap. A utilitarian object of great unreleased energy when set. Symbol of tension, suspense and precise reckoning.

Advertisement. Mousetrap as a symbol for a light-touch pen.
USA 1956 Ken Schmid

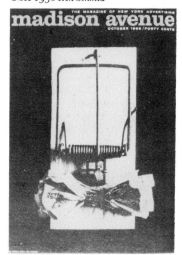

Magazine of the advertising industry.
CURRENCY as bait for magazine article.
USA 1962 Greg Bruno

Moustache. Prime male characteristic. There is a childish obsession with drawing moustaches on other faces both real and printed. This obsession is shared with designers. See also WOMEN WITH MOUSTACHES.

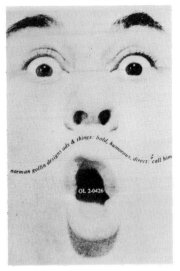

Shock value of GRAFFITI *moustache for self-promotion for designer.*
USA 1959 Norman Gollin

Advertisement for Granada TV. The copy includes the words, '. . . right under the noses of 26,000,000 Englishmen . . .'
UK 1960 George Lois/Tony Palladino

Chaplin's moustache was a symbol for the man. The typographic treatment reminds us of the old moustache in Chaplin's shaven image.
UK 1966 Hans Schleger

Hitler (like Chaplin) was characterised mainly by the moustache. Here the FILM *medium is a symbolic* SUBSTITUTION.
USA 1967 Gary Viskupic

Mouth. Graphics showing the mouth (as in lip-reading diagrams) have the same concentrated impact as the real thing as they can easily be reproduced life size. See also KISS IMPRINT, LIPS.

Expressionistic scream symbolises the horrific opera Wozzek *by Alban Berg.*
Poland 1966 Jan Lenica

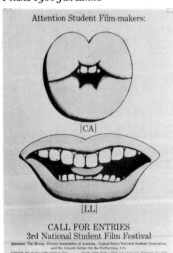

The mouths form the sounds CA and LL. A call for entries to a competition.
USA 1967 Milton Glaser

Mug Shot. The full FACE and PROFILE used in prisoner identification is a device which is readily symbolic of crime. The additional number in STENCIL LETTERING is an added characteristic. See also IDENTIKIT.

Gratuitous use of mug-shot image (of advertising manager) to gain attention. Advertisement to sell space.
UK 1967 Philip Thompson

Murder Victim Outline. The chalk line drawn round the body of a murder victim. A natural graphic symbol for crime but occasionally employed in a humorous context. See also KEYLINE DRAWING, OUTLINE.

Mushroom Cloud. See ATOMIC CLOUD.

Music Stand. Symbol for music.

Book jacket.
USA 1954 Jerome Kuhl

Music stand is an obvious place for book-jacket title.
Italy 1955 Bruno Munari

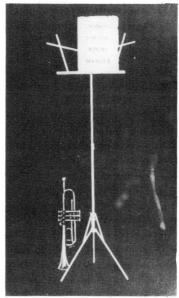

Magazine article, 'Songs for the winter solstice.'
USA 1956 Henry Wolf

Music Stave (Music Staff). The five lines of a musical stave are an immediately understood symbol for music even without the marks for bass and TREBLE CLEF. See also MUSICAL NOTATION.

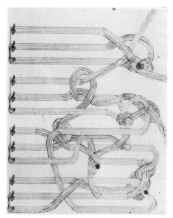

The destruction of the regular stave pattern is an apposite visual equivalent for jazz. See also KNOT.
UK 1960 Bob Gill

Elegant destruction for elegant music.
USA 1966 John Crocker

Christmas card.
UK 1966 Peter Bate

Musical Instruments. Musical instruments are rich in decorative redundancies (like scrolls and calligraphic fretwork) and thus are natural ready-made graphic material. See musical instruments by name.

Condensation of musical instrument on a concert poster.
Switzerland 1950 Donald Brun

See also CUT-UP.
USA 1950 George Krikorian

Poster for a music festival.
Germany 1950 Otto Treumann

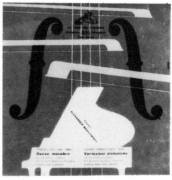

Record sleeve. See also PIANO.
Italy 1955 Bruno Munari

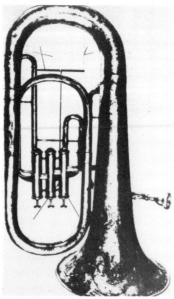

Noisy instrument in contrast to 'Silent Night' sheet music on MUSIC STAND.
USA 1956 Henry Wolf/Ben Somoroff

Musical Notation. Symbol for music. See also MUSIC STAVE, TREBLE CLEF.

Professional score-reader is deafened. See also BODY LANGUAGE, INK POT, QUILL
France 1955 André François

Notation is sometimes susceptible to draughts. See also WIND.
France 1955 Raymond Peynet

N

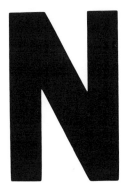

Nail. Being less sophisticated than the screw it has associations with elemental and even shoddy craftsmanship. A useful symbol for brute force. A component of the Chinese PUZZLE (symbol for problem) which has more of the characteristics of a nail when bent rather than straight.

Name and Product. A technique that allows the name and product to stand on its own without additional copy. A kind of arrogant understatement, it is best employed where the merchandise has genuine quality.

Poster.
Germany 1907 Lucien Bernhard

Perfume packaging.
France 1950 J. P. Monteux (agency)

The LABEL *as a symbol of authenticity and quality.*
Germany 1923 Otto Baumberger

Napoleon. Because of his characteristic HAT and stance often used as a symbol for France. Has strong associations with cognac and Josephine jokes.

Publicity for a Corsican restaurant.
Copy says, 'Dine like an emperor'.
USA 1957 Herb Rosenthal

National Stereotypes. Men and women dressed in national clothing can symbolise the relevant country. Sometimes a single article of clothing or a characteristic gesture is sufficient to establish the idea. These are invariably derived from a common fund of myths and misconceptions but which persist in the popular imagination. Sometimes a national stereotype is used to express non-national qualities; for instance, an Eskimo can be used to express the idea of extreme cold and thereby to promote products from frozen foods to thermal underwear.

Image of golliwog at the time was a symbol of good-humour. Hence shopping between rush hours would put one in a good mood.
UK 1929 Austin Cooper

Characteristic French gesture of approval.
Poster for COCA-COLA.
USA 1958 Jack Wolfgang Beck

Needle. A symbol for fashion. Sometimes reference is made to the 'eye' of the needle as the ultimate in small apertures. This usually implies an impossible task.

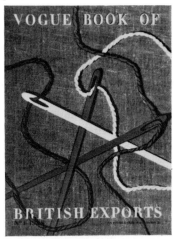

Cover for a fashion magazine.
UK 1948 Paul Piech

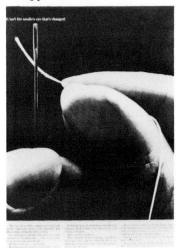

Needle's 'eye', symbolic of the smallest. An advertisement for the Better Vision Institute. See also FINGER.
USA 1963 Len Sirowitz

Negative. The use of the photographic negative as a visual dynamic. See also COUNTERCHANGE.

Poster for photographic exhibition. Germany 1938 Jan Tschichold

Negative for a positive letterhead. See also FILM.
USA 1961 Art Kane

Neon. The manufacturing process of neon lighting gives the lettering its unique style. Sometimes the style is related to the subject (theatreland), at other times it is used for its own sake.

Nest. A natural home symbol.

A change of address card. See also TREE.
USA 1957 Advertising Designers

Nest EGG *as a symbol for saving.*
USA 1958 Lou Dorfsman

Net. The characteristic triangular BUTTERFLY or fishing net shape is a very strong gestalt. As well as symbolising the activities it can be used to symbolise the idea of gentle capture (as in the wooing of a fair maiden). Netting has a strange ambivalence as it covers and reveals at the same time.

Use of butterfly net (network) as a means of capturing potential radio-listeners' ears (see EAR*).*
Luxemburg 1972 Tomi Ungerer

Newspaper. The characteristic look of a newspaper is largely determined by the necessary speed of its compilation and its market (highbrow or popular). Serious newspapers tend to favour black letter mastheads and a certain density in the reading texture. Popular newspapers favour banner headlines and photographs.

Painting. ($72\frac{5}{8} \times 52\frac{5}{8}$ *ins.*)
USA 1961 Andy Warhol

Chocolate packaging. Characteristic black letter and topically titled masthead applied to chocolates (fresh today?). See also TORN PAPER.
UK 1964 Group Design

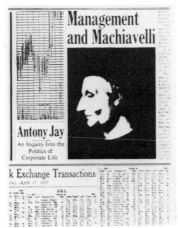

Jacket for a book about the politics of large corporations.
USA 1967 Vincent Ceci

Noose. A symbol for capital punishment or lynching. See also GALLOWS, KNOT, ROPE.

Billy Budd

Poster for Billy Budd. *Noose becomes a symbol for the life and death of the eponymous hero.*
UK 1969 Carolyn Chambers

Notebook. See SCHOOL COPYBOOK.

Number Plate (License Plate). Symbol for motoring.

TV titling for programme about holidays by CAR.
USA 1960 Joe de Voto

Number Symbolism. Since ancient times numbers have been given a particular significance. Number one is the number of the absolute, perfect, unknowable. Two is the combination of opposites; good/evil, black/white, the two-faced JANUS. Three symbolises generative power as in the equilateral TRIANGLE and the trinities; animal/vegetable/mineral, SUN/earth/MOON, faith/hope/charity. Four symbolises justice and order as in the four just men, the four gospels, the quadrangle and barrack square. Seven is the number of harmony and divine grace; the seven days of creation, seven deadly sins, seven colours (see COLOUR SYMBOLISM) of the spectrum, seven ages of man, seven wonders of the world. The sabbath lamp of the Jews has seven branches. There is some dispute about the relative importance of ten and twelve. Both figure in numerical and calendar systems. See also DATE and GENERAL SIGNS.

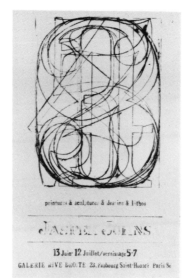

Poster for exhibition of drawings and prints by painters and sculptors. See also STENCIL LETTERING.
USA 1960 Jasper Johns

Christmas card for Stedelijk Museum, Amsterdam.
Holland 1955 Willem Sandberg

A book about junior school-children from ages seven to eleven. See also SUBSTITUTION.
UK 1973 Philip Thompson

Nun. In spite of a recent modernisation of dress the old image dies hard. There are the same general ambivalent feelings about them as monks.

Nut (and Bolt). A symbol for heavy industry.

Number one is the number of the absolute, perfect and unknowable. Inevitably first issues of magazines have a mystical significance. See also BINOCULARS, FILM, GUN, TICKET, TRUMPET.
USA 1961 Henry Wolf

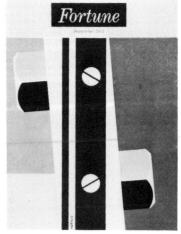

Cover for business and industry magazine.
USA 1951 Walter Allner

From 'Objects count'. A discovery about numerals.
UK 1965 Crosby/Fletcher/Forbes

Oak. Symbol of strength and trustworthiness. Particularly associated with England. See also ACORN.

Occupations. Occupational stereotypes may be identified by a single characteristic item of clothing (the chef's tall hat) or by a single tool of the trade (the doctor's stethoscope). The models for these stereotypes (mad scientist, professor, etc) persist in the popular imagination and are supported in comic books and entertainment. They provide designers with a symbolic language; for instance, a politician favouring economic cuts might be portrayed as a surgeon or a butcher.

Octopus. Mixed historical significance. Its symbolism is generally in the area of bureaucracy and imperialism.

Poster depicting Japanese imperialism. Copy says, 'The Dutch Indies must be freed'.
UK 1944 Pat Keely

Olive Branch. Symbol of peace. Associated with the return of the DOVE to the ARK.

Onomatopoeia. Use of words relating to the sound. For instance, 'chuff chuff chuff' as the copy for a railway poster.

Advertisement for alligator shoes.
USA 1961 Hal Davis

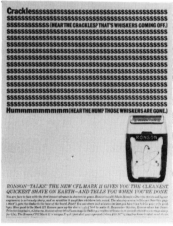

The noise of whiskers.
USA 1961 George Lois

Blasé self-promotion.
UK 1967 Bob Gill

Letterhead for Anthony Hyde.
USA 1968 Herb Lubalin

Poster for breakfast cereal.
UK 1969 J. Walter Thompson

Op Art. Branch of fine ART concerned with optical effects. The graphic processes are sometimes more suitable for reproducing these effects than oil paint.

Advertisement for printer.
Italy 1965 Franco Grignani

Oxymoron. The juxtaposition of contrasting images, for instance wealth and poverty.

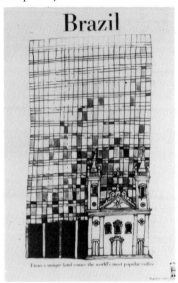

Advertisement for Brazil coffee.
USA 1964 Isadore Seltzer

Oyster. Symbol of high living. Often used showing the pearl.

Pearls of wisdom for a newspaper poster.
UK 1964 John Donegan

Package. See PARCEL.

Paint Box. Pop artists like Clive Barker, Jim Dine and others have been fascinated by paint boxes; literally laying out the TOOLS of their trade. Designers have shared this obsession.

Sculpture, Art Box II. See also KIT,
LAYOUT, PALETTE.
UK 1962 Clive Barker

Trademark for International Wool Secretariat.
Italy 1965 Francesco Sargolia

Ostrich. Has a reputation for eating hard objects which stick in the gizzard. It is also reputed to bury its head in the sand under the impression that it cannot be seen. Although the latter is untrue, the myth is applied to people who delude themselves.

Outline. Device derived from comics where the outline of a person is left in the wall bearing a record of his hurried departure. See also KEYLINE DRAWING, MURDER VICTIM OUTLINE.

Owl. Symbol of wisdom. Associated with the night.

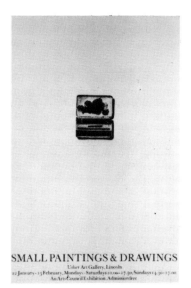

Poster for exhibition of small paintings and drawings.
UK 1971 Margaret Calvert

Paint Tube. Hardy symbol for fine art.

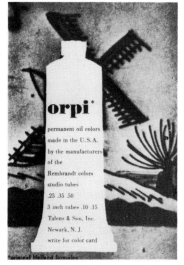

Reference is made to the paintings of Rembrandt. The paint tube is a pun for part of the WINDMILL *(symbolising Holland).*
USA 1942 Paul Rand

Paint tube as a container of art history.
USA 1964 S.Neil Fujita

Visual pun: paint tubes into skyscrapers. Poster for art exhibition; New York School. See also BUILDING.
USA 1966 Louis Danziger

An example of the obsession that the paint tube, PENCIL, PEN, *etc actually* contain the art-work.
France 1967 Savignac

Fusion of graphic (paint tube) and photographic (lens) symbols. See also CAMERA.
Germany 1977 Hansjürgen Hölzer/ Klaus Winterhager

Painting. The use of a specific painting to symbolise something outside of itself. A sort of borrowed symbolism. See also ART.

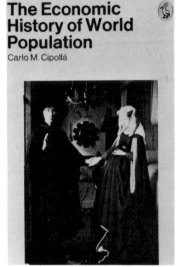

Shot-gun wedding of Jan Van Eyck borrowed as a symbol for world population.
UK 1977 Carole Ingham

Painting by Numbers. A device which started out quite seriously as an aid to the amateur artist acquired such a strong visual character that it is constantly referred to by designers, illustrators and even serious painters. Its symbolism is varied. See also COLOURING IN.

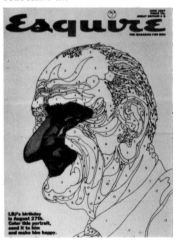

'Colour this portrait of LBJ, send it to him and make him happy.'
USA 1967 Sam Antupit

Palette. A robust symbol for the painter's or poster artist's activity.

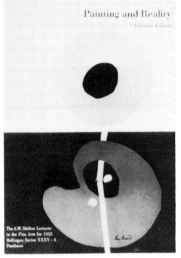

Book jacket for Painting and Reality.
USA 1957 Paul Rand

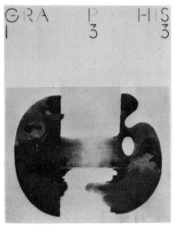

USA 1967 Milton Glaser

Palindrome. A visual equivalent to the figure of speech. See also CARDS, UPSIDE-DOWN FACE.

Soixante-neuf house painters.
France 1949 Savignac

Racial soixante-neuf.
USA 1967 Tomi Ungerer

Palm Tree. Tree beloved by illustrators, children and designers. Immediately establishes exotic locale.

For an article on the South Pacific.
USA 1960 George Giusti

Palmist's Hand. Palmistry, like phrenology, is a somewhat discredited science although its graphics and mythology are a well-established part of our folklore. See also HAND.

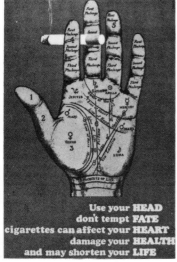

Anti-smoking poster. Copy refers to
head, fate, HEART, health and life.
UK 1960 Eileen Evans/Reginald Mount

Palmist's hand used in foretelling one's
profession. See also CRANIUM.
UK 1960 Tom Wolsey

Paper. See BURNT PAPER, HOLES IN PAPER, PAPER BOAT, PAPER DART, PAPER HAT, PAPER SCULPTURE, PAPER TISSUES, SMASHING THROUGH PAPER, TORN PAPER.

Paper Boat. Associated with childhood. Its symbolism is varied but its fragility is usually referred to. A tentative suggestion.

Paper Clip. Potent image. Symbolic of office procedure and the idea of classification and organisation.

The paper clip as a symbol for 'the
modern office'.
Italy 1958 Franco Grignani

Paper clip supports copy line, 'Passengers
will get attached to the comforts of the
Belgian Airline'. See also MARKS AND
TRACKS.
Belgium 1964 Julian Key

MONOGRAM for Mel Winston Stationers.
USA 1968 Robert Overby

Paper Dart. Potent image with airborne aspirations. Because of its material it has associations with tentative projects.

Notification of flying back to new studio.
USA 1959 William McCaffery

Paper Hat. The paper hat (made in the same way as the paper boat) is a childhood symbol. The commercially produced variety is associated with festivities and false gaiety.

NEWSPAPER *and* EGG *symbolise the day's beginning. Newspaper becomes* HAT *to put on anthropomorphic egg.*
USA 1958 Michael Engelmann/Carl Baker

France 1958 Savignac

Paper Sculpture. A recurring vogue for constructing models in paper and photographing them. They have a sharpness of imagery which photographs well.

Design exploring tactile qualities of paper.
USA 1957 Rudolph de Harak

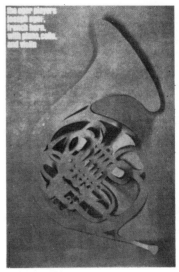

CUT-OUT *of French* HORN *on cover of concert programme.*
USA 1957 Robert Brownjohn

The client's product (paper) determines the graphic technique.
UK 1964 Crosby/Fletcher/Forbes/Gill

Paper Tissues. A symbol of a throwaway society.

Parachute. Imposing shape with a lot of surprise and surreal associations. Allusions are often made to its UMBRELLA shape.

Parcel (Package). A ready-made graphic object which picks up its design element through time and space. Childhood memories of presents and surprises are evoked. It bears traces of its experience. See also ACCUMULATED GRAPHICS, WRAPPING UP.

Passport. Symbol for travel. Also associated with espionage. See also ACCUMULATED GRAPHICS, RUBBER STAMP.

Passport as a symbol of travel.
USA 1955 William Helburn/William Taubin

Credit titles for a film on espionage.
UK 1967 Romek Marber

Pastiche. Using a classic design as a basis for expressing a new idea.

An invitation to celebrate a new TV station: 'Channel 5'.
USA 1973 Zechman/Lyke/Vetere

Patches. In the fine ART of this century there can often be seen arbitrary patches of colour which have gratuitous painterly qualities. These meet a deep psychological and plastic need in both fine artists and designers although they are difficult to account for in rational terms. Invariably there is a direct parallel between the fine and commercial art of the same period.

Arbitrary patches of the 1940s. These were more free and painterly than the regular cut-out patches of the 1950s and echoed the work of contemporary American painters like Clyfford Still.
USA 1948 Paul Rand

The use of arbitrary patches of colour was a formal device obsessively used in the painting and design of the 1950s.
France 1955 Fernard Léger

Arbitrary patches on a poster for a railway museum.
UK 1958 Hans Schleger

Peacock. A pagan and Christian symbol of immortality. In modern usage it is associated with pride and display. A natural symbol for colour registration.

Display bird for a display of posters.
USA 1895 Will Bradley

Peapod. A natural analogy for a community. High recognition when split open.

Photographs of film stars as peas. Copy say they are not 'alike' but have a lot in common.
USA 1955 William Golden

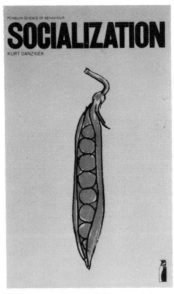

Peas in a pod as a symbol for a social group.
UK 1975 Dennis Bailey

Pelican. The characteristic bill of the pelican is a generous container and its virtues as such are celebrated in doggerel and in many illustrations.

Poster celebrating Father's Day.
France 1950 André François

Pen. The pen (consisting of a pen holder and nib) is quite often used as a graphic pun for a knight's lance. There may be an unconscious connection with the idea of free lance writing. See also FOUNTAIN PEN, PEN NIB.

'Free lance' KNIGHT. See also BLOT, DOG.
UK 1958 Andre François

For an exhibition of drawings, The Poison Pen. *See also* SNAKE.
USA 1968 Milton Glaser

Pen Nib. The decline of letter writing accompanies the decline in elegant HANDWRITING and consequently the nib. The image of the pre-ball-point nib has now a distinctly old-world cultured look. Used as a symbol for literature, the more elegant the nib the more elegant or poetic the literature. See also FOUNTAIN PEN, PEN.

For a school prospectus. The style of nib establishes the pre-ball-point era. See also HANDWRITING, SHADOW.
Holland 1951 Louis Emmerile

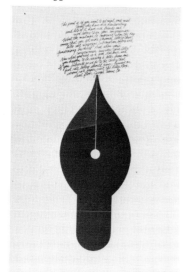

Nib is a symbol for the stationery department of a big store. See also CALLIGRAPHY.
USA 1970 Arnold Varga

Poster in honour of Berthold Brecht's eightieth birthday (pen is mightier than the SWORD).
Norway 1978 Rolf Michaelson

Pencil. A symbol for design thinking or ART. Its side is a natural surface for messages.

Pencil doubles as MOUSTACHE. Poster for National Art Museum.
Sweden 1954 Olle Eksell

Symbol for 1958 AGI exhibition. See also FLAG.
Switzerland 1958 Fritz Bühler

Fourteen pencils; the only sharp one represents outstanding creativity.
USA 1960 Jim Joiner

Exhibitionist pencil poses as BANANA for exhibition of graphic design.
Finland 1969 Unto Jäsberg

Pencil Sharpener. A natural symbol for creativity. The gesture of sharpening a pencil is analogous to a new beginning. The exposed shavings are a strong characteristic.

A symbol for the activity of illustration.
UK 1963 Bob Gill

Penguin. It is regarded with great affection and features as a popular element in illustration and advertising.

The firm's symbol is used architecturally and is also part of the alliterative INITIAL LETTER. *See also* TRADEMARK MANIPULATION.
UK 1967 Gerald Cinamon

Penknife. A symbol for self-sufficiency and versatility. The image is reminiscent of handymen, boy scouts, hikers, etc.

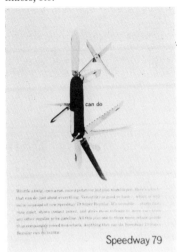

Speedway 79

Advertisement for motor fuel. Copy compares versatility of knife with versatility of fuel.
USA 1959 Saul Bass

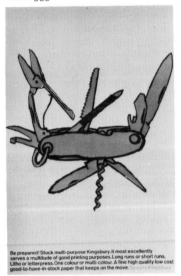

Mailing for a range of new PAPER. *Copy starts, 'Be Prepared'. This tenuous boy scouts' association allows copy to develop versatility theme.*
UK 1963 Bob Gill

Perforation. The graphic DOTTED LINE is an open invitation to tear along it. Simple yet powerful association with the STAMP or SACHET or mail order COUPON. See also CUT-OUT.

TV credit title.
UK 1958 Arnold Schwartzman

INITIAL LETTER *symbol for paper merchants was actually perforated and could be torn out.*
UK 1969 Fletcher/Forbes/Gill

Poster for discount stamps.
Switzerland 1950 Celestino Piatti

Periscope. Voyeuristic associations. It represents the idea of seeing in difficult circumstances. Fascinating because it suggests being in two places at once. See also BINOCULARS.

The Double Bass (a left handed player)

See also MUSIC STAND, MUSICAL INSTRUMENTS.
UK 1955 Gerard Hoffnung

Personification. Attributing human qualities to inanimate objects. As, for example, an orange with a human FACE painted thereon.

Mit der Bahn an die Sonne

Copy reads, 'By rail to the sun'. Ticket inspector's HAT is a prime signal. Hitlerian MOUSTACHE subtly hints at authoritarian nature of job. See also SERVANT.
Switzerland 1958 Herbert Leupin

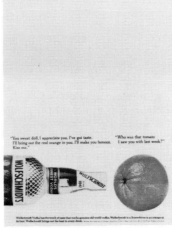

Advertisement for the drink trade. Copy says, 'You sweet doll, I appreciate you . . .' 'Who was that tomato I saw you with last week?'
USA 1961 George Lois

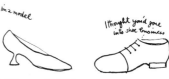

FRUIT *and nut converse.*
UK 1964 Rosemary Oxley

UK 1972 Mel Calman

Harry Barton
Yours Till Ireland
Explodes,
Mr.
Mooney

BLACKSTAFF PRESS

See also MAP.
UK 1973 André François

Perspective. The Renaissance conception of space was translated into ART through the discovery of perspective. These converging lines that defined infinity were rediscovered in a sense by the surrealists of the 1920s and 1930s. This particular formal obsession seeped through into the commercial work of the period and became closely associated with it. It is a device which easily establishes objects in relation to each other in space and is used now to evoke dreamlike situations. See also SURREALISM.

See also CLOUD. *Poster for Shell.*
UK 1944 Hans Schleger

Poster for French Railways. See also STAR.
France 1927 Cassandre

Poster for airline.
UK 1948 Paul Piech

Illusion of perspective by a dramatic change of SCALE *without reference to environment or converging lines.*
Switzerland 1955 Müller-Brockmann

Similar use of contrast in scale to establish space.
USA 1957 Saul Bass

Poster for German section of world fair.
Germany 1930 Herbert Bayer

Revival of converging perspective after a few years respite.
USA 1954 Irving Miller

An experience of recession in type.
Italy 1960 Giovanni Pintori

Phallus. Symbol of life and regeneration. The representation of the male generative organ was used in many ancient religions. A taboo image in our culture, it is however used instinctively and unconsciously throughout the whole of graphic communication.

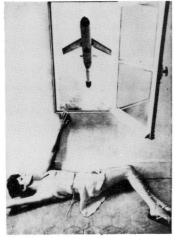

Editorial photograph for Queen *fashion magazine.*
UK 1967 Helmut Newton

Photographer. The full-frontal photographer who is 'taking' the viewer. Sometimes the effect is as disturbing as the real thing. A variation on this is the photographer's model who has assumed the active role and is using the CAMERA.

There is a delayed-action shock because the photographer is partially hidden from view.
France 1952 André François

Early example of role reversal.
USA 1952 Irving Penn

Switzerland 1958 Herbert Leupin

Piano. The PLAN VIEW of the grand piano is a unique shape and a potent image. The grand has associations of high culture, the upright has associations of domestic Victorian interiors and New Orleans jazz halls.

Political duet (Dewey and Truman).
USA 1948 Ben Shahn

The characteristic plan view of the grand piano is inevitably duplicated to express the duo-pianists' art.
USA 1960 Brownjohn, Chermayeff &
Geismar

Piano continued

Transference from piano keyboard to
TYPEWRITER *keyboard. Endorsement*
through associated ideas.
USA 1969 Henry Wolf

Piano Keys. The PLAN VIEW of the
black and white piano keys is a ready-
made graphic symbol for music. See
also TYPEWRITER.

Cover for concert programme. See also
MUSICAL INSTRUMENTS.
Switzerland 1955 Müller-Brockmann

Pictorial Logos. Trademarks of
firms consisting of the name in the
shape of an object connected with the
firm.

For a dog biscuit manufacturer.
UK 1930s Designer unknown

Picture Hook. Memorable object
with old-fashioned associations. A
natural substitute for a painting.

Picture hook as a symbol for ART.
USA circa 1977 Milton Glaser/Seymour
Chwast/Jerry Samuelson

Pie Diagram. See CAKE DIAGRAM.

Pieta. The gesture of the figure taking
down the dead Christ from the cross
is a very fundamental one and a
symbol of caring and compassion.
This is reflected in the cliché of the
bridegroom carrying the bride over
the threshold. The hero carrying the
heroine is a common mythic gesture
in films and often seen on film posters.

Archetypal attitude of caring. Bonus image
of DIVER *with title of record,* Deceptive
Bends.
UK 1977 Hipgnosis

Piggy Bank. Date from Tudor times as money boxes. It is not known whether pigs are provident but it remains a symbol for saving.

Pillory. General symbol for medieval times and customs, or more specifically for punishment, disgrace and humiliation.

Prisoner of the HEART.
UK 1962 Mel Calman

Pilot. The image of a pilot in helmet and goggles establishes the idea of being airborne. The solo pilot is a strong symbol for personal endeavour.

The image of the pre-war pilot flying solo epitomises the idea of solitude.
Word transference : solo pilot to solo pianist.
USA 1966 Paul Davis

Pin-up. To pin up something is to select for approval. The repertoire of facial and bodily gestures associated with the modern female pin-up occurs throughout history.

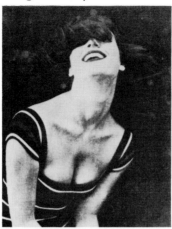

The archetypal attitude of the pin-up.
USA 1956 Henry Wolf/Desmond Russell

A variety of disparate letterforms are pinned up to symbolise a variety of lovely girls (pin-ups).
USA 1957 Henry Wolf

Cover for article on designer's own work.
See also THUMBTACK, TORN PAPER.
USA 1958 Henry Wolf

Editorial spread. 'The girl who hated men.'
The word MEN is pinned up alongside the 'pin-up'. In this case the pinning-up is an act of contempt.
USA 1961 Gene Federico

Pipe. A primary masculine symbol with authoritarian overtones but also indicative of reliability and contentment. Because of the pipe of peace association, the RED INDIAN is often used to promote tobacco.

Male symbol for male magazine.
Switzerland 1954 Fritz Bühler

The pipe represents the boss. See also
PERSONIFICATION.
UK 1955 Henrion

Pirate. The accoutrements of pirates consist of NAPOLEON hats with SKULL AND CROSSBONES, knives between the TEETH, ear rings, eye patches and striped vests. This is a timeless iconography.

The reader makes the connection between copy and image in the case of a popular operetta.
USA 1961 Seymour Chwast

Advertisement for a department store. Copy says, 'We'd even walk the plank for you if we had to!'
USA 1964 Arnold Varga

Pith Helmet. Symbol of exploration, empire building, colonialism and safaris.

Place Setting. A well-established iconography of FORK, knife and plate immediately indicative of the order and ritual of meal-times. High recognition value.

Book jacket, Modern Art in Your Life. *The iconography of a place setting becomes a symbol for everyday life. See also* PALETTE, PLAN VIEW.
USA 1949 Paul Rand

'Don't play with your food.' See also MONK.
UK 1958 André François

Breakfast layout establishes time of day for a morning NEWSPAPER. *USA 1958 Michael Englemann*

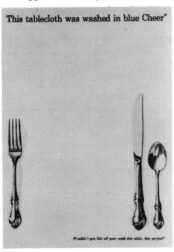

White paper represents tablecloth washed in detergent. The place setting defines the tablecloth in its absence. USA 1959 Frazier Purdy/Arthur Seller

Plan View. The use (particularly in photography) of the plan view of a familiar object like a CAR or BUILDING in order to give a visual shock. See also END VIEW, REAR VIEW, WORM'S-EYE VIEW.

Advertisement for a new cosmetics range. UK 1967 Tom Wolsey

Plug (Electric). Symbol for electricity. More fundamentally, making connections – plugging into a ready-made network.

For an article on automation. The GLOBE *gets plugged in. Italy 1961 Ricardo Manzi*

Advertisement for an 'electrifying' shoe. USA 1963 Gennaro Andreozzi

Trademark. USA 1963 Jerome Gould

Plumb-line. Symbol of building and creative endeavour. Associations of truth, goodness and beauty.

Poster for building exhibition.
France 1936 Jacques Nathan

Plus Sign. See ARITHMETICAL SIGNS.

Pocket. Has much of the same psychological effect as other closed containers. Sometimes the contents are half-observed (handkerchiefs and pencils), at other times they can only be guessed. See also BOX, CASE.

Mailing shot for PKZ.
Switzerland 1930 Designer unknown

See also KANGAROO, MUSIC STAND.
UK 1955 Gerard Hoffnung

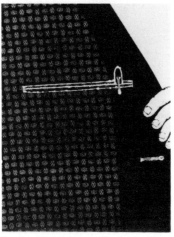

See also INSIDE LINING. *Illustration for* Gentleman's Quarterly.
USA 1957 Henrietta Amellio

Financial page in NEWSPAPER *as background to pocket.*
USA 1963 Morton Goldsholl

Policeman. Kindly father-figure or symbol of authoritarian regime according to the country of origin. Visually, very characteristic and frequently used to symbolise the country or more specifically the capital city, particularly London and Paris.

METAMORPHOSIS *of characteristic truncheon into cigarette. See also* COLUMN.
France 1951 Savignac

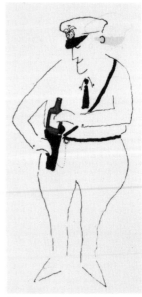

Characteristic holster doubles as hip-pocket. See also JANUS.
UK 1956 Mark Boxer

Characteristic helmet and notebook.
UK 1970 Mel Calman

Poorman. See BEGGARMAN/POORMAN.

Poppy. Symbol of sleep, rest. In UK strong associations with the fallen soldiers of World War I.

Mailing shot to medical profession for morphine.
UK circa 1932 Lewitt-Him

Porthole. The shape of the porthole is the ideal design solution for a WINDOW on a ship. Typical marine shape. Architects of the 1930s designed circular windows for concrete domestic villas; these windows became symbolic of a certain architectural style.

Postcard. The postcard is a ubiquitous and popular form of communication and a natural symbol for worldwide travel. The visual style is very strong; the weather is always idealised in bright colours and the distant horizon is always in sharp focus. The obverse side has a strong typographical style much taken up with the word 'Postcard' and type rules which guide the sender into writing cryptic messages. The style is much parodied.

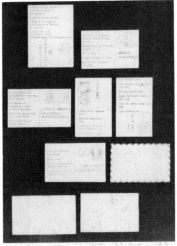

Double-spread from a magazine showing recipes from all over the world.
USA 1960 Henry Wolf

Pound Sign. The libra pound sign is a universal symbol for British CURRENCY and by implication can symbolise economics and fiscal policy in a broader sense. See also DOLLAR SIGN.

Press. The image of a person squeezed in a press is a popular metaphor for taxation.

Newspaper illustration.
UK 1978 Peter Brookes

Price Tag. The price tag with its characteristic domed top is a universal design and a simple symbol for the retail trade or related subjects.

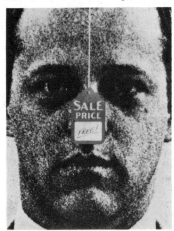

Domed price tag as a general selling symbol. Copy says, 'Don't sell yourself'.
USA 1970 Louis Danziger

Price Tag continued

ECONOMICS OF RETAILING
EDITORS: K. A. TUCKER AND B. S. YAMEY

£1

FRUIT *and vegetable stallholder's lettering becomes a symbol for retailing.*
UK 1973 Michael Foreman

Printed/Real. The visual guessing game of mixing full-colour reproductions of an object (like a bus ticket) with the real article.

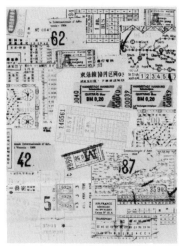

Promotion material for a printer. See also TICKET.
Holland 1959 Willem Sandberg

Printing Press. The diagrammatic rendering of rollers is a ready-made graphic symbol for the print industry.

grafa
international

Poster for exhibition.
Germany 1936 Hermann Eidenbenz

Magazine cover.
France 1953 Fernand Léger/Jean Carlu

The paper and rollers of the press form the INITIAL LETTER *R.*
USA 1959 Rudolph de Harak

Prism. Like the RAINBOW a natural symbol for ART.

Prison Cell. Vertical black rules superimposed on a head or a group are an immediate symbol for captivity. See also CAGE.

Publicity for CBS television programme.
USA 1949 Ben Shahn

Psychological CAGE *for a junkie.*
USA 1955 Saul Bass

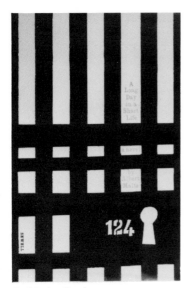

Book jacket. *See also* KEYHOLE.
UK 1963 John Sewell

Profile. The word has associations with the Hollywood ideal of beauty. Like the PIN-UP this becomes a self-parody. The profile as a cliché persists because it is the most characteristic image which identifies the owner. *See also* FACE.

Poster for an evening NEWSPAPER. *See also* PERSPECTIVE.
France 1925 Cassandre

Poster and unofficial trademark for a port wine.
UK 1929 George Massiot

Recruiting poster for women's army. Withdrawn by War Office for being too 'glamorous'.
UK 1940 Abram Games

Poster for UNESCO (human rights exhibition).
France 1942 Jacques Nathan

INITIAL LETTER *used for a concert by Brubeck & Basie.*
USA 1964 Milton Glaser

President becomes his middle name. See also SUBSTITUTION.
USA 1966 Seymour Chwast

Projected Image. The technique of projecting an image onto a three-dimensional object (invariably a female nude because of the necessity to easily identify both images). See also BODY PAINTING.

Moving film projected on gold figures.
Film titles.
UK 1964 Robert Brownjohn

Poster for National Book League. See also
BOOK.
USA 1965 Bob Gill

Mailing shot for an exhibition of 'Big Nudes'.
USA 1966 Milton Glaser

Proof Corrections. The unconsciously graphic SCRIBBLE, ARROW and HANDWRITING on proofs become part or all of the graphic design solution.

Advertisement for a typographer. The uncorrected initials (see INITIAL LETTER) spell the client's name.
USA 1960 Henry Wolf

Punch and Judy. Punch is a priapic fascist monster, Judy is a battered wife. The associations are still with childhood delights and seaside entertainment. The charade remains a potential symbol for macho groups, women's liberationists and marriage guidance counsellors.

Punning Heads. Archimboldo was the master of the punning head. These were heads that were assembled from FRUIT, pots and pans, etc. Dali also uses the device.

Archimboldo head supports the copy 'You are what you throw away'.
USA 1971 George Lois

Puppet. A symbol for a manipulated person. The puppet on a string is a symbol of man as the plaything of others. See also VENTRILOQUIST'S DOLL.

Puzzle. Most puzzles such as the Chinese link have traditional forms and a high recognition quality. They can easily refer to larger social and international problems. See also CROSSWORD, JIGSAW PUZZLE.

Wooden puzzle used as an ANALOGY for combining different skills within a building firm to complete task.
USA 1959 Vance Johnson/Joe Maddocks

Girl manipulates man (Esquire *symbol*).
USA 1957 Henry Wolf

The headline asks 'Gimmick?' Link puzzle by implication becomes a symbol for triviality.
USA 1955 Saul Bass

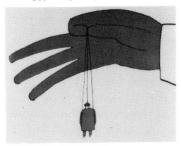

The artist's vision of contemporary man.
Belgium 1965 Folon

For an article on the CIA.
USA 1969 Milton Glaser

Pyramid. The formal configuration of the pyramid is a natural ANALOGY for hierarchies particularly in the areas of business and management. See also SPHINX.

Poster, 'No to bureaucracy'.
France 1968 Atelier Populaire

Book jacket.
UK 1975 Pentagram

Question and Answer. A device which gives news or information about a commodity by asking and answering its own questions.

Advertisement for a CAR.
UK 1962 Derek Birdsall

Question Mark. It is difficult in visual terms to express a negative idea. Similarly it is difficult to pose a question visually. The question mark is therefore a universal and immediately understood typographic sign which modifies the visual material.

Quill. An object associated with literature and poetry. It also signifies the idea of authority as in the signing of a DOCUMENT. See also PEN, PEN NIB.

'Ma griffe is my signature.'
USA 1968 Henry Wolf

Don Quixote. The unmistakable image of the mounted Don Quixote can visually express ideas of a certain eccentric courtesy, romantic idealism and impracticability.

Quotation. A literary quotation in a piece of writing is a kind of cultural name-dropping and gives an authenticity to the writing. Similarly, any quotation which is given an appropriate typographic treatment can be the main constituent of a design and act as an endorsement. See also DICTIONARY.

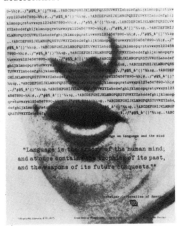

In 'Great ideas of Western man' series the quotation reads 'Language is the armoury of the human mind . . .' See also MOUTH.
USA 1958 Louis Danziger

Twice life-size FACE *as a mailing shot for brand of paper called 'Driven Snow'. Copy is a Shakespeare sonnet which mentions '. . . skin as white as driven snow, black hair,' etc.*
UK 1963 Derek Birdsall

Quotation Marks. The typographic sign for reported speech has an almost audible impact.

Record sleeve. Punctuation as visual speech. See also EXCLAMATION MARK.
USA 1957 Matthew Leibowitz

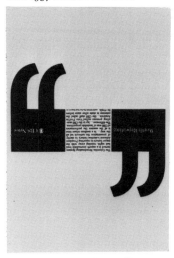

Advertisement for CBS news. Copy says, 'Worth repeating'.
USA 1958 Lou Dorfsman

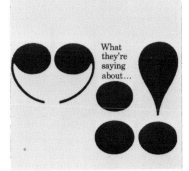

Advertisement for the New York Times.
USA 1958 Louis Silverstein

Rabbit. Rabbits have close connections with magicians and top hats. They have a reputation for unplanned parenthood and timidity but also historically for being a trickster. This is supported by such fictional characters as Brer Rabbit and Bugs Bunny.

Advertisement for a department store. Rabbit out of magician's hat has a surprise element not inappropriate to the needs of advertising. Copy says, 'If it's out of this world it's here'. Rabbit's face is a GLOBE.
USA 1949 Paul Rand

Rabbit continued

*Easter bunny drives one of a new range of
spring shoes on a poster.*
Switzerland 1952 Herbert Leupin

Rain. In real life rain is more ex-
perienced or felt than seen. The
graphic rendering of WATER is a
technical preoccupation of most
artists and children. The simple
shorthand of diagonal strokes corresponds exactly with the sensation of
real rain. Sometimes cats and dogs
are added.

Poster.
UK 1920 Aubrey Hammond

*Drops of rain (see DROP) for a waterproof
garment.*
Germany circa 1932 Herbert Bayer

Rainbow. An indispensable part of
the artist's/designer's/illustrator's iconography. Much employed for its
own sake as a decorative element. As
it literally is a prismatic effect of light
which produces the artist's palette, it
is an inevitably apt symbol for art.
See also PRISM.

Caption says, 'Overdoing things as usual'
(simultaneous funeral and wedding).
*Rainbow as a symbol for the ultimate in
dramatic effects.*
UK 1955 André François

*Rainbow and PALETTE for a school of art
poster. See also CLOUD.*
USA 1964 Milton Glaser

Full-colour rainbow in the service of a full-colour printer.
Germany 1975 Tomi Ungerer

Rat. Associated with the Pied Piper and reputed to leave sinking ships and collapsing houses. Usually the representation of rats is in an uncomplimentary context. Illustrators love them.

Children's book illustration. See also
PRISON CELL.
France 1954 André François

Political rat. Copy says, 'Fascist vermin'.
France 1968 Atelier Populaire

Razor. The open and safety razors are two fascinating examples of low technology which persist without much change in design since their inception. The image of an open razor carries with it feelings of unbelievable sharpness and menace.

Some common objects symbolise the time of the day when they are generally used or seen. Here a razor is a symbol for the morning.
USA 1947 George Krikorian

Poster for sticking plaster. See also
BANDAGE, SMILE.
France 1952 Savignac

Rear View. A particular obsession that derives partly from the paintings of Magritte of the 1920s and 1930s and partly from the universal fear of the unknown. See also BOTTOM, END VIEW, PLAN VIEW, WORM'S-EYE VIEW.

Poster for men's clothing.
Switzerland 1934 Niklaus Stöcklin

TORN PAPER *on a back for an exhibition of*
paperbacks.
USA 1959 Henry Wolf

Fat man covers up the artwork. A poster
for an exhibition of graphic design. See also
CROWD.
UK 1967 Minale/Tattersfield

Rear-view Mirror. See DRIVING MIRROR.

Rebus. The device which substitutes the image for the word in a name or sentence.

Trademark for G. Fisher.
Germany 1881 Designer unknown

The SHELL *was first used in 1900. The*
design shown was developed in 1929 and
was the optimum solution. The failure of
nerve occurred in 1961 when the name
shell was added. This defeated the rebus.
UK 1900 Designer unknown

Black square for black name (Zwart).
Holland 1920 Piet Zwart

Trademark for Bird Pen Inc.
USA 1950 Ernst Roch

Business card for William Bell. See also
PASTICHE.
USA 1959 Gene Federico

Receipt. The DOCUMENT that can stand for the whole activity associated with it. For instance a hotel receipt can represent tourism or a till receipt consumerism.

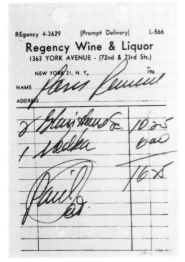

Poster for Paris Review.
USA 1968 Andy Warhol

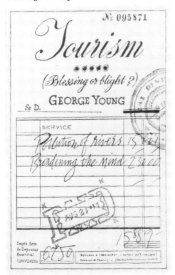

Book jacket.
UK 1972 Philip Thompson

Red. See COLOUR SYMBOLISM.

Red Indian. The characteristic Red Indian article is the chieftain's head-dress. The next most characteristic image is the plaited HAIR and single FEATHER. Sometimes the image of a Red Indian is used ironically to symbolise the guilt in the American Dream.

Fusion of cigarette and head-dress. Strong associations with smoking (pipes of peace and hence cigarettes).
Switzerland 1960 Herbert Leupin

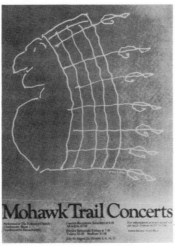

Fusion of MUSIC STAVE and head-dress.
USA 1974 R.O.Blechman

Reflection. The reflected image in the chromium tube, spoon, EYE, shop window, WATER, etc is one of the obsessive phenomena of life and ART. In the last thirty years the reflected image in a pair of GLASSES or SUN-GLASSES has reached epidemic proportions. See also MIRROR.

Painting. The earliest example of the reflecting lenses cliché.
USA 1949 Ben Shahn

Registration Marks. A symbol for accuracy although its use tends to be restricted to subjects connected with printing.

Advertisement for a web-offset printer. See also CROSS.
UK 1963 Robin Fior

Repetition. One of the sacred tenets of the advertising profession. Its banality can only be matched by its effectiveness. It is axiomatic that if something is good it is worth repeating. The psychological effect of a repeated element as in a sheet of postage stamps or an Andy Warhol painting of coke bottles is strong. One's eye rapidly scans the surface as though to spot a discrepancy.

Symbol for Rinascente repeated for wrapping paper.
Italy 1951 Max Huber

C.P.V

have the most original and creative minds .

Infinity of thinking heads as ANALOGY *for creative thought.*
UK 1952 André François

Classic repetition device.
USA 1954 Clifford Coffin

The repetition is a visual equivalent of musical rhythm. Typography to dance to. See also STENCIL LETTERING.
USA 1960 Brownjohn, Chermayeff & Geismar

Advertisement for Sudler, Hennessy & Lubalin.
USA 1960 Herb Lubalin

Reverse. The technique of reversing copy left to right creates the same psychological shock as the MIRROR and other reflecting objects.

The view from the shop. Change of address card.
USA 1960 Bob Gill

Book jacket, The Reactionary Revolution. *See also* INITIAL LETTER.
UK 1965 Philip Thompson

Rhinoceros. No particular symbolism but the armour-plated features of the animal make it a general symbol for the idea of impenetrability.

River. The PLAN VIEW of a river on a MAP has a very idiosyncratic shape and immediately establishes its nature. This flowing line is often incorporated into trademarks or other signs. A natural boundary. It also figures in the life/landscape analogy as a barrier symbol (see LANDSCAPE).

INITIAL LETTER *logotype for Thames Board Ltd who are situated on the river Thames. Treble visual pun for letter T, river configuration and laminated boards. UK 1963 Derek Birdsall*

Road. Like the RIVER it too figures in the idea of life as a landscape. It represents the individual's personal journey through life, successive horizons are one's aims and objectives. See also LANDSCAPE, PERSPECTIVE.

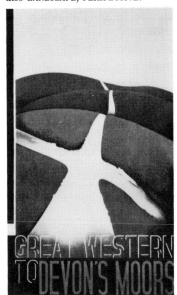

Travel poster. USA 1932 McKnight Kauffer

Travel poster. The classic PERSPECTIVE and distant MOUNTAIN range appeal to a universal, primitive sense of adventure. Switzerland 1935 Herbert Matter

Road Sign. In Europe the system of signs for road traffic is a mixed one consisting of self-explanatory marks and icons with signs whose meanings require learning. They are sufficiently part of the common visual language to be incorporated into communication not primarily connected with traffic. See also SIGNPOST.

Example of a graphic understatement. See also EXCLAMATION MARK. '. . . instead drink Eptinger.' Switzerland 1948 Herbert Leupin

Magazine cover. USA 1966 Folon

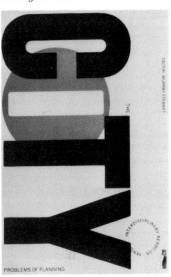

Book jacket. See also SUBSTITUTION. UK 1972 Philip Thompson

Roller Skate. Symbol of childhood and childish independence. Sports such as these are subject to the whim of fashion and are therefore reminiscent of a particular time.

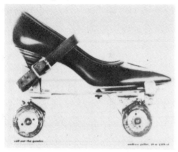

Promotion for a shoe called 'Gamin'. Word association with street urchins and their method of transport.
USA 1961 Gennaro Andreozzi

Roof. The pitched roof is the characteristic shape and the one that says 'HOUSE'. The view of Paris rooftops has strong romantic associations.

Reference is made to what 'Frenchwomen are wearing'. Paris roofs are a strong signal for the capital city.
USA 1962 Ken Duskin

Rope. The texture of rope is very idiosyncratic with strong marine associations. In general a symbol of BONDAGE and limitations (the boxing ring or the tether). Also a useful tool for securing (the industrial CRATE) and for gaining access (the rope bridge, ladder, etc). See also KNOT, NOOSE.

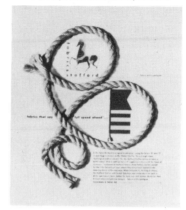

A naturally flexible graphic element. Here the rope's marine symbolism supports the copy, 'Fabrics that say full speed ahead'. Flags spell out 'advance' (see FLAG). See also CODE.
USA 1944 Paul Rand

The classic rope trick. A much copied device to symbolise tension.
USA 1951 George Olden

Rope as a measuring tool. Example of OXYMORON; contrast of opposites.
USA 1962 Roy Kuhlman

Rorschach Blot. Symbol for psychology or psychiatry.

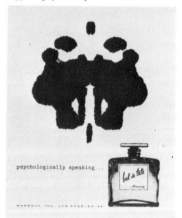

Copy says, 'Psychologically speaking . . .'
USA 1956 Jack Roberts

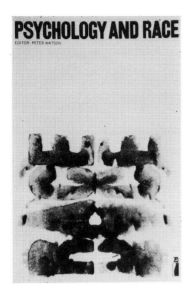

Book cover.
UK 1973 Philip Thompson

Rose. Symbol of beauty and the national flower of England. Poetic and amorous associations.

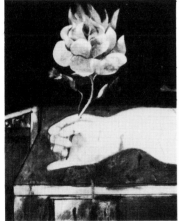

Magazine illustration. The THORN *is the price of the rose's beauty. See also* BLOOD, FIRE.
Germany 1964 Heinz Edelmann

Rosette. The symbol of allegiance or prizewinning excellence as in prizes at a show. See also BADGE.

Rosette as a first prize. Copy says, 'First in TV, first in merchandising'. See also EYE.
USA 1958 William Golden

Roulette Wheel. A symbol of chance.

Roundabout (Carousel). The roundabout is a symbol of life (the wheel of life) in the sense that patterns of behaviour are repeated to a point of monotony, particularly in the area of affairs of the HEART. See also FAIRGROUND.

Rounded Corners. A peculiar formal device popular in the 1960s. The cliché was also expressed in the windows of certain examples of modern architecture (see WINDOW).

The cliché taken to its ultimate conclusion including the holes.
UK 1967 Derek Birdsall/Harri Peccinotti

Rubber Stamp. The image of a rubber stamp or of the mark that it makes is highly evocative. A fitting symbol for official authorisation or in the case of many rubber stamps, bureaucracy. See also ACCUMULATED GRAPHICS, FRANKING, PASSPORT, RECEIPT.

Ruler. A symbol for any trade that uses a rule but also in a more general sense a symbol for the idea of accuracy or scrupulous honesty.

Ruler as an ergonomic symbol.
France circa 1952 Peter Knapp

Poster for General Dynamics. Ruler as an indication of tidal movement.
USA 1969 George Tscherny

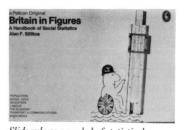

Slide rule as a symbol of statistical analysis.
UK 1970 Mel Calman/Philip Thompson

Rules. Undecorated rules of various lengths and thicknesses are design constraints in many graphic design problems.

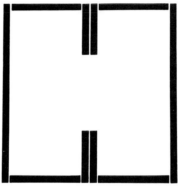

A flexible trademark made from rules for a modular furniture manufacturer, Holtzapfel. See also INITIAL LETTER.
Switzerland 1958 Gerstner + Kutter

Illustration (Book 4a 1961).
Iceland 1961 Dieter Rot

Russian Doll. The idea of a large BOX containing smaller boxes ad infinitum is a fairly obsessive one. Strong childhood associations but the idea persists into adulthood and emerges in colloquial phrases like, 'in every fat person there is a thin one trying to get out'. See also IMAGE ON IMAGE ON IMAGE.

Personal Christmas card.
France 1966 Savignac

Drawing.
UK 1969 Mel Calman

Russian Roulette. The game played with a revolver (see GUN) containing one BULLET. A symbol of foolhardiness and risk-taking.

Advertisement. Copy says, 'Don't gamble – call . . .'
USA 1965 Tomi Ungerer

S

Sachet. The visual characteristics of the modern plastic sachet are the crimped outer edges and the cut off corner. It is a symbol for instant convenience. A naturally condensed and thus potent image.

'Instant vin rouge' – an ironic symbol for France. The characteristic snipped end contains the symbol. See also GLASS.
USA 1958 Henry Wolf

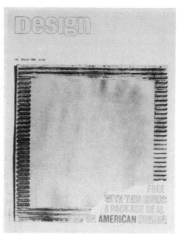

Giant silver sachet on magazine cover supports copy, 'Free with this issue . . .'
UK 1964 Derek Birdsall

Sack. Essentially a crude, tough container. It is associated with portability and heavy-duty use and thus exports. STENCIL LETTERING is the characteristic adjunct. 'The Sack' was a mid-1950s style of dress cut on basic lines.

Big sack equals big mail. See also HYPERBOLE.
UK 1946 Tom Eckersley

Symbol for minimal living. See also BARREL.
UK 1964 Colin Millward/Arthur Parsons

Safe. A symbol for security.

Safety Pin. A useful joining device. Associated with babies' nappies (see BABY).

Symbol for a baby show. See also SEAL (NOTARY).
UK 1961 Bob Gill

Safety pin as a joining device for two musicians who share a common name.
USA 1964 Stanislaw Zagorski

Saints' Symbolism. Some of this symbolism is absorbed into the common currency of communication. A specialised iconography. See also HALO.

Based on the 15th century painter Castagno's St Sebastian. Muhammad Ali was a conscientious objector and was 'martyred' for his Muslim beliefs.
USA 1968 George Lois/Carl Fischer

Sand Castle. A general symbol of holidays and childhood. On a different level it has slightly less innocent associations of staking a territorial claim. It can also be a symbol for projects that crumble.

Sandwich Board. A primitive channel of communication. Used for low-budget advertising and prophecies of doom.

Cover for Show *magazine.*
USA 1961 Henry Wolf

Santa Claus. Derived from an amalgam of St Nicholas, father figure and benevolent MAGICIAN, he is a symbol of the Christmas spirit.

Santa Claus in the guise of a six-armed Indian god is thus capable of circulating a great many French encyclopaedias.
France 1957 Jean Carlu

Ironic Christmas cover. Notorious 'bad-man' Sonny Liston models 'good-man' Santa Claus.
USA 1963 Carl Fischer/George Lois

Sardine Tin. Sardines in the tin are analogous to overcrowding in housing and travelling. The characteristics of the tin are the KEY and the roll top when the tin is half open.

Saxophone. Because the saxophone is not generally used in symphonic scores its image suggests jazz in general and swing music of the 1930s in particular. See also MUSICAL INSTRUMENTS.

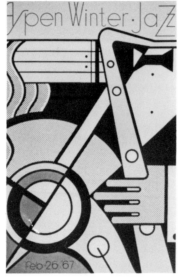

Poster for jazz festival.
USA 1960 Roy Lichtenstein

Scale. The dramatic contrast of scale in two or more objects which suggests infinite pictorial space. This is usually effected by inverting the *actual* scale, e.g. car WHEEL is bigger than human being, etc.

Poster for a shipping line.
France circa 1932 Cassandre

Mailing prospectus for CBS TV.
USA 1956 William Golden/Kurt Weihs

Suggestion of infinite space by a dramatic contrast in scale. In both these examples the typography and type RULES become part of the 'landscape'.
Italy 1958 Franco Grignani

Editorial photograph for an article on patriotism. See also STARS AND STRIPES.
USA 1962 Art Kane

Scales. Symbol of justice and fairness.

Illustrating problems of management in balancing staff and money.
UK 1962 Mel Calman

Effectiveness of TV programme established by good measure.
USA circa 1963 Lou Dorfsman

Scarf. A powerful signal for allegiance. Associated with schools, colleges and sports clubs. See also SHIELD, TIE.

For an article on students.
UK 1967 Ron Sandford

School. For clear communication it is sometimes necessary to use an obsolete pictorial form. Despite the advance in school architecture the characteristic British school is still Victorian gothic, the characteristic American school, New England clapboard.

Archetypal American school elevation with PRICE TAG *attached for article on school costs.*
USA 1962 Tony Palladino

School Copybook (Notebook). The marbled school copybook as immortalised by Roy Lichtenstein and Steinberg is a nostalgic and evocative image and a suitable symbol for primary education and related subjects.

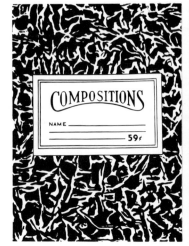

Painting.
USA 1964 Roy Lichtenstein

Scissors. One of the many anthropomorphised tools. As scissors appear as an appendage to mail order COUPON advertisements their image is an incitement to action. Cutting the tape is a symbol for a new enterprise.

PHALLUS-like scissors to open an exhibition.
USA 1968 Claes Oldenburg

Scissors as a symbol for cutting railway fares.
Switzerland 1975 Herbert Leupin

Screw. The SPIRAL is a symbol of progressive development. The image of a screw has a feeling of energy. See also NAIL, TOOLS.

Scribble. An involuntary and obsessive activity from which few are immune. The fine-art climate of the 1950s and 1960s permitted large areas of CONSPICUOUS WASTE (as in the paintings of Rothko) and this filtered through to the world of publicity. See also COLOURING IN, DOODLE, GRAFFITI.

The copy says, 'Get the lead out of your ads'. Here scribble is equated with non-creative thinking although ironically it constitutes ninety-nine per cent of the advertisement.
USA 1960 Herb Lubalin

Advertisement for a ball-point pen.
Switzerland 1961 Ruedi Külling

Poster for a coffee house. See also COFFEE POT.
UK 1963 Bob Gill

A back and front cover for a magazine The American Institute of Graphic Arts. *Scribble is the primal graphic form.*
USA 1965 Chermayeff & Geismar

Designers' own trademark.
UK 1967 Minale/Tattersfield

Script. The 18th century copperplate script has strong associations of gentility and gives a feeling of orthodox respectability to wedding and christening invitations. See also CALLIGRAPHY, HANDWRITING.

Advertisement for a store. The copy refers to 'the elegant understatement . . .'
USA 1967 Arnold Varga

Scroll. A motif popular in memorial art since Roman days. The unfolding of a scroll is likened to life. A much parodied symbol.

Scythe. Symbol of time and death carried by FATHER TIME.

Sea-horse. Appears on the coats of arms of many seaside towns. Used a lot at one time on posters and publicity for seaside towns.

Seal. Symbol of authenticated ownership and contracts. A personalised mark like the MONOGRAM. Strong associations with the power of the state and the church.

Seal on end of paper immediately transforms it into a legal DOCUMENT.
UK 1970 Mel Calman

Sea-lion. The sea-lion as a JUGGLER has many of the qualities and associations of the human juggler. Much used at one time in the role of an announcer of messages usually written on the balanced BALL.

Poster for a beer.
UK 1935 John Gilroy

Circus poster.
Switzerland 1957 Herbert Leupin

Section. The use of a cut-through section to describe a characteristic aspect of things like FRUIT, cables and TREE TRUNKS.

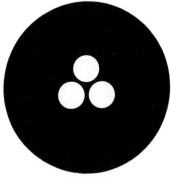

Trademark for cable manufacturers. Holland circa 1926 Piet Zwartz

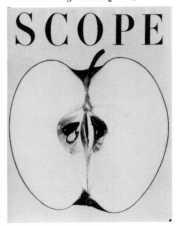

Section of APPLE *is the most characteristic viewpoint.*
USA 1955 Will Burtin

Booklet for Pirelli cables.
UK 1967 Crosby/Fletcher/Forbes

Seek and Find. See HIDDEN ELEMENT.

Servant. The livery of butlers, chauffeurs, door porters or bus conductors defines a hierarchic society. In advertising and on packaging images of butlers and servants offering us lemonade, cigarettes, coffee, etc., have been for years a popular substitute for the real thing. The idea of the servant in UNIFORM is an appealing one and is an important element in the corporate identities of hamburger chains and garages.

Poster for COCA COLA.
Switzerland 1954 Herbert Leupin

Railway poster. 'Swiss National Railways – always at your service.'
Switzerland 1959 Donald Brun

The idea of personalised service applied to a lithographic company.
USA 1960 Seymour Chwast

Sex. Traditionally, sex (particularly the female BODY) has sold everything from seaside holidays to recruitment.

Sex sells recruitment for the US Navy. *USA 1917 Howard Chandler Christy*

Gratuitous strip-tease to advertise department store.
Japan 1929 Tsunetomi Kitano

One of a series of coolly sexual advertisements for stockings. Copy says, 'Any woman who pays 12/11 for a pair of stockings ought to have her legs examined'.
UK 1963 Robert Brownjohn

Sex Signs. The astrological signs of Mars and Venus which are the same as the botanical signs for male and female bloom. The sign for Venus is also the chemical sign for copper which is supposed to derive from the material from which the MIRROR of Venus was made.

SHAMROCK *becomes an Irish sex symbol.*
UK 1969 Derek Birdsall

Shadow. In the interpretation of dreams the shadow represents the dark side of the individual; the suppressed part of his nature. The shadow image carries sinister feelings of the unknown. Alternatively, the shadow establishes the season or the time of day.

See also BALL, PATCHES.
USA 1953 Rudolph de Harak

Shamrock. National emblem and symbol of Ireland. A general symbol of good luck.

Sheep. Its secular association is with the easily-led masses, sleep and docility.

Sheep as a sleep symbol.
UK 1955 Gerard Hoffnung

Shell. A form in nature that demonstrates the SPIRAL. A protective part of many creatures such as the tortoise, SNAIL and turtle. A popular symbol for the seaside because of shellfish.

Shell as a seaside symbol. Overtones of hermit crabs. See also IMAGE ON IMAGE ON IMAGE.
France 1958 Siné

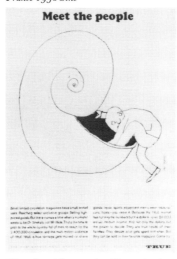

The colloquial expression, 'Retreating into one's shell' is given a visual treatment and refers to advertisers who don't take advantage of large circulation magazines.
USA 1964 Tomi Ungerer

Shield. Symbol of allegiance and protection. Derived from heraldry but now associated with schools, universities and clubs who wear them emblazoned on the POCKET. See also ARMOUR, SCARF.

Ship in Bottle. A symbol of high craftsmanship. Tantalising in its apparent impossibility.

Shirt. The starched shirt is a symbol of formality and propriety.

Change of address notice. Writing on the shirt cuff is a synonym for 'making a note'. More conceptual than real. Here the idea is made visual.
USA 1959 Gene Federico

Signature. Symbol of individuality.

The signatures of the conductor and composer on the programme cover personalise the event.
USA 1952 Paul Rand

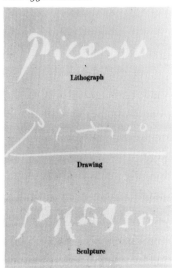

Different versions of a signature become the design for a gallery poster.
USA 1960 George Tscherny

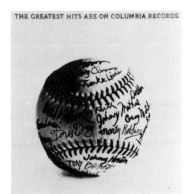

Transference of baseball players' signatures. BALL *supports the word 'hit' in copy headline.*
USA 1961 Larry Miller

A petition opposing the proposed introduction of admission charges to London's galleries. Signatures include those of Van Gogh, Leonardo da Vinci, Rembrandt, etc.
UK 1970 Pentagram

Signpost. A strong visual characteristic of the road communication system. The dynamic ARROW is a recurring feature. See also CROSSROAD, ROAD SIGN.

Direct mail advice to clients moving to a new city.
USA 1957 Roy Kuhlman

Artists plus name of jazz venue on signpost for a record sleeve.
USA 1958 Emmett McBain

*Name of town is the name of drink.
Switzerland 1964 Herbert Leupin*

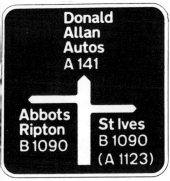

*Characteristic motorway lettering and
signpost as a basis for a garage house style.
UK 1978 Howard Waller*

Silhouette. See PROFILE.

Skeleton. A medieval symbol for
death.

*Sowing the seeds of death. Anti-fascist
poster.
Germany circa 1932 John Heartfield*

Skittles. In common with coconut
shies the figurative meaning is often
to do with debunking. See also
FAIRGROUND.

Skull. Symbol of death from about
the 16th century in England. Much
used in the 18th century on memorials
and tombstones and expressed the
pessimistic religious spirit of the age
and its ideas on the corrupt nature of
man.

*Accident prevention poster.
Poland 1957 Waldemar Swierzy*

Skull and Crossbones. PIRATE
symbol. Immediately understood as a
warning sign on poison bottles or at
dangerous traffic junctions.

Smashing Through Paper. A popular device in graphics which has the
same emotional effect as the real
thing (CLOWN jumps through paper
HOOP, etc). A general symbol for
surprise. See also PAPER.

*Hitler breaks through the non-aggression
pact.
USSR 1941 Designer unknown*

*Copy reads, 'Breaking through the white
barrier'. Lena Horne speaks on the negro
revolt.
USA 1963 Henry Wolf*

Smile. Not unreasonably advertisers wish their products to be associated with happy looking people. The laughing or smiling purchaser of goods is one of the hardiest of clichés. Pedlars of merchandise use images of misery at their peril. See also FACE, TEETH.

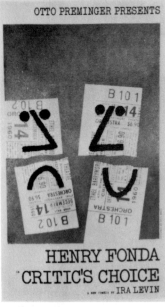

Smile and grimace as a symbol of critical appraisal on a theatre TICKET.
USA 1960 Saul Bass

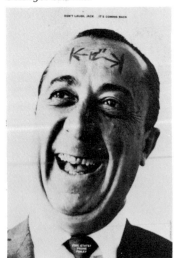

A measured smile from a supplier of photostats. See also DIMENSIONS.
USA 1960 George Elliot

Process engraving good enough to make an art director smile.
USA 1961 Norman Gollin/Tommy Mitchell

Advertisement for rye bread.
USA 1963 William Taubin

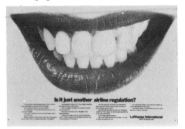

Genuine smile from Lufthansa stewardess.
UK 1968 Neil Godfrey

Smoke. Historically a symbol of purification, it represents the soul's journey from earth to heaven. In modern thought it is sometimes a welcoming signal from an occupied HOUSE or associated with a heavily industrialised landscape. Like WATER, its graphic representation is a perennial technical challenge.

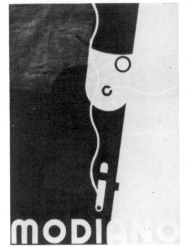

Poster.
Hungary circa 1924 Robert Berény

ROSE *and smoke symbolise art and industry.*
France 1925 Charles Loupot

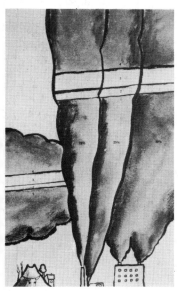

Comparative bar diagram treated as a free illustration.
France 1969 F.Constantin

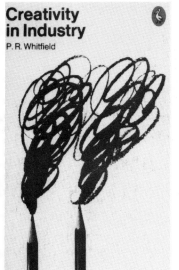

Creativity in Industry
P. R. Whitfield

Book jacket. See also PENCIL *and* SCRIBBLE.
UK 1975 David Pelham

Smoke Ring. Usually indicative of extreme contentment.

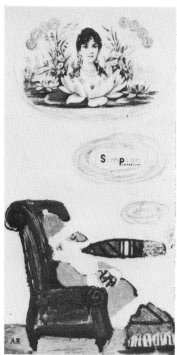

A contented SANTA CLAUS *for a Christmas catalogue cover.*
UK 1955 André François

Snail. Extremely characteristic SPIRAL configuration makes for immediate identification. They are creatures regarded with a mixture of caution and affection and are occasionally eaten. As food, they are associated with haute cuisine. Otherwise the associations are with tardiness and mobile housing. See also SHELL, TORTOISE.

BY A SNAIL
PAR L'ESCARGOT

Envelope sticker to celebrate a go-slow among mail workers. See also AIRMAIL STRIPES.
UK 1972 Philip Thompson

Snake. After its long history as a symbol of wisdom and good, its development in Christianity reversed its attributes. Then it became the symbol of evil and temptation (in Hindu religion serpents and phalluses were identical). Its ambivalence together with its decorative and flexible form make it a popular symbol.

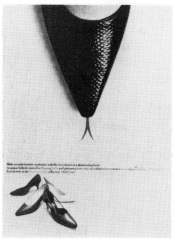

Advertisement for snakeskin shoes. See also FORKED EMBLEM.
USA 1963 Mike Cuesta

Snake forms MONOGRAM *(CP) for pharmaceutical firm.*
USA 1971 John Massey

Snake continued

Eve uses the serpent as a sexy SAXOPHONE: *a poster for a music publisher. The copy reads, 'Paradise for love-songs'.*
USA 1977 Tomi Ungerer

Snapshot. The essentially amateur photograph sometimes with a DECKLE-EDGE is associated with holidays.

'Me at sea.' Lone yachtsman Sir Francis Chichester snaps himself in mid-Atlantic. Authenticity overcomes essentially amateur qualities.
UK 1967 Sir Francis Chichester/ Michael Rand

Snowflake. The crystal structure of a snowflake is a symbol for winter.

Poster for winter holidays.
Switzerland 1958 Peter Andermatt

Snowman. A symbol for Christmas or winter.

Association of snow and babies' woollens with softness.
Switzerland 1955 Herbert Leupin

Soap Box. Symbol for political activities particularly in the area of electioneering speeches.

UK 1976 Carole Ingham

Social Perspective. The habit (as in medieval drawings and Indian miniatures) of drawing people at a SCALE appropriate to their social standing.

Space Frame. The space frame which was a cliché of the 1940s and early 1950s exhibition design was also a cliché in its two-dimensional form. The style belongs firmly to its period.

Outdoor advertisement.
Italy 1950 Giovanni Pintori

CRATE *on* Fortune *cover.*
USA 1953 George Giusti

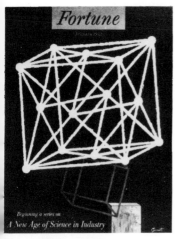

Furniture advertisement.
USA 1956 Herbert Matter

Spanner. A popular device in the 1930s and 1940s symbolising industry.

'America's answer! Production.' See also
SUBSTITUTION.
France 1942 Jean Carlu

Magazine cover.
USA 1954 Walter Allner

Spectacles. See GLASSES (PAIR OF).

Speech Balloon. Derives from the language of comic books. Totally absorbed into the common currency of communication. See also THINKS BUBBLE.

Advertisement for pop-art exhibition.
USA 1964 Ivan Chermayeff

Sphinx. Unofficial symbol for Egypt. Often used to suggest mystery or inscrutability. See also PYRAMID.

Spiral. Historically one of the most popular of decorative elements. It is a pattern of the universe, representing the cosmic forces in nature. Deriving from climbing plants and spiral schemes found in nature, it is a symbol of progressive development. The spiral is a universal symbol, turning and revolving and generating energy, for the most part creative, but in the form of a whirlwind, destructive. See also SHELL, SNAIL.

War poster. 'Your talk may kill your comrades.'
UK 1943 Abram Games

Use of spiral motif to suggest an infinity of paints and varnish.
France 1948 Savignac

The squared spiral, symbol of man's (as opposed to nature's) progressive development.
Italy 1957 Bruno Munari

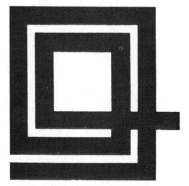

Squared spiral. Symbol for Olivetti.
Italy 1957 Marcello Nizzoli

An appointment CALENDAR. Cover for the Museum of Modern Art. See also CALLIGRAPHY, DOODLE.
USA 1957 George Tscherny

Symbol for Ulster carpet mills. The calligraphic swash on the U derives from Celtic ornament.
UK 1963 Ivan Dodd

Wood shaving expresses itself characteristically.
Finland 1963 Jukani Suna

Industrial spiral. Record cover entitled Cordon Bleu.
UK 1976 Hipgnosis

pliced Image. An image made up
rom disparate sources that is suffi-
iently disturbing to give the viewer
certain frisson. Used for comparing
hings or people with similar charac-
eristics.

A visual comparison of Roger Vadim's
women. See also FACE.
UK 1964 Brian Haynes

Old and new furniture supported by old and
new typography.
UK 1964 Churchill/Holmes/Kitley

Surreal image (see SURREALISM) for film
company publicity.
UK 1967 Bob Gill

Spliced Lettering. The technique
whereby lettering is spliced horizont-
ally and the top and bottom halves
derive from different letterforms. A
disturbing image.

The two halves of a PIANO duo come
together to form the name.
USA 1958 Brownjohn, Chermayeff &
Geismar

The changing type-face reinforces the title.
USA 1958 Ivan Chermayeff

Spool. See COTTON REEL.

Spotlight. Used to focus attention on
some aspect of excellence.

Spring. A very potent image of unreleased energy. See also SPIRAL.

Child's TOY used as a symbol for colonic
spasm.
USA 1958 Herb Lubalin

Spy. The spy is a useful device for
witholding information or teasing the
reader with intriguing half-facts.

The copy says, 'Internationally intriguing'.
The pun on the word 'intrigue' affords the
characteristically furtive image of the spy.
USA 1956 William Taubin

Square. See GENERAL SIGNS.

Stairs. The symbolism is universal in iconography. The meaning is concerned with hierarchies, gradation (and hence status, excellence and authority) and ascension. See also MOUNTAIN, PYRAMID, ZIGGURAT.

Fusion of stairs and line GRAPH. INK POT, PENCIL, RAZOR *blade are symbols of creativity.*
USA 1957 R.O.Blechman

Stairs as a three-dimensional chart that registers accummulation of money.
Savings Poster.
USA 1977 Milton Glaser

Stamp. Postage stamps have associations of authority, legislation and authenticated contracts. This idea of legality is passed on to other forms of stamps like trading stamps. The PERFORATION is the characterising visual element and a regular DOTTED LINES grid establishes the idea immediately. See also ACCUMULATED GRAPHICS, FRANKING.

Cover of Esquire *magazine.*
USA 1956 Henry Wolf

Record sleeve : Sweden in the War Years. *The back of the* ENVELOPE *and the arcane nature of the stamp suggests in some subtle way Sweden's neutrality in World War II.*
Sweden 1966 Bergentz/Falk/Lenskog/ Roos

Book jacket for Sociology of Marx. *UK 1975 John McConnell*

Star. In Christian symbolism th[e] star is associated with the birth [of] Christ. In language and in its graphi[c] form it suggests ideas of supremac[y] and excellence. One of the hardie[st] components of the graphic languag[e.]

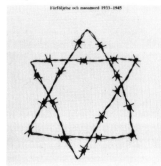

Record sleeve. Star of David from BARBED WIRE.
Sweden 1966 Falk/Bergentz/Lenskog/ Roos

Trademark for Mercedes-Benz. Designed by early pioneer of the motor car, Gottlieb Daimler, whose engines operated on land, sea and air – the three points of the star. Germany pre-1900 Gottlieb Daimler

Stars and Stripes. One of the most robust of flag designs. More than any other it withstands the maximum of condensing and distortion without any loss of identity.

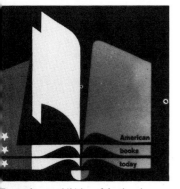

Poster for an exhibition of the American BOOK.
Switzerland 1954 Müller-Brockmann

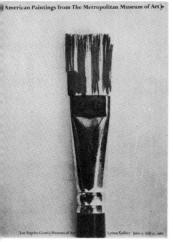

Fusion of BRUSH *with* FLAG.
USA 1958 Louis Danziger

Cover for Print *magazine. See also* DISTORTION.
USA 1961 Rudolph de Harak

Magazine cover. See also ARROW.
USA 1963 Rudolf de Harak

Poster. See also STENCIL LETTERING.
USA 1969 Jasper Johns

Poster for exhibition in USSR on American graphic arts. See also PEN NIB.
USA 1963 Chermayeff & Geismar

Catalogue of exhibition of paintings on the disappearance and reappearance of the Image in American painting. The single STAR (*the ultimate condensed image of the* FLAG) *expresses this dilemma.*
USA 1969 Chermayeff & Geismar

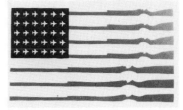

Poster. See also GUN.
USA 1970 Designer unknown

Statue. To erect a statue to somebody is the ultimate act of veneration, respect and honour. To put someone on a pedestal figuratively is the same. See also COLUMN.

Steering Wheel. Symbol of motoring. The characteristic steering wheel has three equidistant struts from the centre to the rim.

Steering wheel establishes ambience. France 1930 Cassandre

Stencil Lettering. A particular letterform frequently associated with the industrial CRATE and SACK, hence export. In fact it can be used in a multitude of applications with absolute neutrality.

Symbol for Théatre National Populaire. France 1953 Marcel Jacno

Book jacket. USA 1955 Paul Rand

Early use of commercial application of concrete poetry (see EXPRESSIONISTIC TYPOGRAPHY*). USA 1957 Roy Kuhlman*

Cover for magazine of industrial art. USA 1957 Matthew Leibowitz

Special issue on design for export

The characteristic lettering on a CRATE for a magazine article on exports. UK 1968 Crosby/Fletcher/Forbes

Stitching. The marks of stitchin[g] establish the material (as in jeans). [A] fascinating drawing substitute.

tocking. The associations are fairly subjective but usually has a high erotic content. See also GARTER.

CHRISTMAS STOCKING *is made of silk for a fashion magazine.*
USA 1957 Lester Bookbinder

NUN *adjusts stocking on a mailing shot for a photographer.*
USA 1968 George Adams

Stork. Ancient symbol of parenthood and filial affection.

Advertisement. "Birth of a new Ford car.'
USA 1957 Chauncey F. Korten

Infertile Marriage
Robert Newill

Callous stork on a book jacket.
UK 1975 Mel Calman/Philip Thompson

Straw. Associated with iced drinks and a natural symbol for summer.

Two bent straws become an evocative symbol for American girl teenagers.
USA 1955 Art Kane

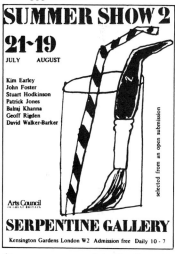

Straw as a summer symbol. Advertisement for summer art exhibition. See also
BRUSH, GLASS.
UK 1979 Philip Thompson

Street Sign. The street sign is an example of functional design where clarity is of prime importance. Highly evocative of a place or particular country. See also SIGNPOST.

The name 'Wall Street' is an immediate signal for suicide.
UK 1970 Mel Calman

String. String has a peculiar fascination as it is in fact a three-dimensional line with all the possibilities and implications of drawing in space. A ball of string has the visual potential of a pencil – it contains lines. On another level it has strong associations with binding and tying-up (see TIE) and shares some of the symbolism of ROPE.

Calendar for a hand typesetter. The tying-up of hand-set metal is made a chief characteristic. Real DATE pad attached.
Switzerland 1958 Siegfried Odermatt

Strip Cartoon Form. It has its own peculiar form and is analogous in some ways to the FILM. Jump cuts, dramatic changes of SCALE and viewpoint and the possibility of transgressing the bounds of the frame are some of its possibilities. See also CHARACTERISTIC STYLE.

The style of pulp-fiction romance applied to a sophisticated market.
UK 1970 Carol Annand

Strong Man. Part of the iconography of the circus, the strong man is often called upon to uphold and endorse things which have qualities of strength like beer or glue. See also TATTOO.

Typical strong man attitude suggests that the CHAIR is child-proof.
USA 1955 Herbert Matter

Substitution. The technique of substituting an appropriate image for a letter in a word.

Advertisement for CBS TV.
USA 1955 Lou Dorfsman

Booklet cover for an insurance company.
USA 1956 Herb Lubalin

um. A device whereby the facts are broken down and laid out as an arithmetical sum.

Holland 1933 Piet Zwart

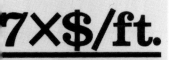

Rubbermaid can bring department stores seven times the sales per counter foot.'
USA 1957 Arnold Varga

Poster against drinking and driving.
Holland 1975 C. Van Rij

Sun. Pre-Christian object of worship. Used as a metaphor by Christianity. The sun's habit of setting and rising again corresponds to Christian sentiments. A much used graphic device. See also SUNRISE/SUNSET.

Sundial. Together with the HOUR-GLASS and SCYTHE it appears in churchyards and gardens as a general symbol for the temporal nature of man and the passing of time.

Lecture by Milton Glaser (founder member of Pushpin studio) begins at 8 pm.
THUMBTACK *(symbol for designer) casts*
SHADOW.
Canada 1977 Robert Burns

Sunglasses. A prime symbol of summer but with sinister overtones. Used to preserve anonymity and thus associated with the SPY and the rich and famous. See also GLASSES (PAIR OF), REFLECTION.

Sunrise/Sunset. The colour establishes the sunrise and sunset as the configuration is identical. The sunrise is associated with optimism and freshness, the sunset with contentment and happy endings. The sunset is one of the great popular ideals of beauty in nature and ART. See also LANDSCAPE.

Magazine cover. See also EGG.
USA 1973 André François

Magazine cover. See also APPLE.
USA 1979 Pierre Le-Tan

Superman. Typical of a whole range of modern MAGICIAN figures that can symbolise a variety of ideas and qualities.

Poster. Copy says, 'Amaze your friends . . . quote Newsweek'. HYPERBOLE: a graphic exaggeration. See also FLASHER. USA 1966 Bob Dunning/Phil Shulman

Superman as a symbol of a world power. Poland 1967 Roman Cieslewicz

Surrealism. The predominant art movement of the 1930s and the one (with to a lesser extent Constructivism) that has most influenced publicity and advertising design from that time to the present. There is something in the compelling and apparently irrational imagery of Surrealism that is appropriate to the needs of selling and marketing goods and ideas.

Coat advertisement deliberately using surrealist props and PERSPECTIVE. Copy says, 'It's a dream it's Harella'. UK 1942 Ashley Havinden/Henrion

Suspenders. See BRACES.

Swallowing. The act of swallowing little fish by larger fish can be a symbol for totalitarianism, or the take-overs that occur in business monopolies.

Take-over of small nations by large one. Germany circa 1932 John Heartfield

Swastika. The swastika is an ancient symbol in many countries for the SUN and hence for ideas of revival and prosperity. Despite this it would seem that the symbol can never be dissociated from Hitler and the Third Reich.

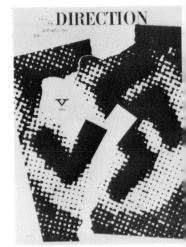

Magazine cover. See also TORN PAPER. USA 1941 Paul Rand

See also ARROW, X MARKS THE SPOT. USA 1963 Rudolph de Harak

Sweep. Popular symbol of good luck especially at weddings.

Sweep sits on wedding present.
USA 1955 Herbert Matter

Sword. Symbol of power, protection and knighthood. The sword unlike many other weapons has associations of positive virtues such as justice and vigilance. In many cultures it signifies penetrating intellect and insight; victory over ignorance. Seen on such things as disinfectant bottles which purport to protect one against germs. The sword of Damocles is a symbol for ever-present danger and retribution. See also DAGGER.

Table. The table is at the centre of many symbolic dramas in life and death (altar, operating table, gaming table). In still-life paintings the table is an important device on which the gifts of nature (wine, FRUIT, FLOWERS), and symbols of the intellectual life (MUSICAL INSTRUMENTS, BOOK) appear. See also DESK.

Tablecloth, clothes and CIGAR define ambience.
France 1930 Jean Carlu

Poster for a FISH restaurant.
France 1935 Cassandre

Tablecloth is a natural surface for menu.
UK 1971 David Hockney

Table 225

Tap. The tap is typical of a whole range of mundane objects which have psychological overtones beyond their apparently neutral character. Installed as a household fitting it gives us access to a vast network of servicing technology.

See also ARROW.
USA 1937 Lester Beall

Magazine cover.
USA 1954 Walter Allner

High Speed Gas is lots of hot water!

See also BATH, HYPERBOLE.
UK 1969 Mel Calman

Tape Measure. The idiosyncratic appearance of the tape measure is determined by its function. The moulded metal end and hole prevent fraying and enable it to be hung in a workshop. The design of the letterform has optimum legibility when distorted. Such things change their design rarely if at all because the ideal design has been attained.

Copy plays on words associated with health, slimming (product) and sales:
'...Healthy sales figure' etc.
USA 1956 Lou Dorfsman

Letterhead for fashion designer.
UK 1965 Churchill/Holmes/Kitley

Dramatic change of SCALE *for a men's suit store advertisement.*
UK 1971 Richard Dearing

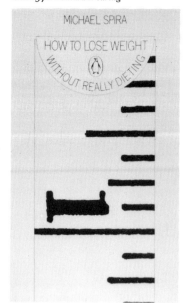

For a slimming book.
UK 1975 Penguin Books

Target. The roundel target of archery and fairgrounds (see FAIR-GROUND) is a powerful graphic signal in its own right and is used widely purely as a formal element. The meaning is invariably in the area of objective or achievement. The target in the shape of a human being has become a kind of symbol for police training and by implication the fighting of crime.

'Can paper board stop a shell?' Advertisement for Container Corporation. USA 1942 Man Ray

The image is a visual transference from the literal meaning of 'score'. See also BULLET HOLES. USA 1947 Paul Rand

Target as an aid to inept duellists. See also DUEL, GUN. France 1950 André François

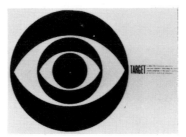

CBS 'eye' as a target. Copy refers to 'objective' (large audience). See also TRADEMARK MANIPULATION. USA 1956 William Golden

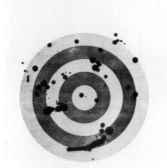

Cover for Print magazine. BLOT (substitute for graphics) being more or less effective (finding the target). USA 1962 Chermayeff & Geismar

Cover for house organ. DOG retrieves target. USA 1962 Tomi Ungerer

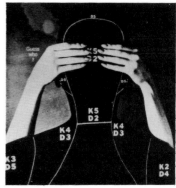

Self promotion for a photographer. See also GUESS WHO? USA 1969 Henry Sandbank

Tattoo. An exotic and bizarre practice which has a highly characteristic appearance because of its texture, soft colour and limited subject matter. Associated with the STRONG MAN in particular and sailors in general.

Sentimental and 'homely' tattoo style adopted for colouring the home. USA 1957 Phil March

Advertisement for a ball-point PEN (popular tool for self-tattoos). France 1957 André François

Tear Drop. An emotive graphic shape with great tension similar to the DROP.

Formally identical to the DROP. *In relation to an* EYE *it unequivocally expresses the idea of sorrow.*
USA 1956 Saul Bass

The UMBRELLA *has a propensity for getting lost. This one sheds tears. Classic English poster. See also* LUGGAGE LABEL.
UK 1945 Tom Eckersley

Sad CAT *appeals to lazy packers.*
UK 1954 Tom Eckersley

TROMPE L'OEIL *effect of printed page and 'real' hand.*
USA 1964 George Lois

Teeth. Feature in dreams, psycho-analysis, fantasies and a great deal of figurative language. See also SMILE.

Telegram. The condensing of syntax in telegrams due to economic necessity gives the literary style a poetic ambiguity. In general the visual, verbal and audible forms have strong associations of urgency, requiring immediate action. The passive associations are with condolences or congratulations. See also CHARAC-TERISTIC STYLE.

Poster describing the Lidice atrocity where the entire male population was killed is spelt out in telegraphese. The matter-of-fact style emphasises the horror. See also HOOD.
USA 1943 Ben Shahn

Congratulations telegram as a wedding symbol. A cover whose meaning at the time was conjectural. See also BOUQUET.
USA 1958 Henry Wolf

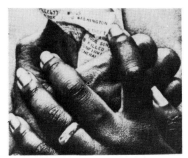

Editorial illustration for 'A son dies'. Hands crumpling the paper is a characteristic attitude of grief. See also BODY LANGUAGE.
USA 1962 Herb Lubalin/ Art Kane

Telephone. Like the PIANO it features a good deal in surrealist situations. Dali was obsessed with both. Like the TAP it enables one to be plugged in to a vast technological network with no great effort.

Advertisement for Olivetti. The telephone is a substitute for the client. See also PERSONIFICATION.
UK 1955 Henrion

Potential advertisers' link from telephone to radio. See also MICROPHONE.
USA 1957 Lou Dorfsman

Christmas conversation for a Christmas issue.
USA 1958 Richard Avedon/Henry Wolf

Typographical conversation links telephones. See also EXPRESSIONISTIC TYPOGRAPHY.
Switzerland circa 1965 Siegfried Odermatt/Rosemarie Tissi

Telescope. Associated with retired sailors and yachting men. The idea of forecasting weather conditions is often applied to forecasting prospects in a wider sense.

Copy says, '. . . the visibility is good . . . Three million ready travel prospects in view . . .' (space is converted into time). Advertisement to sell advertising space. See also END VIEW.
USA 1959 Malcolm Mansfield

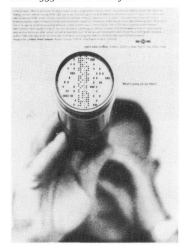

'What's going on out there.' Advertisement to keep data processing business informed.
USA 1961 Louis Danziger

Telescopic Sight. The CIRCLE and CROSS superimposed on a photograph is a popular device with subjects relating to hired assassins, espionage and violence in general.

EYE *on TV credits.*
USA 1952 George Olden

Advertisement aimed at advertisers to spend their money wisely: Aim your millons well. (An example of HYPERBOLE *a poetic exaggeration.)*
Italy 1963 Robert Riccuiti

Television. The image of a television set or the characteristic screen has as hypnotic an effect on the eye as the real thing.

'His master's voice.' De Gaulle dominates the medium.
France 1968 Atelier Populaire

Tent. In general the associations of the tent are with boy scouts, bedouins and armies on the move. For the nomadic Israelites their sacred tent was the HOUSE of God. Tent-like structures occur frequently in church architecture as in the ciborium (the canopied shrine which houses the Eucharist) and the tented dome of Liverpool cathedral and other churches around the world.

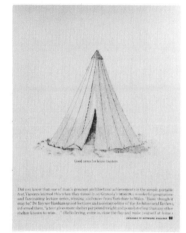

For a TV lecture on architecture (the merits of the tent as a classic structure was one of the subjects). Copy says, 'Good news for house hunters' – tents being synonymous with temporary residences.
UK 1962 Kurt Weihs

Test Tube. Symbol of chemical research. See also FLASK.

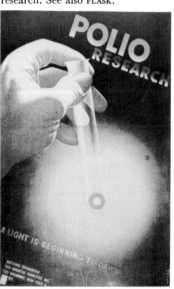

Poster for polio research.
USA 1949 Herbert Bayer

Thermometer. The most elementary of medical instruments. The thermometer for taking the temperature of the environment is similar in looks and symbolic potential.

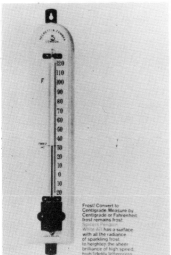

A real thermometer on walls of shops and railway stations that was an advertisement for ink. The dual-purpose copy says, 'For all temperatures'.
UK circa 1930 Designer unknown

Advertisement for a paper called *Penguin*. The mercury is suitably at freezing point.
UK 1963 Fletcher/Forbes/Gill

Thinks Bubble. A characteristic CLOUD shape derived from the language of comic books. Like the SPEECH BALLOON a universally accepted shorthand.

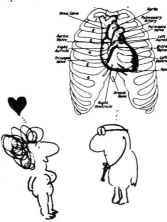

Doctor maintains his Hippocratic oath under pressure. See also HEART.
UK 1962 Mel Calman

Thonet Bentwood Furniture. Although a cheap and ubiquitous furniture its essentially spare and radical classic qualities have endeared it to architects and designers.

Elegant prop for elegant merchandise.
USA 1959 Gene Garlanda

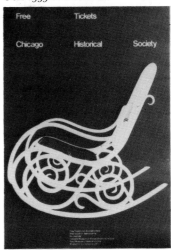

Poster for the Chicago Historical Society.
USA 1977 Bill Bonnell III

Thorn. Tactile image. The original model for BARBED WIRE with which it shares many associations and the antithesis of the ROSE. A symbol of Christ's passion and by implication any human suffering.

Three dimension. There is a popular belief that three-dimensional things and effects are somehow better than graphic ones. Hence 3-d films, laser projections and so on. TROMPE L'OEIL effects are commonly admired and applauded.

For the Container Corporation.
USA 1958 Ralph E. Eckerstrom

Three-dimensional bleach out.
UK 1959 Alan Fletcher

Trademark for a chain of hotels suggesting infinite expansion.
USA 1960 Norman Ives

Publicity for an exhibition of sculpture in the 1960s.
USA 1966 Louis Danziger

Thumbtack. A visually characteristic object which has the advantage of being reproduced same size. A natural symbol for plotting (as in planning a war or a market research campaign). It is an essential visual adjunct to the PIN-UP and is an unofficial symbol for designers.

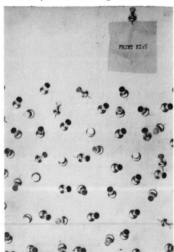

For an article on the designer's work.
Pinned up – that is, selected. Cover for
Print. See also PATCHES.
USA 1957 Henry Wolf

Tick. The graphic demotic mark is associated with the marking of the SCHOOL COPYBOOK and thus teaching. It can suggest the affirmative in a much wider sense and is sometimes applied (with the CROSS) to ideas of morality.

The BLACKBOARD *right and wrong signs*
for correct English usage.
UK 1969 Derek Birdsall

Ticket. A licence to partake in an activity for a limited period. Rather ambivalent image as it is at once valuable and expendable. The graphic portrayal usually emphasises the processes through which it goes – punching, clipping, endorsing and tearing and so on. Symbolic of the particular activity; theatre, travel, FILM, etc.

Book jacket. The story of the Group Theatre and the 1930s. See also EXCLAMATION MARK.
USA 1941 Paul Rand

Typographic punching.
Switzerland 1961 Roger Geiser

Characteristic tearing of theatre ticket supports the copy line, 'Front row centre on the world. Every week'. See also TRADEMARK MANIPULATION.
USA 1964 K.V. Studio

Cloakroom ticket CALENDAR.
UK 1966 Bob Gill

Book about a man who finds peace on Paddington station. The whole platform ticket forms the jacket, the punched hole (see HOLES IN PAPER) permits the book title printed on the front board to show through.
UK 1967 Nicholas Thirkell

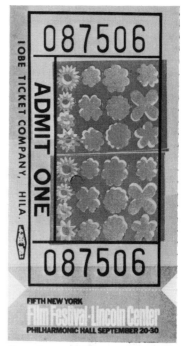

Poster for an exhibition of posters.
USA 1967 Andy Warhol

Fusion of numeral and SNAKE on a book jacket.
UK 1969 Penguin Books

Ticket continued

Book jacket.
UK 1973 Peter Davenport

Tie. An essentially male article of attire. Has some of the symbolism of BONDAGE; a mark of submission to an institution. Its symbolic use in communication is more concerned with the emblematic aspects. Can be a symbol (like its brother image the SCARF) for school or university life and for the idea of allegiance generally. See also ROPE, SHIELD.

Gifts for men inevitably associated with unwanted ties.
USA 1963 Arnold Varga

Tiger. Generally associated with strength, majesty and speed.

Association of animal with fashion stripes.
USA 1963 Arnold Varga

Condensed image (tail represents whole animal) of tiger as a symbol of speed and strength.
USA 1964 Tomi Ungerer

Tightrope Walker. From the microcosmic world of the circus. Advertisers have always favoured circus performers as a vehicle for merchandising for the simple and effective reason they have your undivided attention. Even in the graphic interpretation they are compulsive viewing.

Time Bomb. Unequivocal symbol of anarchy or dissent.

Comment on Olympic Games assassination.
UK 1973 Mel Calman

Tongue. Mixed significance. Associated (depending on the degree of exposure) with feelings ranging from coquettishness to dissent.

Large LIPS and tongue for Rolling Stones record label. Symbol of youthful dissent.
USA 1972 Andy Warhol (idea)

234   **Tie**

Tools. They are a natural extension of man's own TEETH, HAND, BRAIN, etc. With our habit (unconscious or otherwise) of creating such things in terms of human and animal morphology, it is reasonable that such tools can easily be returned to the source of inspiration.

To the new typographic dynamic of the 1920s was added the imagery of mundane objects. The circular saw has a particularly tactile quality and is also an INITIAL LETTER *O.*
Holland 1922 Van Doesburg

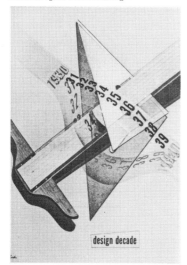

Cover for Design Decade. *See also* DATE.
USA 1940 Will Burtin

See also SPIRAL.
USA 1951 George Giusti

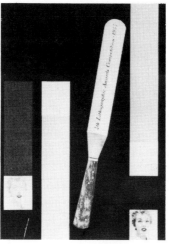

Advertisement for Litho Awards Competition. Colour-mixer's palette knife and four progressives of a girl. See also SEX.
USA 1954 Lester Beall

Composing stick for a printer's advertisement.
USA 1956 Bob Gill

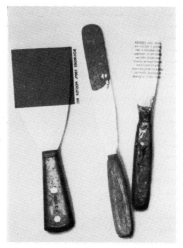

Advertisement for printing ink firm.
USA 1956 Bob Gill

Part of an annual report. Symbol for a mining corporation. The shape of the spade is used as a 100 per cent diagram with subdivisions of information.
USA 1963 Joe Weston

Tools continued

Drill as an instrument of CALLIGRAPHY.
UK 1970 Mel Calman/Philip Thompson

CORKSCREW *as a pain substitute. For an
anti-noise poster. See also* EAR.
Poland 1977 Andrzej Krajewski

Torch. The Greek torch is a pagan symbol of immortality, in the sense of handing on civilised values. Superseded by the Christian lamp which symbolised wisdom and guidance in addition to spiritual immortality. There is some confusion in modern usage which requires the heroic torch to express ideas of wisdom, etc (it was once the sole image on the British ROAD SIGN for 'School'). It is a more powerful gestalt than the lamp which accounts for its popularity. See also ICE CREAM.

*British road sign in use for sixteen years.
UK 1933 Designer unknown*

*Advertisement. Copy says, '. . . 48 states
light the road to world peace and
commerce.' Big business rides on the back
of world peace.
USA 1946 Paul Rand*

Torn Paper. From a purely technical viewpoint torn paper has a graphic quality which is unique. Part of the pure language of graphic marks which include cut paper, frottage, the BLOT, BURNT PAPER, etc. Its prime meaning is in connection with such subjects as war and divorce which are literally accompanied by the tearing up of contracts and treaties. Can obviously imply rifts of a much less serious nature.

*Mailing shot for an exhibition of
paintings by Howard Simon.
USA 1959 Bob Gill*

Poster for exhibition of designers' work making CAPITAL OUT OF ERROR: mis-spelt addresses to group of designers on ENVELOPE pieces.
USA 1960 Brownjohn, Chermayeff & Geismar

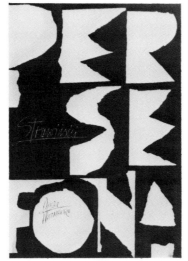

Mock Greek/Brutal Modern style of lettering reflects the style of Stravinsky's Persephone.
Poland 1961 Roman Cieslewicz

Jacket for book on revolution.
USA 1964 David November

Robert Bloch
An Inner Sanctum Mystery

The technique of tearing the title of the FILM exactly parallels the psychopath's state of mind.
USA 1960 Tony Palladino

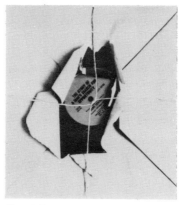

Record sleeve.
USA 1962 Ralph Casado

The use of torn paper as an extra dynamic.
USA 1965 Saul Bass

Torn samples for a PAPER firm.
UK 1963 Fletcher/Forbes/Gill

Tortoise. Affectionately associated with a reliable slowness. Like the SNAIL it also characteristically carries its own HOUSE around.

Tower. Unofficial symbol of impregnability. Associated with incarcerated damsels and hence with proposals of marriage. Used frequently by insurance companies and house brokers. See also CASTELLATION.

Magazine cover. Copy refers to '. . . let-creative-people-alone-week'. Here a 'creative' person constructs his ivory tower. See also AUTO-CREATE.
USA 1962 Tomi Ungerer

Toy. A natural symbol for childhood. Children playing suggest their future development. Sometimes warlike toys (tin soldiers and tanks, etc) are used as a EUPHEMISM for the real thing. See also toys by name.

Comparison of toy soldiers in war GAMES *with use of SDC computer in simulated nuclear attack.*
USA 1961 Louis Danziger

Trademark Manipulation. The simple expedient of cutting, fragmenting or otherwise distorting (see DISTORTION) the logotype or trademark as a design solution.

One of the characteristics of Esquire *covers was the ingenuity with which the symbol could be woven into the design. Here it becomes the back of a* CHAIR.
USA 1955 Henry Wolf

Magazine cover.
USA 1959 Henry Wolf

See also STEERING WHEEL.
France 1960 André François

Advertisement for Benton & Bowles.
See also REBUS.
USA 1963 Irene Egan

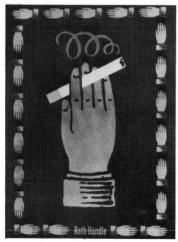

The trademark (HAND) smokes one of its own cigarettes. See also LINE/LINES, SMOKE.
Germany 1975 Herbert Leupin

Train. See LOCOMOTIVE.

Transparency. The image of the mounted transparency has become an acceptable symbol over the last decade or so for the amateur PHOTOGRAPHER and thence to associated ideas of holidays. At one time the object would only have been seen by professional photographers when it would have seemed esoteric. Typical example of a specialised image gradually gaining wider acceptance.

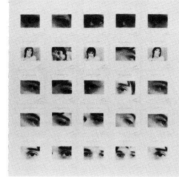

Record sleeve with transparencies and
MAGNIFYING GLASS.
USA 1972 Andy Warhol

Trapeze Artiste. Trapeze artistes are part of the circus iconography through which ideas of wider implication can be expressed.

Death-defying routine ensures that merchandise gets maximum attention.
France 1957 André François

Trashcan. See DUSTBIN.

Tray (In/Out). A simple indication of work load. It is in fact a natural BAR DIAGRAM which measures work and effort.

'In' and 'Out' meaning in with a chance (of selling your goods).
USA 1961 Lou Dorfsman

Treble Clef. A hardy symbol for music. Often seen without the MUSIC STAVE.

Poster for Ambler Music Festival.
USA 1968 Milton Glaser

Treble clef for fat sound.
UK 1965 Bob Gill

Tree. One of the most extensively used symbols throughout history. Tree worship occured among the ancient and early historic peoples of India, Greece, Egypt and China, as well as the Celtic, Teutonic and Scandinavian races. The architecture of Gothic churches is said to have been inspired by tree forms, as was much eccelsiastical decoration. The tree is a universally accepted symbol of life, knowledge and wisdom. Roots of a tree are a perfect ANALOGY for a process which takes nourishment at the source and expresses itself in the full flowering of the branches.

Symbol for PAPER. *Tree as* ARROW. *Picture shows tree on tree.*
USA 1950 Lester Beall

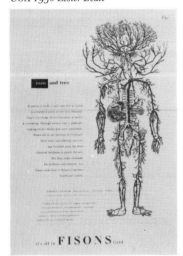

Morphological ANALOGY *of man and tree. (Chemicals for man and the soil.) UK 1954 Hans Schleger*

Trademark for Finmar, a Swedish furniture firm whose chief feature was its characteristic use of wood. The tree was thus a natural symbol and was also an INITIAL LETTER *F. UK 1955 Hans Schleger*

Tree Trunks. Because printed images can and are taken from the tree SECTION they have ready graphic qualities. A natural symbol for time as the age of the tree is recorded by the rings.

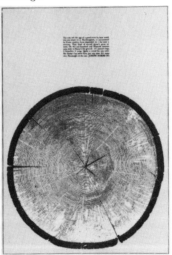

Advertisement for department store. Copy refers to age, branches, growth and so on. USA 1964 Arnold Varga

Tree into PAPER *equals print. Booklet cover for a Japanese printer. Japan 1964 Shigeru Akizuki*

Triangle. See GENERAL SIGNS.

Trident. Symbol of the sea. Held by the Roman Neptune, the Greek Poseidon, the Hindu god Siva or BRITANNIA it symbolises ascendancy over the sea. Also held by the DEVIL.

Trombone. Although within the literature of classical music trombones are accorded majestic parts, the image of the trombone is often associated with clownish antics. This is partly due to the jazz musicians' influence. See also MUSICAL INSTRUMENTS.

Folder cover for a FILM *about jazz. USA 1952 J. Chris Smith*

Trompe l'Oeil. The style of painting that is primarily illusionistic. One that has been consistently practised throughout history and one that consistently fascinates. The only criterion is to delude the EYE. See also THREE DIMENSION.

Classic smack in the EYE.
France circa 1936 Cassandre

Photograph steps out of its FRAME into another environment, causing spatial ambiguity.
1941 A. Shitomirsky

Large ENVELOPE with life-size ARM.
USA 1965 Bernie Zlotnick

Trumpet. An announcing symbol, popular with angels (see ANGEL). The trumpet was at one time popular as a symbol for the advertising trade. See also MUSICAL INSTRUMENTS.

Editorial photograph. 'Requiem for jazz.' Reference to the Last Post which is usually played on bugle or cornet. Artistic licence permits the image of a trumpet.
UK 1965 Art Kane

Turban. An indispensable part of the fantasy world of harems. Also the characteristic headgear of the Sikh Indians. See also NATIONAL STEREOTYPES.

Poster for razor blade. Close shave makes a Sikh SMILE.
UK 1945 Tom Eckersley

Poster for soap flakes. The black FACE contrasts with the newly washed turban. The diamond emphasises the idea of brilliant WHITE.
France 1960 Savignac

Typewriter. The image of a typewriter or part of it has surreal overtones in much the same way as a PIANO. In both cases one depresses keys (see PIANO KEYS). The typewriter is capable of producing deathless prose, the piano music of the spheres. The object and the image have concentrated feelings of potential energy. The symbolism of the typewriter is usually associated with journalism or popular fiction. A favourite device is to type the copy for the poster or book jacket on the paper in the typewriter.

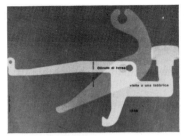

See also IMAGES OF MOVEMENT.
Italy 1949 Albe Steiner

Copy reads, 'Going back to school'. See also PEN NIB.
USA 1939 Paul Rand

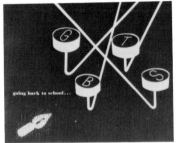

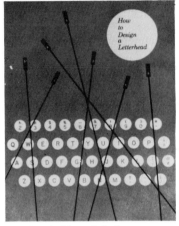

Cover for a booklet on designing letterheads.
USA 1952 Lester Beall

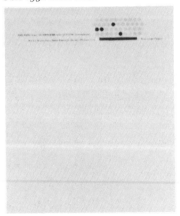

Letterhead for National Secretaries Association. Each INITIAL LETTER *in a different colour.*
USA 1957 James P. Camperos

Typewriter Type. A condensed version of the typewriter. Popular as a symbol for a secretary.

Record sleeve. See also BLEED.
USA 1957 Reid Miles

TV credit titles. Private secretary shows her experience with characteristic style. See also CAPITAL OUT OF ERROR.
USA 1959 Bob Gill

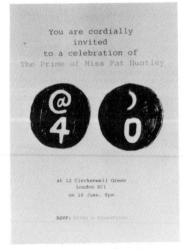

Invitation to a secretary's fortieth birthday party.
UK 1979 Philip Thompson

Typewriter profile and PAPER CLIP *as symbols for business.*
USA 1940 Lou Dorfsman/William Golden/Ray Komai

Umbrella. A general symbol for protection in the widest sense. Sometimes with the BOWLER HAT and briefcase closely associated with the typical Englishman (see NATIONAL STEREOTYPES).

Rainy days with protective umbrellas as a poverty symbol.
USA 1952 William Baldwin

Advertisement for pharmaceutical firm. Umbrella as a protection against illness. See also RAIN.
France 1954 Raymond Peynet

Rain represented by typographic dotted leaders (see DOTTED LINE).
USA 1954 Gene Federico

Advertisement for shoes. Image of umbrella supports the idea of weatherproof shoes.
USA 1957 Art Kane

Umbrella as a sun-shade used as a symbol for summer.
Switzerland 1966 Herbert Leupin

Uncle Sam. A mythical figure representing the USA. Derived from the initials US.

Poster. The American version of the KITCHENER call to sacrifice.
USA 1917 J.M.Flagg

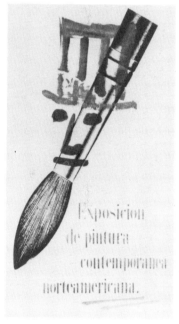

Fusion of beard and BRUSH. See also HAT, STARS AND STRIPES.
USA 1941 Paul Rand

Uncle Sam continued

Illustration for 'Americanisation of Paris'.
See also PERSONIFICATION.
USA 1960 Tomi Ungerer

Pastiche of a KITCHENER *pastiche.*
USA 1963 George Lois

Poster as a protest against Vietnam war.
Bad breath is equated with bad
international image due to Vietnam
involvement.
USA 1967 Seymour Chwast

Unicorn. A mythical beast having
the legs of a buck, the tail of a LION,
the head and body of a HORSE and a
single WHITE, RED and BLACK horn in
the middle of its forehead. A symbol
for Britain. See also FABULOUS BEASTS.

Uniform. A hierarchy-defining device. An immediate signal for authority and responsibility. It gives
licence to the wearer to indulge certain fantasies in the form of irrational
decoration, medals (see MEDAL), in-
signia, etc but which are contained
within certain strictures. See also
SERVANT.

The uniform that defines the marital status.
For a pharmaceutical product that
combats fear and anxiety.
Belgium 1955 Siné

Showcard for a beer. Copy says, 'Guinness
the order of the day'. Beer LABEL *is visual*
pun for MEDAL.
UK 1960 Donald Smith

Real book matches pasted on drawing.
USA 1965 Tomi Ungerer

Union Jack. National banner of Great Britain and Ireland. It consists of three crosses, St George for England, the saltire of St Andrew for Scotland and the CROSS of St Patrick for Ireland.

For COLOUR CORRECTION *by Dye Transfer firm. Union Jack is in* BLACK *and* WHITE.
UK 1963 Fletcher/Forbes/Gill

Trademark for British Rail international publicity. Fusion of Union Jack with British Rail ARROW.
UK 1970 Peter Davenport

L'idée et la forme-
design en Grande-Bretagne
Centre de Création Industrielle
107 rue de Rivoli, Paris I
1 avril - 31 mai 1971

Condensed image of Union Jack in RED *and* BLUE *for a poster publicising British graphics in France.*
UK 1971 Colin Forbes

Upside-down Face. A sort of visual PALINDROME consisting of a head which reads upright and upside down. Rex Whistler was famous for his drawings of these heads. This technique was carried further by Gustave Verbeek who devised complete stories in STRIP CARTOON FORM which were first read straight, then turned upside down and read to their conclusion. The technique is part of a vast repertoire of visual trickery (HIDDEN ELEMENT and so on) that appears in children's comics.

Vagina. A DOOR in the body-as-house (see HOUSE) ANALOGY. The substitution of lines of type for the pubic triangle is a popular device particularly in invitations to art exhibitions.

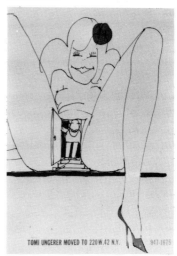

Change of address card.
USA 1967 Tomi Ungerer

Vagina continued

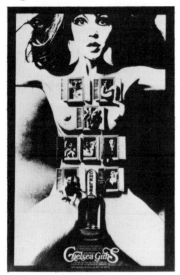

Poster for Andy Warhol's Chelsea Girls.
UK 1968 Alan Aldridge

Photomontage.
UK 1975 Penny Slinger

Vase. The image of the Greek amphora has strong associations of things Greek and therefore high ART. In general terms vases symbolise whatever they contain.

Poster. Vase as a strong culture signal.
France 1957 Jean Carlu

Veil. Veils are somewhat ambivalent as they cover and reveal at the same time, and are associated with the qualities of innocence and seductiveness. See also NET.

Logotype as veil distorts FACE.
Holland 1960 Pieter Brattinga

Venetian Blind. A natural interference pattern. The EYE compensates for the parts that are obscured and reads the whole image. There is a certain tantalising aspect to the Venetian BLIND similar to other objects (like the VEIL) that at once reveal and conceal.

Voyeur takes cover on record cover.
UK 1976 Hipgnosis

Ventriloquist's Dummy. Features considerably in films and popular fiction as a sort of doppelganger figure or alter ego. In graphic communication it is often used as a symbol for the idea of manipulation in politics or business. See also PUPPET.

Poster for GPO. SPEECH BALLOON *comes from badly packed* PARCEL.
UK 1966 Tom Eckersley

Gatefold cover that makes possible delayed action effect. Copy says, 'I have known for sixteen years, his courage, his wisdom, etc.' 'You tell 'em, Hubert.'
USA 1966 George Lois

Vice. One of the vast armoury of TOOLS with a function so specific that it can easily be accepted as a symbol for an equivalent function or idea.

Vice as a synonym for physical pain.
USA 1963 Tomi Ungerer

Pharmaceutical advertisement. HEART *in a vice-like grip of angina.*
Switzerland 1964 Hans Schweiss

Contrast of brutal and precious objects. See also JEWELLERY, OXYMORON.
Spain 1969 Jose Maillo

Vice Versa. The game beloved by illustrators whereby the roles of the protagonists are reversed thereby revealing hidden truths.

The BULL *as butcher. From a series entitled 'The World Upside Down'.*
Italy 1955 Antonio Frasconi

Violin. Used greatly in the 1930s and 1940s as a symbol for classical music. An adaptable image as it is also associated with square dancing, Irish fiddlers, and street musicians. Full of extremely characteristic details such as the bridge and sound-board with f-shaped holes. See also MUSICAL INSTRUMENTS.

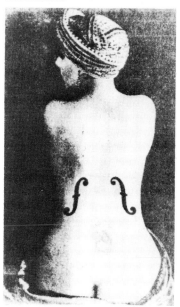

'Violon d'Ingres.' The classic and much copied photograph.
USA 1919 Man Ray

Violin continued

For a Schubert Festival. Symbol of high culture.
Germany 1928 Max Buchartz

The violin also has poverty-stricken associations. See also HAT, ROSE.
UK 1958 André François

Volcano. A symbol for ideas of potency, uncertainty and tension.

Wall. A symbol of defence or division. In general the symbolism is associated with a sudden problem or as a division of opinion, political or domestic. See also BRICK WALL.

Wand. The fairy's wand is a symbol of transformation and fulfilled wishes.

Watch. See CLOCK.

Water. Symbol of birth, purification and regeneration. We are born in water and it is our chief constituent. Historically and in modern thought a symbol for life. Like the other elements of air, FIRE and earth, its graphic representation creates technical problems. The Egyptian hieroglyph for water is the WAVY LINE (W) adopted unconsciously by children. See also FOUNTAIN, RAIN.

Wave. WATER in agitation, its graphic representation is explicit. The engulfing wave is a symbol for a disaster. The famous giant wave by Hokusai is often gratuitously used for its decorative value. More imaginatively used as a symbol for Japanese world exports.

Poster for a shipping line.
UK 1921 F. C. Herrick

Pastiche for an article on 'The teeming world of Japanese films'.
USA 1962 Henry Wolf/Gyo Fujikawa

Wavy Line. A kind of structured DOODLE. A natural symbol for WATER or sound waves. See also LINE/LINES.

Trademark for Plessey, telecommunications and electronics firm, using an oscillograph as a basis.
UK 1959 Norbert Dutton

Record sleeve, Sounds from the Alps. The line suggests the shape of an alpine horn and also sound waves.
USA 1963 Rudolph de Harak

Weathercock. A symbol of changeability. Sometimes used to support the points of the compass. See also COCK.

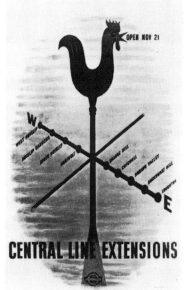

Fusion of weathervane with east to west railway line extensions.
UK 1949 Tom Eckersley

Weathercock as a symbol of spring. Advertisement for a department store. Copy reads, 'If it's out of this world it's here' and reference is made to spring collection. See also ARROW, GLOBE.
USA 1949 Paul Rand

Web. Images of formal or organic networks (like spiders' webs) are indicative of inextricable situations. See also SPIDER.

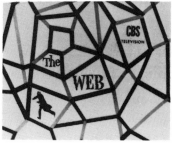

Poster for TV thriller.
USA 1954 George Olden

Wedding Cake. The design of wedding cakes belongs to an immutable tradition (along with biscuit and confectionery design). The tiered CAKE structure is a simple ANALOGY for marriage with a natural propensity for crumbling.

Weight. The image of the weight (that accompanies scales) can be used effectively to convey the idea of the quality of weight.

Advertisement for a typeface demonstrating its range of 'weights' (degrees of boldness).
UK 1963 Herbert Spencer

Whale. A general symbol for enormity.

Wheat. A universal symbol for man's staple food. The image of an ear of wheat is a stronger gestalt than bread in the same way that grapes and a vine are a more suitably graphic way of representing wine.

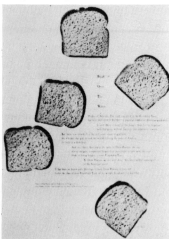

Advertisement in praise of Drew Pearson's efforts to provide food in post-war Europe. Compare sliced bread with wheat as an icon.
USA 1947 Paul Rand

Archetypal image of wheatfield. For a CBS television promotional folder.
USA 1949 William Golden/Ben Shahn

For a book about the rural poor of 1830 who burnt down ricks.
UK 1973 John McConnell

Wheel. An ancient Greek and oriental symbol for the SUN, its spokes indicating the rays. At times a symbol for change, fortune and the idea of onward motion.

Symbol for London Transport. An intuitive design based on the wheel.
UK Designer unknown

Wheel as a condensed symbol for travel.
France 1932 Cassandre

Wheel as a condensed symbol for office procedure. Advertisement for Olivetti office machines. The wheel is on the leg of an office CHAIR. *See also* ARROW, KINETIC IMAGE.
Italy 1947 Walter Ballmer

Condensed image of a sports CAR *wheel used as a symbol for an article on automobile classics.*
USA 1959 Henry Wolf

Pirelli logotype used as a substitute for spokes of a sports car. See also TRADEMARK MANIPULATION.
Italy 1963 Bob Noorda

White. See COLOUR SYMBOLISM.

Wind. Visually the wind can only be described through some agent such as cherubs with bulging cheeks or through bellows.

'Lipstick, the light flourish'. The SPIRAL *as a graphic synonym for air.*
USA 1959 Henry Wolf

Windmill. A piece of low-technology with a concentrated picturesque value. For Europeans it is an unofficial symbol for Holland.

Advertisement for a Dutch mink.
USA 1962 Onofrio Paccione

Magazine cover. Comment on the ecology craze in America.
USA 1979 R.O.Blechman

Window. The means by which we
assess reality, etc. In general the view
from a window suggests limitless
opportunity. Sometimes there is an
association of freedom (supported in
the view from the PRISON CELL
window). Opening a window suggests
letting in a fresh opinion. The image
of windows viewed from the outside
of a BUILDING is a popular device for
describing disparate activities. Voyeuristic overtones. See also HOUSE.

*The ubiquitous shop window sign used to
inform clients of a designer's holiday.
UK 1960 Alan Fletcher*

*Man opens window/newspaper. Window
as an early morning symbol. Poster for a
morning NEWSPAPER.
France circa 1963 Savignac*

*Advertisement for man's fashion shop. A
typical cliché of thriller films. Voyeur's-eye
view of man in need of fashion advice.
Copy says, 'Crime in room 608 . . . man
putting on old-fashioned clothes' etc.
USA 1959 Lee Batlin/Wingate Paine*

*Poster: 'Winter Aid 1962'.
Switzerland 1962 Peter Hajnoczky*

Closed window as holiday symbol. See also
HANDWRITING.
Switzerland 1965 Donald Brun

Advertisement for Ladies Home Journal.
GROUP PHOTOGRAPH *of ladies in
windows of building. Popular device in the
1950s for showing the entire staff of a
particular firm.
USA 1959 Ormond Gigli/Martin Stevens*

Bereavement
Studies of Grief in Adult Life
Colin Murray Parkes

Darkened window on book jacket as a symbol of bereavement.
UK 1973 Ireland/Jones/Thompson

Wings. In various cultures wings are associated with supernatural messengers whether attached to ANGEL, HORSE or FABULOUS BEASTS. In general a symbol of freedom and associated with flying fantasies. See also AEROPLANE.

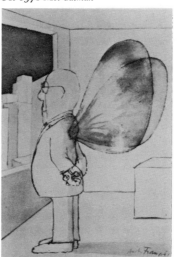

This may be slower than the Jumbo—but there's a lot more privacy

UK 1970 Mel Calman

The Icarus impulse. Poster for a plane-hire firm.
France 1973 André François

Witch. To the repressive early Christian church female sexuality and temptation took the form of a new sexual monster to accompany the DEVIL; the witch. They were thus required to be depicted as crones instead of the attractive females they probably were. The witch is also the archetypal 'bad mummy' figure. See also MEDUSA.

France 1955 Siné

Wolf. In modern thought he is associated with chaos, artfulness and naked terror.

The new Fiat 132.

Poster for CAR. 'Wolf in sheep's clothing.'
Verbal cliché made visual.
UK 1977 Neil Godfrey

Women with Moustaches. Primary sources of this obsession are Marcel Duchamp's amended MONA LISA of 1919 (L.H.O.O.Q.) and certain scenes in Bunuel's *Un Chien Andalou*, but graffiti artists (see GRAFFITI) have probably been active in this area since pre-history. The object in most examples is to emphasise the female nature by adding a MOUSTACHE, a primary male characteristic.

The corrected 'ready-made' L.H.O.O.Q. was a reproduction of the MONA LISA to which the artist had added a moustache and beard in pencil. This together with the French pun in the title were iconoclastic gestures aimed at the attitudes and values of the bourgeoisie (whom the Dadaists held responsible for World War I). It is a prototype for the manipulation of one artist's work by another and has influenced painters and designers alike. USA 1919 Marcel Duchamp

Poster for a serious NEWSPAPER. UK circa 1960 Patrick Tilley

The men's shop at Ohrbach's is symbolised by the characteristic graffiti of a Van Dyck beard and moustache. The elegance of the whiskers' style reflects the elegance of the shop. USA 1961 Sydney Myers

This habitual coquettish gesture is used as a symbol for a male cologne called 'Moustache'. USA 1963 Lou Mousachio

For an article on the masculinisation of the American woman. The femininity of the model is enhanced by the typically male impedimenta and gesture. USA 1965 George Lois / Carl Fischer

For an article on Stalin's daughter
Svetlana.
USA 1967 George Lois

*A piece of promotional material for a
photographer. The 'pencilled-in'
moustache, reminiscent of eye-liner, is a
typographic refinement and serves to
emphasise by contrast the feminine ideal.
See also* EXPRESSIONISTIC TYPOGRAPHY.
UK 1968 Derek Birdsall

*The already manipulated Mona Lisa of
Marcel Duchamp is once again appropriated
by a design studio to celebrate twenty years
work. The logotype is substituted for
Duchamp's ironic moustache. See also*
TRADEMARK MANIPULATION.
USA 1976 Pushpin Studio

*More Duchamp allusions. For a book on
hormones.
UK 1974 Penguin Books*

Wood Letter. The three-dimensional
(see THREE DIMENSION) image of a real
wood letter is occasionally employed
for its architectural quality. As they
are similar to CHILDREN'S BRICKS they
naturally simulate a BUILDING.

Acoustic WALL *made from wood letter for a
symphony orchestra.
USA 1959 Brownjohn, Chermayeff &
Geismar*

Worm's-eye View. One of a series of
fresh viewpoints to revive old subject
matter. See also END VIEW, PLAN VIEW,
REAR VIEW, SECTION.

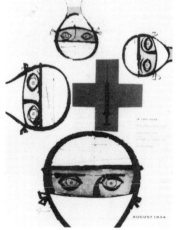

Patient's view of hospital staff. See also
CROSS.
USA 1954 George Giusti

Wrapping Up. The act of wrapping up gifts or guessing the contents of wrapped objects by their shapes evokes feelings of childhood. These feelings of suspense and re-discovery by wrapping are played on by fine artists like Christo and Magritte and by designers. See also ACCUMULATED GRAPHICS, GUESS WHO?, PARCEL.

Poster. Wrapping paper as a strong signal for a gift. See also CIGAR.
USA 1954 Paul Rand

Greetings card for Vogue. CUT-UP logotype turned into gifts.
USA 1956 Lester Bookbinder/Richard Loew

Advertisement for a Saarinen CHAIR.
USA 1957 Herbert Matter

Copy says, 'All wrapped up'. Wrapped-up film CAN as an announcement of the completion of a FILM. See also LUGGAGE LABEL.
USA 1961 Saul Bass

Booklet cover for Volkswagen CAR in mail SACK.
USA 1963 Murray Jacobs

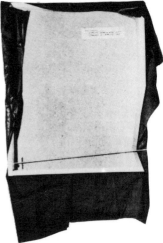

Front and REAR VIEW of a free-standing poster for an exhibition of sculptor Christo's work.
USA 1968 Christo

Display outside HMV shop during redecoration. See also TRADEMARK MANIPULATION.
UK 1979 Carole Ingham

X. Visually a CROSS, it has all the associations of the cross including the cancellation meaning. (See CANCELLATION MARKS.) The Roman numeral for ten, the mathematical sign for the unknown quantity (see ARITHMETICAL SIGNS), part of the Chrisnom XP (see MONOGRAM), its mystery and ambiguity are reflected in its many graphic interpretations.

X for affirmation.

The electorate's cross as a symbol of affirmation on a book jacket.
UK 1971 Mel Calman/Philip Thompson

X for cancellation.

X cancels the need to diet and exercise.
For an article on slimming.
USA 1957 Michael Wollman

Magazine spread on Marilyn Monroe. Copy reads, 'She was one of the most unappreciated people in the world' and reflects the spirit of the art director's cancellation (see CANCELLATION MARKS) of the unwanted NEGATIVE. See also FILM.
USA 1962 Herb Lubalin

X marks the spot.

Magazine cover. Stylised MAP of New York: Empire State Building establishes orientation. X marks the spot where client has taken new address.
USA 1945 Paul Rand

X-ray.

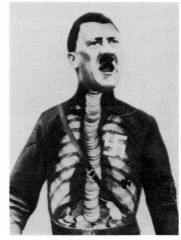

Poster. 'Adolf, the superman : swallows gold and talks tin-plate.' (Tin-plate is a German synonym for trash or trivia.)
Germany 1932 John Heartfield

Cover for Show. *Copy refers to Opera Valentine. See also HEART.*
USA 1960 Henry Wolf

Y Z

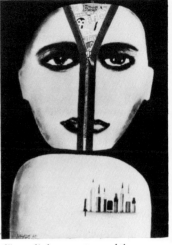

Yard. See GARDEN.

Yellow. See COLOUR SYMBOLISM.

Yoke. Wooden cross-piece fastened over necks of two oxen or to go over the shoulders of a milkmaid from which to suspend pails. A yoke is thus a symbol of submission and a powerful image.

Yo-yo. A plaything similar to the PUPPET. Its symbolism is associated with easy manipulation as of a fluctuating economy. Because of the skill involved the performer (like the ICE SKATER) has an air of nonchalance.

The Yo-Bow. Child's toy becomes a difficult instrument to master. See also MUSIC STAND.
UK 1950 Gerard Hoffnung

Zebra. A striped quadruped regarded with a mixture of affection and awe. The CAMOUFLAGE aspect of the stripes is sometimes referred to. Useful as the ultimate symbol of the ALPHABET.

Ziggurat. A man-made MOUNTAIN popular with designers, sculptors, painters and architects purely as a formal device although architects have used the principle for designing blocks of flats. See also PYRAMID.

Zip. Superseding the BUTTON in fashion it is not capable of symbolising (as the button is) the fashion industry. The image of the zip is as dynamic and sexual as the real thing; it reveals and conceals at great speed.

TROMPE L'OEIL *record sleeve with real zip.*
USA 1971 Andy Warhol

Zip applied to FACE *to reveal the* BRAIN. *Illustration on the future of design. See also* PENCIL, POCKET.
Italy 1965 Riccardo Manzi

Zodiac. The imaginary zone of the heavens that the ancient Greeks divided into twelve equal parts. In popular thought the symbolism is associated with the prediction of personal fortune. See also FABULOUS BEASTS.

ZZZZZ. The sign denoting sleep that derives from the shorthand of STRIP CARTOON FORM. ONOMATOPOEIA for a gentle snore. Firmly entrenched in graphic symbolism.

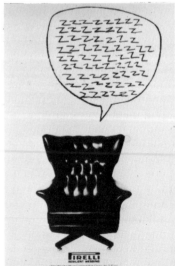

Advertisement. SPEECH BALLOON *recommends a comfortable* CHAIR.
UK 1965 Bob Gill

Index and Credits

Every possible effort has been made to trace and contact all those people whose work has been selected to illustrate our thesis, and we have striven to attribute and date all pieces of work correctly. We apologise for any inaccuracies that may have occurred, through lack of available information or other reasons beyond our control.

Bruno, Greg Mousetrap
Buchartz, Max Violin
Bühler, Fritz Boomerang, Pencil, Pipe
Burns, Robert Sundial
Burrell, John Ball
Burtin, Will Section, Tools
Byfield, Brian Alphabet

Calman, Mel Analogy, Armour, Bed, Blindman, Bowler Hat, Boxer, Brick Wall, Case, Cash Register, Chess, Cloud, Coffin, Column, Cripple, Crossroad, Crystal Ball, Devil, Dollar Sign, Duel, Ear, Fairground, Father Time, Games, Hourglass, Igloo, Janus, Joined-up Numbers, Knight, Knitting, Mask, Maze, Medusa, Monument, Personification, Pillory, Policeman, Ruler, Russian Doll, Scales, Seal, Stork, Street Sign, Tap, Thinks Bubble, Time Bomb, Tools, Wings, X for Affirmation
Calvert, Margaret Paint Box
Camperos, James P. Typewriter
Carlu, Jean Fireman, Printing Press, Santa Claus, Spanner, Table, Vase
Carruthers, Roy Book on Book
Carter, Larry Chess, Cork, Dustbin
Casado, Ralph Torn Paper
Cassandre, A. M. Arrow, Compass, Kinetics, Perspective, Profile, Scale, Steering Wheel, Table, Trompe l'Oeil, Wheel
Causer, Martin Blackboard
Ceci, Vincent Clapper Board, Newspaper
Celiz, Robert Film
Chambers, Carolyn Noose
Chermayeff, Ivan Blackmail Lettering, Cannon/Cannon Balls, Clock/Watch, Collage, Dove, Speech Balloon, Spliced Lettering
Chermayeff & Geismar Atomic Cloud, Date, Ear, Film, Heart, Mosaic (Photographic), Scribble, Stars and Stripes, Target
Chichester, Sir Francis Snapshot
Christo Wrapping Up
Christy, Howard Chandler Sex
Churchill/Holmes/Kitley Spliced Image, Tape Measure
Chwast, Seymour Anvil/Hammer, Art, Camouflage, Case, Comb, Flattened-out Perspective, Initial Letter, Picture Hook, Pirate, Profile, Servant, Uncle Sam
Cieslewicz, Roman Bottle Top, Superman, Torn Paper
Cinamon, Gerald Penguin
Coffin, Clifford Repetition
Colin, Jean Daisy, Lighthouse
Collins, Angela Braces
Constantin, F. Smoke
Cook, Roger Envelope
Cooper, Austin National Stereotypes
Coppiello, Leonetto Bull
Corso, Fischer Matchstick
Courtos, Tom Arrow, Characteristic Style, Christmas Bauble
Crocker, John Music Stave
Crosby/Fletcher/Forbes Blood,

Burnt Paper, Embossing, Graffiti, Holes in Paper, Number Symbolism, Section, Stencil Lettering
Crosby/Fletcher/Forbes/Gill Before and After, Diary, Dovetail, Paper Sculpture
Cuesta, Mike Snake
Curtis, Bob Inside Lining

Daimler, Gottlieb Star
Daly, Tom Body Painting
D'Amato, George Halo
Danziger, Louis Bow, Egg, Eye, Fork, Globe, Hammer, Paint Tube, Price Tag, Quotation, Stars and Stripes, Telescope, Three Dimension, Toy
Davenport, Peter Eye, Ticket, Union Jack
Davis, Hal Body Language, Key, Onomatopoeia
Davis, Paul Art, Devil, Fairground, Handshake, Pilot
de Harak, Rudolph Dot, Expressionistic Typography, Heart, Paper Sculpture, Printing Press, Shadow, Stars and Stripes, Swastika, Wavy Line
de Voto, Joe Number Plate
Dearing, Richard Tape Measure
Deighton, Len Ink Pot
Delacrétaz, Olivier Ear
Delaney, Brian Cigar
Design Research Unit Arrow
Dexel, Walter Exclamation Mark
Dickens, Frank Building
Dodd, Ivan Spiral
Dodson, John Characteristic Style
Doebele, H.P. Barbed Wire
Donegan, John Oyster
Dorfsman, Lou Apple, Bracket, Chair, Characteristic Style, Conspicuous Waste, Cranium, Cut-up, Dimensions, Ear, Franking, Games and Battles, Graph, Guillotine, Kinetics, Map, Microphone, Nest, Quotation Marks, Scales, Substitution, Tape Measure, Telephone, Tray (In, Out), Typewriter
Duchamp, Marcel Women with Moustaches
Dudovitch, Marcello Chair
Dunning, Bob Superman
Duskin, Ken Roof
Dutton, Norbert Wavy Line
d'Ylen, Jean Fountain, Horse

Eckersley, Tom Candle, Clock/Watch, Cog, Eye, Lighthouse, Sack, Tear Drop, Turban, Ventriloquist's Dummy, Weathercock
Eckerstrom, Ralph E. Three Dimension
Edelman, Heinz Rose
Egan, Irene Trademark Manipulation
Egensteiner, Donald Expressionistic Typography
Eidenbenz, Hermann Printing Press
Eisenman, Stanley Doodle
Eksell, Olle Pencil
Elliot, George Smile

Emmerile, Louis Pen-nib
Englemann, Michael Paper Hat, Place Setting
Erni, Hans Atomic Cloud
Errol Body
Ettinger Bird
Evans, Eileen Palmist's Hand
Evans, John Date

Facetti, Germano Brain
Federico, Gene Ampersand, Bicycle, Capital out of Error, Diver, Fireman, Hammer, Honeycomb, Ice Skater, Juggler, Model, Pin-up, Rebus, Shirt, Umbrella
Feiffer, Jules House of Cards
Feurer, Hans Hair, Housewife
Fior, Robin Ball, Registration Marks
Firle, Otto Bird
Fischer, Carl Building, Saints' Symbolism, Santa Claus, Women with Moustaches
Flagg, J. M. Uncle Sam
Fleming, Allan Expressionistic Typography
Fletcher, Alan Expressionistic Typography, Handwriting, Heads/Middles/Tails, Three Dimension, Window
Fletcher/Forbes/Gill Ampersand, Case, Electrical Symbols, General Signs, Heads/Middles/Tails, Perforation, Thermometer, Torn Paper, Union Jack
Folon, Jean-Michel Arrow, Building, Car, Clockwork, Family Tree, Jigsaw Puzzle, Maze, Puppet, Road Sign
Forbes, Colin Calendar, Jigsaw Puzzle, Kit-layout, Union Jack
Foreman, Michael Price Tag
François, André Abacus, Adam and Eve, Aerial, Animals, Antlers, Apple, Bandage, Bed, Bee, Beggarman/Poorman, Bicycle, Bird, Blot, Body Language, Bottle, Breasts, Bullfighter, Bus, Butterfly, Cat, Christmas Stocking, Cloud, Clown, Cog, Collage, Conductor, Dance, Driving Mirror, Easel, Elephant, Fabulous Beasts, Face Substitute, Fan (Handheld), Flasher, Flowers, Franking, Funnel, Gallows, Guardsman, Gun, Heart, Horse, Ink Pot, Knight, Laurel, Lion, Mask, Medal, Musical Notation, Pelican, Pen, Personification, Photographer, Place-Setting, Rainbow, Rat, Repetition, Smoke Ring, Sunrise/Sunset, Target, Tattoo, Trademark Manipulation, Trapeze Artiste, Violin, Wings
Frasconi, Antonio Vice Versa
Frazier, Charles Coca Cola Bottle (Collection Dr and Mrs Leonard Kornblee)
Freedman, Carl File
Freeman, Robert Code
Froshaug, Anthony Cancellation Marks, Map
Fujikawa, Gyo Wave
Fujita, S. Neil Bag, Kit-layout, Paint Tube